IN MY ELEMENT

Life lessons from the world's
toughest solo ocean race

PIP HARE

T0357411

**ADLARD
COLES**

LONDON · OXFORD · NEW YORK · NEW DELHI · SYDNEY

ADLARD COLES
Bloomsbury Publishing Plc
50 Bedford Square, London, WC1B 3DP, UK
29 Earlsfort Terrace, Dublin 2, Ireland

BLOOMSBURY, ADLARD COLES and the Adlard Coles logo are trademarks of
Bloomsbury Publishing Plc

First published in 2024

A catalogue record for this book is available from the British Library

ISBN: PB: 978-1-3994-2049-5; ePub: 978-1-3994-2048-8; ePDF: 978-1-3994-2051-8

2 4 6 8 10 9 7 5 3 1

Typeset in Sabon LT Std by Deanta Global Publishing Services, Chennai, India
Printed and bound in Great Britain by CPI Group (UK) Ltd, Croydon CR0 4YY

To find out more about our authors and books visit www.bloomsbury.com
and sign up for our newsletters

CONTENTS

DEDICATION

Writing this book has been quite a tonic for me. Too often we get dragged down into the day-to-day struggles that life throws our way. Head down, trying to get through the quagmire, is a stance into which it is all too easy to fall. In writing this book, I have been reminded of why it is incredible to be a human being. It has forced me to employ my own technique of zooming out to take in my journey, to recognise and acknowledge the pure joy of my achievements. It has refuelled my soul for what continues to be a tough path to the top of my sport.

I have also been reminded of the many people who have made this all possible. One of the greatest revelations of my Vendée Globe journey is that other people want me to succeed. The gratitude I still feel towards every person who donated to my crowd fund, bought a sponsorship package, turned up to one of my talks, volunteered their time to work on the boat or wrote a kind or encouraging comment on my social media post is immense. For all the people in my life who have told me I was not good enough or it was not possible for someone like me to compete in the Vendée Globe race, there are literally thousands more who backed me simply because they wanted me to succeed.

This book is dedicated to every one of you. You are and always will be a huge part of my success. Your trust and faith humble me.

A NOTE FROM THE AUTHOR

Hello, I am Pip Hare, author of *In My Element* and currently the full-time skipper and CEO of the Pip Hare Ocean Racing Team. Thank you for buying this book. I hope you will enjoy my story of how I created and then delivered the greatest sporting achievement of my life.

Despite being based around one of the greatest sailing races in the world, I do not think this book is about sailing. For me, it's about the human journey that many of us make over and over throughout our lifetimes, in both big and small ways. I was inspired to write this book by the many questions people ask me about my life alone on the ocean. Seldom, if ever, does anyone ask, 'How do you hoist a sail?' or 'How do you navigate?' Not even the sailors are eager to know those details. Instead, I am asked over and over about the human challenges: 'Don't you get lonely?', 'Aren't you scared?', 'How do you stay motivated?', 'How do you prioritise what to do?', 'How do you manage with so little sleep?'

These questions really pique interest because they relate to problems we will all face at some point, often many points, in our own lives, whatever path we choose. When I started the Vendée Globe race, I had no idea how it would end, whether I would finish, or what kinds of problems would be thrown my way during my 95 days at sea. I had to rely on the basic human skills I had learned throughout my life to make it through the hard times, as the hardest challenges were more in my head than in the water around me.

I shared my race and some of the build-up online, via our social media channels, @piphareoceanracing. For every chapter in the book, you will find corresponding video diaries, blog entries, explanatory videos and social media updates online. If you are left curious or wanting more, you can look back through my channels to find those key moments and experience them in the moment.

Even better, I will be racing around the world again on 10 November 2024, writing my name on the ocean in a whole new way. Once again, I have no idea how that race will end. As you read the book, there will be an opportunity to watch my new race unfold, taking in the race tracker and my regular updates as I deal with new challenges, triumphs, pains and happiness. I will employ my own tools to get me through the hard times and maybe find new ways to survive and thrive.

I hope some of what I have written about will resonate with your own challenges and perspective on the world. If you have the time or inclination to share your own experiences regarding some of the topics I cover, I'd love to hear from you via social media channels or by email through our website. Whatever your chosen path in life, whatever you are striving towards, I wish you luck and your very own definition of success.

The Pip Hare Ocean Racing Team competes in both solo and crewed ocean racing and manages every aspect of high-performance sport, from both a technical and human development perspective. We offer high-value sponsorships to companies looking to demonstrate their own values and attributes through the power of high-performance sports. To find out more about our team, the Vendée Globe, and other races, explore sponsorship opportunities or learn how to get involved with the team, visit our website: www.piphare.com or find us on social media channels @piphareoceanracing on YouTube, Facebook, Instagram, LinkedIn, X and TikTok.

PROLOGUE

I look out to an empty horizon from my vantage point on the back of the boat. The sky is uncharacteristically blue, a welcome change from days of grey clouds that hid the sun from view. My boat *Superbigou* twitches, gathering itself up for a sprint. It is a feeling I know well. A slight pause as the wave picks up the back of the boat, and in that tiny moment – a microsecond that I've come to notice from the days and nights I've sailed alone on it – I can hear and feel the vessel load up under the power of the wave. The boat heels, the sheets holding the sails tighten, and the autopilot moves the rudders to a hard angle. It is braced – I am braced – and then we go, charging down the face of the wave. *Superbigou* rumbles. The sea roars around me. Everywhere I can see and feel power. The boat, though old now, is the interface between human ingenuity and the power of nature. It was designed to be fast and strong, to interact with the huge winds and immense waves of the Southern Ocean, to harness the untameable power of nature in a bid to help its skipper become the fastest human being to race around the globe by water.

I cling on to the backstay, knuckles white with the bitter Southern Ocean air, and a wall of water – literally a tonne – barrels down the deck towards me. Thigh high, it slams against my body, whipping my feet out from under me. Although I am clipped on with a harness, I struggle to regain my footing as the wave washes under my feet. *Superbigou* is heedless now, charging headlong, absorbing the boost of speed from the wave. The whole boat is shaking, while all around a cacophony of creaking, slamming and roaring deafens me. I am addicted to the speed; it feels incredible. I imagine eating away at the lead of my competitors, but with every noise, jerk and slam, a bolt of adrenaline stabs my chest. What if I break a sail? How would I wrestle 120 square metres of flogging material out of the sky? What if the autopilot fails, turning us sideways to the oncoming 6-metre waves? We'd be knocked down for sure. What if the mast snaps, leaving me stranded a thousand miles from shore? If I fall over the side, I will surely die: the water is a freezing six degrees and no other human is within 100 miles of my position. *Superbigou* picks up another wave and surfs again, faster this time, deafening. My eyes are streaming, sore from the icy wind that throws spray in my face. And over the top of it all I can hear my own laughter. I feel powerful, strong. I am sailing *this* boat, *this* fast, in the middle of the Southern Ocean, and I cannot believe it. I am a thousand miles from land in one of the world's most dangerous environments. Alone and free.

PIP'S VENDÉE GLOBE RACE ROUTE 2020–2021

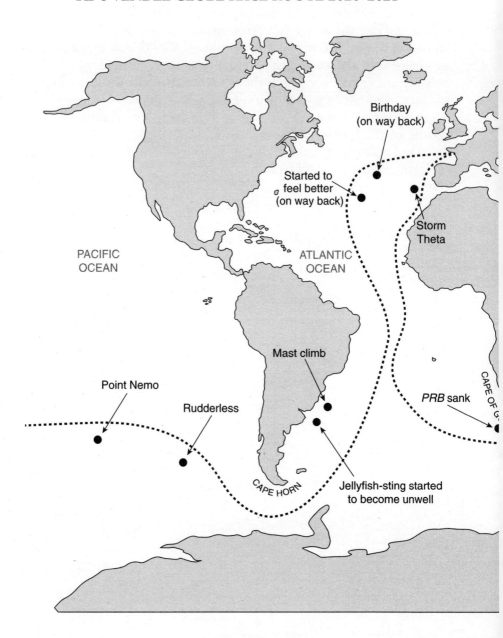

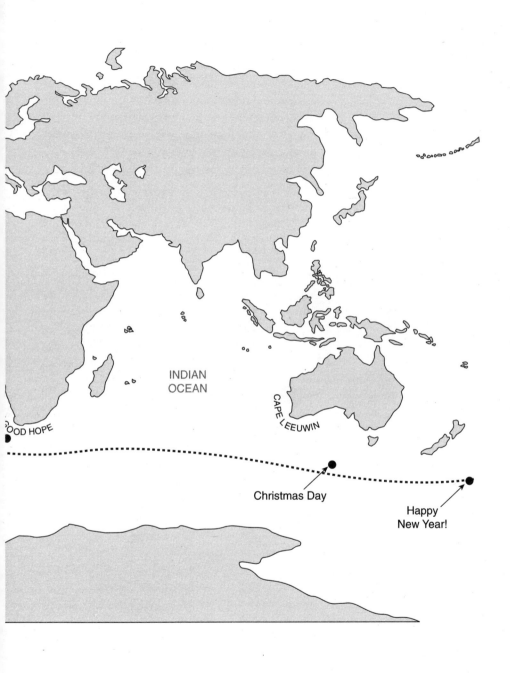

SUPERBIGOU

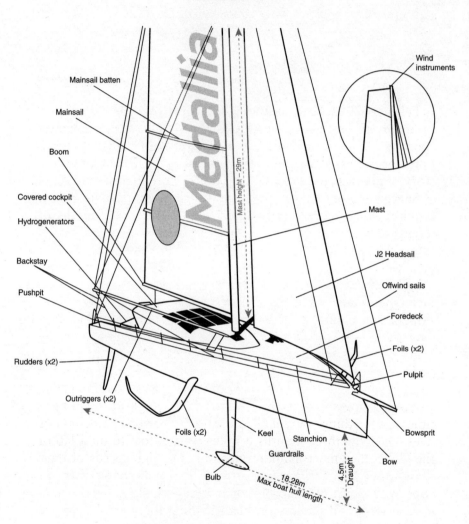

Wind instruments

Mainsail batten

Mainsail

Boom

Covered cockpit

Hydrogenerators

Backstay

Pushpit

Rudders (x2)

Outriggers (x2)

Foils (x2)

Keel

Stanchion

Guardrails

Bulb

Mast height ~ 29m

Medallia

Mast

J2 Headsail

Offwind sails

Foredeck

Foils (x2)

Pulpit

Bowsprit

Bow

4.5m Draught

18.28m Max boat hull length

I

DREAMING BIG

In February 2021, I became the eighth woman and the 79th person in history to finish the Vendée Globe race. One of the toughest sporting events in the world, its rules are simple: single-handed, non-stop, no assistance, one lap of the planet. This book tells the story of my race, but it is about so much more than sailing.

Surviving alone on the ocean in a high-pressure environment requires much more than nautical expertise. Three months of racing around the world through extreme weather systems a thousand miles from land, surviving on only 30 minutes of sleep at a time, will stretch a human being until their mental and physical resilience is wafer thin. The race requires skippers to face innumerable challenges entirely alone. With both boat and skipper descending to increasingly depleted states of exhaustion over the course of the race, they are tested and pushed to the brink of failure over and over again because mother nature has no favourites. Though the race is concerned ostensibly with the sport of sailing, at its core it is about surviving as a human being. Having to find solutions and the strength to fight through hard times is something we will all encounter at various points in our lives. Over the three months it takes competitors to do a lap of the globe, they must maintain not only the high speeds of their vessels, but also the positive attitude that will enable them to cope with physical and emotional isolation, sleep deprivation, fear, anxiety and endless problem-solving; these challenges are common to all humans in all walks of life and they are what underlies this uniquely tough mental and physical trial. In this book I hope to share, alongside the story of my race around the world, the techniques I used to overcome difficulties, drive performance and maintain a mindset that allowed me to stay focused, happy and optimistic for 95 days. Alone.

Solo ocean racing is one of the most complex and open-ended sports on Earth. The racetrack is vast, with no lanes to follow or a final whistle after a preordained number of laps. Instead, we cover thousands of miles across the surface of our planet, the largest racetrack there could possibly be. We are accountable only to ourselves; we own the solution to our problems and the potential to do better, as well as the responsibility for underperformance or mistakes. When I look out over an ocean, I see a limitless expanse without boundaries, where I can choose my own route, where I will never be contained. Alone on a boat in the middle of the ocean, I feel limitless opportunities to develop as a person. No one will tell me I am not capable, nor is there anyone to take a job out of my hands when my confidence fails. Being forced to make every decision, face every fear and solve every problem alone has made me a stronger person in every way. Moreover, the lessons I have learned through managing myself on the water have helped me to deal with my life on land.

The Vendée Globe race was born in 1989. It was designed to provide the toughest sailing challenge imaginable for those willing to take it on. Since its inception, the race has been run every four years, and has represented the pinnacle of achievement for solo sailors the world over. It is a sporting event like no other, where athletes are required to perform 24/7 for weeks on end. Over the course of the race, competitors must brave weather conditions that range from the extreme heat of the Earth's equator to snowstorms and towering waves in the Southern Ocean, all the while sleeping, eating, carrying out repairs and maintenance on a wet, wildly moving platform. As pilots of the high-tech, innovative boats, which sometimes travel in excess of 70 km/h as they fly above the ocean's waves, we must be responsible for every aspect of life on board. We must navigate, read the weather, strategise, generate and manage power, make water, monitor and repair our vessels, all while maintaining speed and performance. The boat is entirely managed by one multifunctioning person, capable of winding winches, pulling ropes, dragging 70- or 80-kilo bags around the deck, hoisting sails to the top of a 30-metre mast and performing any number of onerous duties, many of which would be a full-time job on a fully crewed racing boat. We solitary sailors live in sparse conditions, with no furniture below decks. We sleep on beanbags on the floor, taking the shortest of naps lest conditions on deck change. During its three months at sea, the boat will be under constant stress. Parts of it, and its equipment, can and will break, sometimes with catastrophic consequences.

You could say I started my Vendée Globe campaign at the age of 16, the day I opened a magazine and read about the French sailor Isabelle Autissier, then competing in the round-the-world BOC Challenge. Although living in a landlocked town in the east of England, I had already fallen in love with the sport of sailing. I'd taken part in a youth sailing scheme one summer, led by young people for young people, and had been captivated by the agency I was allowed at the helm of the sailing boat and the possibilities that an open horizon offered. After that, I'd devoured books about ocean racing, gobbling up tales of the fully crewed Whitbread race, where huge boats circumnavigated the world in stages. Even to think there might be a career in racing yachts seemed to me wonderful; the fact that I knew no sailors and nothing of the industry didn't seem a problem, although I was painfully aware that there were no women among the pages of my books. Then, in that second-hand magazine picked up at a charity shop, I came upon the article about Isabelle. I had never heard of solo ocean racing before and was immediately captivated. The BOC Challenge was a circumnavigation, in legs, like the Whitbread, and in a boat of a similar size. But, this time, the sailors were racing alone. It seemed audacious, outrageous, to push the limits that far. Here was one woman, racing as an equal, talked about as an equal. She gave me the green light, and although I was still at school, I decided then and there that it was the sport for me. It seemed there was nothing more challenging in the world that I could do.

I started my Vendée Globe campaign proper in November 2018 with a £25,000 bank loan and a crowd fund. For my whole adult life, sailing had been my career, and for the previous ten years I'd been climbing through the ranks of solo sailing. Although it is not the subject of this book, suffice it to say that my route to the top of the sport has not been easy. I've had to forge my own path every step of the way. When I first started sailing professionally, in 1992, fewer than three per cent of yacht-racing participants were women. Today, it is just over 15 per cent. There was no performance pathway to follow, and for a shy girl with no contacts or experience, opportunities were scarce. I determined that I would have to make my own way, so I set goals and planned how I might best gain skills and experience. I devised campaigns, raised funds, delivered training programmes, set up and maintained boats, and inched my way on to the international stage. Because each race campaign took years to deliver, I had to earn a living while training, so I took on short contracts, coaching other sailors, and wrote articles for sailing magazines. At the end of each campaign, I would map out my next steps, always asking the same questions of myself: 'Am I capable of more? Do I want to continue? Have I got the energy to go on?' I made a promise that if the answer to any one of these questions was 'no', I would hang up my boots and walk away.

I accepted that my campaigns would never be perfect. Time-poor and on a meagre budget, I couldn't devote myself to training, unlike many of my competitors. At times it was hard to turn up at the start line feeling down at heel, and I had to keep reminding myself that although my kit wasn't the best, and I wasn't the most prepared, at least here I had the opportunity to become a better sailor. And with each race my results improved, and my hunger to compete continued to grow. I always knew I had more to give. So much of my energy was eaten up with bringing each campaign into life – imagine what I could do if I was allowed just to be a sailor?

By 2018, at 44 years old, I finally believed I had acquired enough knowledge and experience to race around the world alone. The problem was always going to be finding the funding. In the world of ocean racing, the Vendée Globe is the equivalent of Formula One. The IMOCA-class boats are 18.28-metre-long (60-foot) immaculately built carbon racing machines. The latest designs have foils fitted to the hulls that, when extended like wings out of the side of the boat to trail in the water, lift the hull clear above the surface of the sea so that the boat is flying. A new-build IMOCA costs around £5 million, and the running costs for a top team come in at around £20 million over a four-year cycle. You might be the best sailor in the world, but if you don't have the funding to secure a boat, and cannot get a team together, you will never have the chance to compete.

With the next start scheduled for 2020, I knew this could be my last opportunity to enter the Vendée Globe. As yet, I had nothing to offer except experience. I could enter the race with an older boat, but even to charter one would cost in excess of £100,000 per year. I had never managed to raise sponsorship even close to that amount. Just as I was wondering if I had reached the end of my journey, a friend told me about an old IMOCA-class boat, *Superbigou*. It had a history. In 1999, it had been designed for and built by Swiss solo legend Bernard Stamm for the 2000 Vendée Globe. Since then, the boat had completed four circumnavigations, one of which it won, and it had also set a transatlantic speed record. Most recently, it had raced in the 2016 edition of the Vendée Globe, skippered by another Swiss sailor, Alan Roura, who at 23 was to become the youngest sailor ever to finish the race. After that, however, *Superbigou*'s fortunes had gone downhill. It had been chartered by another Vendée hopeful who had run out of funds, and for several months the boat had been left uncared for in France. I contacted the owner and asked if there might be an opportunity to take over the charter. I knew the boat was in very poor condition, and by modern standards far from competitive. I reminded myself that this was about creating the opportunity to become the athlete I wanted to be, and if I had to accept a less than perfect boat, it would still give me a platform to perform. The charter fee was set at just €2,000 a month, with the understanding that instead of hiring a fully functioning ready-to-race boat, I had to take it as it was. I would be responsible for upgrades, repairs and ongoing maintenance, all of which I knew would come at huge cost. I was given ten days to decide.

As I was coaching in the States at the time, I called my great friend Paul Peggs, a solo sailor himself who had competed in the Mini Transat. Paul agreed to travel to Brittany to inspect the boat and make the call on my behalf if I decided to go ahead with the charter. In the meantime, I set sail for the Azores. Paul emailed me five days later when I was in the middle of the Atlantic. 'It's knackered,' he reported back. 'It will need a lot of work. It's unloved and uncared for. But it is strong. This is it. Go for it.' It was just what I needed to hear. Without setting eyes on the boat, I said yes.

Back in the UK, I arranged a £25k loan that would cover the first few months of the charter and initial set-up costs, giving me a very short runway to generate more income. It was, on paper, a crazy plan to take this project on alone and unfunded. I knew I was battling the odds, but I also knew that the only way I would ever get to compete in the Vendée Globe race was if I forced my own project into existence. I promised myself that every day I would work as hard as I possibly could. I would never stop, no matter how futile a task might seem. Only that way would I demonstrate to others that I was worth investing in and would have the confidence and integrity to stand in front of prospective sponsors. I wasn't daunted by the boat. I knew I had the skills and seamanship to manage, even though I had never set foot on one of these 60-foot IMOCA beasts before, let alone sailed one solo. I told myself it was like other boats, just big. Like the whole project. The most daunting task – the mountain I had no idea how to climb – was getting the funding. In order to refit my tired old boat and cover running and race entry costs, I would need to raise a minimum of £1 million.

I had received help and donations from private individuals throughout my sailing career, which, alongside small sponsorships, had helped me to the start line of each event. These donations had always been offered unsolicited, a result of my meeting people and telling them about what I was doing. I have always believed in working hard for what I want, and like many of my generation, the concept of a crowd fund did not sit comfortably with this philosophy. It seemed OK to ask for sponsorship – a commercial deal – but I struggled to see why individuals would want to invest in my campaign. It seemed presumptuous to even suggest it. Several of my friends sat me down and told me that I had to give people the chance: they had the right to make up their own minds, and there was no shame in raising funding this way.

I opened my crowd fund in November 2018, feeling a little sick, ready for a torrent of abuse. I thought I'd be accused of being overprivileged, of taking donation money when there were people in the world who deserved it far more than me. But all I got back was kindness. People wished me well and wanted me to succeed; they offered to help in a multitude of ways. I continued to share my story and its developments online and the momentum quickly spread. Sailing friends came to help me train with the boat during those first months, and although none of us had sailed an IMOCA before, we learned together. On my dock days, volunteers would turn up to help move equipment, clean and maintain the boat, and when we took *Superbigou* to the Southampton Boat Show, some even drove all the way down from Cumbria to support me. The community around the campaign kept growing, both online and in the flesh, and I was continually surprised by how happy people were to donate their time and money. It was hard at first to step out of the shadows and share my ambitions. I felt exposed, fearful that people would judge me unworthy or incapable of the challenge ahead. But I figured that if I was honest and shared the truth – the mistakes as well as the achievements – I could hold my head up, whatever the outcome.

Through 2019 I raced as a one-woman team. We had to complete three international IMOCA-class races to qualify for the Vendée Globe. The average spend of an IMOCA team over one competition year is £1 million, and in 2019 I delivered my entire programme on £150,000, raised through our crowd fund, credit card borrowing, and donations in kind. Starting with small corporate sponsorships at local level, we began to attract some business investments to the campaign. Other than meeting the cost of entering and competing in races, every penny went into fixing and maintaining the boat. My volunteers and I must have looked a ramshackle bunch beside the inscrutable uniformed teams and immaculate boats of my competitors. On one occasion, while working on the back deck with an angle grinder, we were told to be quiet: the elite Banque Populaire team behind us were trying to conduct interviews with their young protégé Clarisse Crémer and their previous Vendée winner, Armel Le Cléac'h. Although sometimes we were regarded with raised eyebrows, we always finished every race, and we were never last.

There were many times during that first year of campaigning when I honestly had no idea how we would get through the next month. I was racing, training, fixing the boat, looking for funding, running my own comms and marketing campaign, as well as managing the race programme. I didn't feel I could let others know how tough I was finding it, because I had chosen this path myself. Some days I was so stressed by the impossible hill I had to climb and the lack of progress I was making that I would be physically sick. I sold everything I could, regularly eBaying items to get me through the next month. I borrowed money on credit cards, paying off the interest each month. Every item on the boat was tired and old, and with every race I knew that something critical would break. I had a good background in 'make do and mend', and spent evenings on the boat taking defunct electronics apart and sticking sails back together with glue and tape. So often, I thought I'd come to the end of the road, but every time, as if by a miracle, someone stepped forward to help me over the hump. Despite the enormous stress I felt on land, however, whenever I sailed that huge 60-foot boat on my own, I knew it was where I belonged. I was good at this – in my element – and given the chance, I'd get even better. Knowing that gave me the energy to carry on.

By the end of 2019, completely against the odds, I was announced as one of the 33 sailors who had qualified for the Vendée Globe. With a place secured, my biggest hurdle now was ensuring my boat would make it around the world. We needed to do a big refit, impossible without serious sponsorship, so I continued to fundraise as if my life depended on it. My first sponsorship breaks of the campaign had come from local people in early 2019, starting with the Poole Harbour Commissioners, who offered to give my boat and my campaign a home. Until then, Poole had never housed any elite offshore racing team, and our presence at the marina quickly sparked interest and pride. A syndicate of local sponsors formed around us, each of whom made monthly contributions in exchange for branding and shared media and networking events. Finding larger lumps of funding was slower going, but I soaked up marketing advice from our generous local partners and honed my presentation skills at every opportunity. Other businesses soon joined as supporters, offering equipment, vehicles, labour, storage, and locations for refits. I can never thank them enough. My acknowledgements list in the back of this book is meagre recognition for what their contributions have allowed me to do.

Chasing the big money always seemed like an impossible task. So many blind alleys, so much waiting – and almost always for nothing. I found myself celebrating when someone actually bothered to reply with a 'no'. The only way to get noticed was to march on regardless, putting everything I had into making the campaign happen anyway. With every race I finished, always against the odds, I demonstrated my worth. In the words of the suffragettes, though with less militant intent, 'deeds not words' is a core belief. Our first big sponsor came on the back of a successful performance in the 2019 Fastnet Race, my second in *Superbigou*. Double-handed, the race also marked an exciting new partnership with my co-skipper, the tall, wiry Australian Paul Larsen, who with his Swedish wife, Helena Darvelid, became linchpins of our Vendée team. Paul was and is the outright world speed sailing record holder, a feat he achieved in 2012 in a boat he had designed and built with Helena's help. It was lucky for me that both of them understood the value of aiming high with what you had. It didn't faze them that *Superbigou* was an old boat, and it was clear that they believed in me. This marked a turning point in my campaign, and I proceeded with this new injection of confidence. Despite having the oldest boat in the fleet and being ranked last in class on paper, 24 hours into the 600-mile course Paul and I were leading that Fastnet Race, ahead of not only all the IMOCAs but the entire fleet of bigger yachts as well. Paul and I proved that if you put yourself out there, anything can happen. People following the race went crazy. I was messaged by journalists, friends and competitors on other boats, all of whom found it incredible that we were leading this fleet of multi-million-pound boats and their paid crews. A triumph for the underdog. Paul and I couldn't stop laughing. By the time we reached the Scilly Isles, the wind had filled in and we could hold off our rivals no longer, but still the glow of success remained. As they passed us, one of my heroes, Sam Davies, and her co-skipper, Paul Meilhat, came out on deck to give us a thumbs up. Another great endorsement, which filled me with hope and courage. We arrived to an incredible welcome on shore. Immediately after the race, we were contacted by the founder of Yondr, a company that supplies infrastructure to big data business. He had followed the race, loved our story, and felt that it resonated with the journey his own business had taken. We had a sponsor.

At the beginning of 2020, with my place secured in the race, we could delay the refit of *Superbigou* no longer. Once again, Poole came to my aid. I was able to use the cranes and trucks at the commercial port to lift the boat out of the water, and WQI Marine offered me the use of their shed as well as donating labour. I had managed to raise a meagre budget to spend on the refit, and decided to enlist an expert to manage the work and help me prioritise. I had first met Joff Brown in a crowded bar before a Route du Rhum race, where he'd been introduced to me as 'the most experienced technical director in Vendée Globe history'. Unlike most of his peers, he was British-based, so I decided to seek him out. Over the history of the Vendée, Joff had prepared boats for four British sailors and one American, each of whom had completed their race. Considering the average finishing rate of the fleet was 55 per cent, these were numbers that could not be ignored. Happily, Joff agreed to take on the project, while I supplied labour and sourced materials. We started work in January 2020. Volunteers came to the shed to help at weekends, giving up their free time to don a pair of overalls and drive an orbital sander or pull vinyl from the hull. The incredible Mark and Julie Bestford made a 1,400-mile round trip, bringing spray guns and a compressor to antifoul the bottom of the boat. We were making progress, but I was painfully aware of what we were lacking.

Then the events of 2020 changed everyone's lives. The COVID pandemic was starting to rumble away at the beginning of February, and by March we were hearing of countries going into lockdown. I was still working on the boat and pushing hard to find sponsorship, with a number of conversations progressing well. When Britain went in to its first lockdown on 26 March 2020, everything stopped. I remember going to the deserted shed to pack everything away. The boat was sitting in pieces, hull stripped bare, rudders out, all equipment stripped off the deck ready for painting. The keel was outside on a pallet, the mast in a car park on the other side of the port. I looked at the bare boat, taken apart like a giant Meccano set, and for the first time I felt beaten.

By the time restrictions were relaxed, I knew that I had run out of options. The boat wasn't mine; I had signed a charter agreement until 2021; I couldn't stay in the shed indefinitely; and with the social distancing rules, volunteers were unable to help. The only thing I could do was put the boat together again in a basic fashion, crane it back into the water, and finish the job once it was on its mooring. At minimum, I needed to vacate the borrowed shed and return the boat in a similar condition to that in which I had found it. To make matters worse, my personal income stream had been based around sailing, a sport no longer viable in lockdown. In April, I had to acknowledge my situation was grim; bankruptcy was the next step. With no way of getting a job in the current climate, there was no other option but to register for state support, something I had never done in my life. Then, just as it had happened in the previous year, at the eleventh hour a call came from the team at Yondr, who were wanting to know if the Vendée Globe was going ahead. If it was, they were still committed to their bronze-level partnership and our basic refit could continue.

And indeed, the Vendée Globe was still happening. It was our good fortune that the race was uniquely adapted to COVID times. We could compete in isolation and spectators would watch the race online from their own homes, so there was no risk involved. As the race organisers and the French government were quick to agree the race would go ahead, all of a sudden I saw opportunity. As possibly the only sporting event to take place that year, it had to spark some interest. I contacted a journalist at the *Telegraph* who had covered my campaign the previous year, and he published a piece about how I was still searching for sponsorship. We put the story out there, carried on working, and hoped that someone would notice. At the end of May, I received a one-line email from Leslie Stretch, CEO of Medallia, an international customer insights business with headquarters in the US: 'Are sponsorship opportunities still available?'

Within a week of that email, Medallia had verbally agreed to be the title sponsors to my campaign. The contract was signed within the month, and the course of my Vendée Globe race changed forever. Leslie Stretch, a no-nonsense Scot, was both friendly and formidable. During our first Zoom meetings I was terrified by his questions and straight talking, but as I got to know him, I realised that I could talk straight back. I didn't need jargon: all I had to do was tell him in my own words what I had to offer, what I would do with funding, and what I would give in return. It is hard to quantify the immense gratitude and respect I have for the decision he made to back my campaign. To this day he has championed me in a way that has allowed me to achieve the potential I always believed I had.

Hot on the heels of Medallia, another business joined the family. US software company Smartsheet joined us as a silver-level sponsor. Now, with the necessary budget achieved, I was finally able to invest heavily in *Superbigou*. Joff and I planned all the work we could sensibly complete in the timeframe, and started to order parts: new sails, rigging, autopilot and instruments, for starters. For the first time, too, I could employ a team to work on the campaign, and I was thrilled to be able to offer a full-time job on the campaign to Paddy Hutchings, one of the young volunteers who had donated their time for free in 2019. Though the majority of our spend would be on the technical side of the programme, I was also able to staff the administration and business side, starting with offering my right-hand woman and volunteer, Lou Adams, a paid part-time role. I had met this medic and kindred spirit years before – the wife of a colleague who constantly told me how scarily alike we were: both of us driven women who would not allow others to define our goals. How right he was.

With just four months left to the start of the race, we had a team and had pimped the boat. I was even able to get out and train. Eighteen months of the hardest work I had ever done in my life had paid off.

There were many people who have influenced me and given me the strength and courage to continue through these difficult years. I would love to mention them all by name, but the list is too long. I feel privileged to have had a unique insight into the incredible positive, selfless generosity of human beings and I am unequivocal in my acknowledgement that I did not get where I am on my own.

2

KNIFE TO A GUNFIGHT

There was little fanfare as we arrived at the entrance to the harbour of Les Sables d'Olonne – a fishing port on the Atlantic coast of western France that would be our home for the next three weeks – just Joff, our technical director, telling me to head back out to sea for a sail. It was low tide, impossible to enter the harbour with a keel as deep as mine, and the fear was that if we loitered about waiting, the boat might get rammed – and that would be the end of that. We hadn't spent the last nine months kitting out *Superbigou* only to have our Vendée Globe chances shattered by a collision. We all remembered the VG of 2008 when *Hugo Boss* was dismasted after a collision with a fishing trawler in just such circumstances.

Eventually, in the early hours of the morning, there was enough water for me and Paddy Hutchings, our young team volunteer, to bring *Superbigou* into the harbour. I was happy that we could motor up the channel under the cover of night. I hate having my picture taken at the best of times, always self-conscious under scrutiny, and right now I was failing to get my head around the fact that I was here at all. I had expected that after all the years of fighting to get to the Vendée I would be hit by a huge wall of emotion as we entered the harbour – this was hallowed ground, after all – but as we made our way down the canal in the darkness it felt unreal, almost flat. It was as if I'd stepped into someone else's life. We were met on the dock by my small shivering team, who had come out ahead of us in vans loaded with kit. They were grinning like maniacs: 'This is it, Pip. You've made it!'

In France, the Vendée Globe race is the most popular sporting event after the football World Cup, the Olympics and the Tour de

13

France. My name, along with those of the other 32 sailors taking part in this extraordinary competition, would soon be familiar to millions. The average in-person attendance at the race village alone would normally exceed three million people in the three weeks running up to the race. It was hard to get my head around any of this. Figures like that were still just stats I had regurgitated at sponsorship pitches. I was soon to discover the reality. Staring down at me from one of the vast industrial buildings overlooking the race village was a huge mural. Among the head-and-shoulders portraits of the 33 skippers who would be setting off to circumnavigate the world, there was a giant, painted, grinning me. The mural had been copied from a photo of one of my first training sails on *Superbigou* where I was winding a winch and smiling for the camera. I looked carefree and happy, but I remember the moment of that photo well: the ball of stress in my stomach; the desperate aversion to being on camera; the little demon on my shoulder telling me I wasn't good enough. Only one thing was going to conquer that demon, and that was completing this race successfully.

I arrived early at the race village the next day, before the crowds, to give myself a chance to take it all in. As I walked down the gangway to the long dock, I saw ahead of me a row of 33 IMOCAs ranged either side of the pontoon, extreme 60-foot race yachts gleaming in the grey light of the autumn morning. I was overcome by awe, all at once feeling a humble fan again. These sleek thoroughbreds would be taking on the toughest oceans of the world at the greatest speeds possible in a single-hulled race yacht. Over half the fleet had foils – the latest development in race boat design – which extended like wings out of the side of the boat. When trailed fast enough through the water, these foils would lift a 10-tonne boat clean out of the sea to fly about 2 metres above the surface. The technology on show here – the dedication, the daring to make it happen – was simply mind-blowing. In the past I would happily have blended into a long queue of fans to view just one of these boats up close, but here I was making my way along the pontoon to *Superbigou*, the old-timer of the bunch and my rag-tag hero. The boat had undergone a Cinderella-like transformation, but through the lens of my insecurity she seemed to me smaller than the other boats.

It wasn't the first time I'd felt insignificant in such circumstances, like the kid sister on her trike pedalling madly to keep up with the big boys on their two-wheelers. Throughout 2019, I had turned up to events feeling like a have-a-go amateur, my boat covered with mismatched stickers, the sponsor brands on its worn sails painted over with Dulux. Was it an affront to the other competitors that I dared to believe I could qualify for the VG with a 21-year-old boat and no serious funding? Perhaps it was. Deep down I knew I had as much right to be here, but nothing changed the fact that, in my eyes, these sailors were legends, and I was well aware that I still had to prove myself. I'm ambitious. I have drive. I aim high. But I wasn't here because I wanted to be a hero or receive any accolade. I believed that I had accumulated the skill and strength required to race single-handed, non-stop around the world, and I wanted to know how well I could do it, old boat or not. It is true that I never feel the finished article – and I'm sure I never will. I had, and still have, a huge amount to learn, but that excites me. I'm lucky there is so much more to achieve and that I have the desire to do it. None of us starts life on an even playing field. There is no such thing as equality of opportunity. We all need role models who have achieved great things against the odds, who have battled inequality, bad luck or bad circumstances to become the best at what they do. A great achievement will always be impressive, but when a person has managed to accomplish something significant despite having a lack of support or opportunities, it is a level above and beyond. I was proud to be in that race village. I'd got there against the odds, and it had taken every part of me – reserves of strength I didn't know I possessed – to make it happen.

Many sailors who set their cap at this trophy fall by the wayside: in the VG race village of previous years, a scattering of sailors desperate to gain last-minute funding would display on their boats a giant question mark; others would work through the night in an eleventh-hour sprint to make their vessels race-worthy, only to have their hopes dashed when they weren't accepted or couldn't raise the funds. By no means every sailor who puts in their application makes it to the starting line. I'd battered on door after door to get here. I could not have worked harder. But now that I'd burst through and was on the other side, I had to confess to feeling tired, old, and more than a little outgunned.

I tried to blinker out the race village as much as I could during that first week. We still had much to do, including the final scrutiny of safety officials and class IMOCA – the two groups that decided which boats were allowed to race in the event. Our small team turned up every day to work, either on the boat or in the communal team offices ashore. We would arrive before everyone else, and were usually the last to leave. We weren't the only ones with work still to do. On the dock there was a mix of activity from the lower-budget teams, who like us were working round the clock. It was an exciting bustle – flags flying, interviews, inspections, last-minute jobs, people up masts, in the water, on the end of foils – while the public wormed their way through a one-way system of separate walkways, taking photos and consulting their race guides. It was notable that the fully sorted teams weren't present at all. They had arrived, washed their boats, put the covers on, and left a skeleton crew to make daily checks while the skipper and core crew went home to relax, isolate themselves from COVID, work on weather strategy, eat good food and get plenty of sleep and gentle exercise before the off.

There was an amazing solidarity among those of us bustling about the dockside, tackling our never-ending job list. Although we didn't have much time to stop and talk, each day my surroundings felt more like home. I shared racing history with a few of the sailors. The Spaniard Didac Costa and Swiss Alan Roura were both on their second VG race, and I had competed against them both, in different years, racing in the Mini Transat (a transatlantic race in tiny 6.5-metre pocket rockets with very limited comms and tech allowed on board). I didn't know it then, but Didac would be my most constant racing companion for the next three months (though not within sight), and during the Vendée I was always happy to know he wasn't too far away.

The more time I spent in the race village, the more I realised that I was not alone. Other teams were fighting the same battles, and each of us was determined to make the most of what we had. Miranda Merron, a 52-year-old British sailor based in France, was an invaluable presence. Quietly confident, she was a source of sage words when I did not quite know where to turn. She was someone I'd always looked up to, who had worked hard to get this far. Like me, Miranda had entered Vendée qualification late in the cycle and, though she'd had a sponsor from the beginning, she too was working with meagre funds.

With COVID in the mix, there wasn't the same degree of relaxed milling that the crowds had enjoyed in the past. The race village was managed meticulously. Every five days, teams were tested; masks were worn at all times, both in and out of doors. Briefings were by video conference, and all official engagements had been cancelled. Across the rest of the world, we could see restrictions tightening again as the second wave of the pandemic started to take its grip. We had been promised that the race would go ahead no matter what, but with every day it became more incongruous that the crowds were allowed to mingle so closely. Eventually, after the first week, it was announced that the race village would close. France was shutting its borders to foreign travellers, once again going into lockdown. With two weeks to go, my closest friends and family would be unable to travel for a send-off, and I finally had to confront the sad inevitability that I would not be sharing my race start with the people I cared about most in the world. The idea of setting off into the unknown without my close friends' and family's support felt hard. I envied the French sailors who were already surrounded by their nearest and dearest or had gone home to wait out the final weeks in familiar surroundings. But it seemed churlish to make a fuss when so many people were much worse off. We had a lot to be grateful for. As athletes, we knew we were lucky to even be able to compete. I only had to think of the Olympians, who like us had trained over a four-year cycle for the event and had suddenly lost their chance. For some, it would never come again. We were lucky. We could still race.

Meanwhile, there was plenty to do. We still had to test new kit, fit some sails, install and then verify software updates. It is never ideal to make changes on a boat so close to a race start, but we had no choice. Doing this meant we would have to take *Superbigou* off the dock to road-test our improvements so we could put things back to how they were if they didn't work. It was risky but necessary work. Before taking the boat out, we first had to get permission from the race committee, detailing why we wanted to leave the dock and how long we'd be out there, as only five boats were allowed out at any one time. By week two we'd gained permission to make a few test sails, and we would head out with a long tick list of things to try, coming back into the dock late and relieved that things were starting to take shape.

Over the previous five months, Joff and I had worked to ensure I would have comprehensive redundancy across all boat systems – the concept of redundancy is a 'belt and braces' approach to boat preparation. If one critical component, such as my GPS system, fails during the race, I need back-ups for the back-ups to keep both competitive and safe. I had been out and tested my spares, practised changing over pilots, plugged in my spare computer, swapped data feeds and satellite domes. There was no point in having a spare if it didn't work and I could not change it over quickly. The one item that had not been road-tested was the spare rudder, which had been a last-minute purchase just six weeks previously. I knew breaking a rudder was a real risk – Alan Roura had done exactly that in *Superbigou* during his 2016 race. I also knew changing a rudder alone would be a hugely difficult task. We normally took the boat out of the water and then performed the job with two people underneath the boat on a scissor lift, and two above on the deck.

I knew that I needed to practise the change, but had struggled to find the time or the headspace in our race to the line. As we ticked items off the list in the race village, this job loomed over me, until finally I bit the bullet and told Joff I would like to practise on an early cold and murky morning, before the public began to arrive. The team assembled and laid out the ropes and pulleys on the deck, while Joff explained how the change would be made. Our biggest problem was that the rudder would float, so I had to sink it down underneath the boat using 50kg of anchor chain packed into a container to act as a counterweight. If I had to change the rudder for real I would do it from on board the boat, but in this case we agreed I would get in the water to guide the rudder stock into the boat, thus avoiding damaging anything this close to the start. I listened to instructions and manoeuvred the huge rudder over the back of the boat, pulling it beneath the surface.

The team watched from the dock, making suggestions and giving encouragement. I could see a couple of them really wanted to get on board to help me, but I knew I had to feel what it was like to do this alone. My arms and legs were following instructions, but was I taking anything in? Would I be able to replicate any of this in the ocean alone? My brain was a tangle of spaghetti. I was self-conscious in my wetsuit, its fabric clinging to my body. I didn't look or feel like an athlete about to take on one of the world's hardest sporting challenges – just a tired middle-aged woman being told what to do. The whole process was, and still is, a complete blur, but I remember thinking at the end: 'There, at least it's done. Let's just hope I never have to do it for real.'

3

STRESS-TESTING

'The race has such a diverse range of boats on the same start line with the same rules. Superbigou *is one of the oldest in the fleet, it's racing against the latest foiling boats with no handicap system, so in many ways it's a knife to a gunfight.*

'Everything on an IMOCA like this is largely custom built, the pieces that go on it take a lot of design time, they come from all over the world and building them is complicated, so putting that all together in a short amount of time and when the world has been shut down has been a challenge.

'... it's also challenging working with a boat when you don't really know its history. This is a 20-year-old boat with not a lot of records, so that makes it difficult to know what's old and what's not, so anything we haven't been sure of we've changed for peace of mind...'

Joff Brown, technical director,
7 November 2020

There has been a lot of debate about whether extreme sports enthusiasts have a physiological need for the adrenaline and dopamine highs associated with their sport. Some scientists have theorised that we have a particular genetic profile that has led to extra-large dopamine receptors, in common with drug-takers and gamblers. But any argument that we have a reckless need for thrills is belied by the reality that most of us willingly undertake months of relentless and often tedious preparation for our event. In the case of the Vendée Globe race, I was engaged in the detailed slog for years before the event. It's a strange dichotomy in our make-up, I guess.

Many who embark on a difficult enterprise talk about taking a leap of faith, but for me that sentiment applied less to crossing the start line and more to my initial decision to charter *Superbigou* and enter the Vendée Globe. Once Medallia, Smartsheet and Yondr had collectively secured enough funding to refit my boat, our approach in the run-up to the race became about meticulous tick lists rather than blind faith, as my team and I prepared for every possible eventuality. 'Expect the best, prepare for the worst' is a common mantra to many, but in the IMOCA world our attitude is more a case of 'expect the worst and be ready for it'. It's important to understand that having 'the worst' in mind isn't a case of pessimism, it's simply another tool to make success possible. When I set off around the world, I knew that half the battle would be recovering from unwanted events, breakages, mistakes and failures. Joff once told me that the race would be a 'round-the-world DIY trip', and he was right. Over the course of my 95-day race I reported 105 technical problems, a rate of over one per day. It would be naive to have any other mindset than 'shit happens – we need to be ready for it'.

Any person who sets sail across an ocean, whether alone or with a crew, needs to be prepared to deal with every eventuality. It is accepted as basic seamanship that in leaving the shore you are walking away from the safety net of help that surrounds us in our everyday lives. A thousand miles from land, and you must become the solution to your problems. I had to be equipped and trained for every worst-case scenario, and I performed drill after drill prior to the Vendée. Before each race and training session I would check every item of safety kit, and I underwent regular sea survival and emergency scenario training. As a solo racer, I was accustomed to the idea that everything would rest on me: that included managing my own medical problems as well as the boat. I had to be prepared to treat all manner of injuries and ailments, including stitching up cuts and administering injections. My team medic, Lou Adams, carefully considered the physical challenges I might have to face during the three months alone at sea and gave me training in how to self-diagnose and self-treat. We broke my body down, much as we did the boat, imagining all the damage that could occur, from cuts (which can easily become infected) to bruises and broken bones. It's no simple thing when you're trying to insert a needle into your own vein on a giant bucking bronco. Lou and I spent evenings together, in the lead-up to the race, practising on medical manikins, cuts of raw meat, and eventually myself. I learned to suture different profiles of laceration, using chicken thighs and pork trotters. I even practised suturing a head wound in a mirror with a pork trotter clingfilmed to my forehead, although we were never able to stress-test the procedure in an erratic, moving environment. The important thing was I had the tools to look after myself, because the moment I had to call for help I would be out of the race.

Any competitor in the Vendée Globe, or any other endurance racing challenge, will display much the same attitude of can-do resilience. When outside help is neither available nor allowed, your definition of an emergency changes. The skipper of a boat dismasted close to the shore may call for help immediately, whereas if it happens in the middle of an ocean they must clear the debris, make the hull safe, and then build a jury rig to get them to shore, or to the finish line. If finishing a race is even a vague possibility, then that is what we do. In 2017, I ran the last five miles of the final leg of the 'Three Peaks Yacht Race' – a multi-discipline running and sailing event – on a fractured ankle. In our 2020 Vendée Globe race, French sailor Alexia Barrier would eventually finish the race with two fractured vertebrae, so that, following her final walk off the boat with a stick, she had to go straight to hospital. And it's true, we have schooled ourselves to be Kevlar: prepared to take on anything, fix anything ... and endure.

Preparing a boat to sail around the world is a rigorous job. It requires a sharp eye for detail and a huge amount of experience. In the prologue to his book *Close to the Wind*, Pete Goss, winner of the Légion d'honneur for his heroic rescue of Raphael Dinelli in the 1996 Vendée Globe, outlines the principles enshrined in good seamanship: 'If you see that a job needs doing, do it;

when you do the job, do it well; and accept no standard but the highest. At sea you never know when you might need to call on your equipment in a crisis and you can't afford to have it let you or anyone else down. Don't get caught in a corner, always plan well ahead and make sure that you have an alternative plan up your sleeve.' – Good advice, to which every one of the skippers preparing for the race would subscribe.

As I would be racing for three months in a boat full of moving parts that would wear away with every mile it covered, it was essential that we spent the months leading up to the Vendée Globe – and are currently engaged in doing the same in preparation for the 2024 race – under the direction of Joff, my technical director, taking *Superbigou* apart, servicing and stress-testing every item on board. We checked and rechecked, determined that the boat should hit the start line in pristine condition. Once the race began, I'd need to know that I had enough tools and spares, and the necessary skills, to fix every single thing that might break, from sails to electronics. The volume and weight of every item loaded on to the boat had to be minimised so as not to compromise the boat's performance. The example often cited is of skippers cutting their toothbrush in half to save on milligrams, although in reality this is not a smart thing to do – it is hard enough to brush your teeth on a wildly moving platform without taking away the control of a long handle – but it illustrates the point. Imagine packing your cabin bag for a cheap flight, where you endlessly put in items only to take them out again in an attempt to meet the weight limit. Now picture that on a massive scale. With *Superbigou*, even the spanner set had to be analysed, spanner by spanner, so that only the ones that served the size of nuts and bolts on my boat were included, which in turn meant we had to know, and streamline, the size of every nut on the vessel.

Over the decades, death or disaster in sailboat racing has often been caused by a rushed or incomplete preparation of the vessel. If a sailor joins their newly equipped boat only three days before the race and isn't, for whatever reason, familiar with every single part of it, the odds will be against them when something goes wrong. It is not uncommon for competitors to have to return to port early in the Vendée Globe race, often after experiencing tough conditions in the Bay of Biscay, when a part of their boat fails. And while turning back to Les Sables d'Olonne doesn't disqualify you from the race (though stopping for repairs at any other port will), it puts you behind the pack, thereby losing both your sporting potential and the security that comes with sailing in close proximity to others.

If you don't have exactly the right kit and the systems in place to carry out complex repairs in the dead of night when you're wet, cold and tired, on deck or in cramped spaces, it's unlikely you'll get across the Southern Ocean and back home again. It was important that I went through every possible disaster scenario. For example, imagine my alternator belt were to break at night in rough weather and I was bashing along at speeds in excess of 20mph, deafened by the noise of wind and waves. In that scenario, I'd need to be able to act quickly and efficiently in the darkness. My batteries might have less than ten per cent charge remaining and I'd risk losing power to the autopilot. I would be minutes away from losing control of my speeding boat. That's when all those weeks of training and checking would come into their own. The better prepared my boat, the faster I would find that new belt, tools and head torch to get the job done. I knew the tools would work, I knew the belt would be dry, the correct size and brand new. However, just putting the equipment on the boat was not enough; how it is packed and stored is important too. Water is our enemy at sea; it imperils everything it touches. It rusts tools and destroys electrical components. All items needed to be individually vacuum bagged, padded and packed to survive the roller-coaster ride around the world.

Some of this work, often mundane and repetitive, was really a series of rehearsals. As with an actor, the more you rehearse the less likely you will be to fluff your lines on the first night, when you're dazzled under the stage lights. In preparing for the race, my training and checking procedures were physical activities, and yet it wasn't only that. As I named and addressed all the things that could go wrong, I became mentally prepared. If I expected to have certain problems, it would come as less of a shock when they arrived: I had already created the confidence in myself that I was ready to deal with them – I had given myself the power to diminish emotionally an alarming and stressful situation. Visualising negative outcomes may not seem like a conventional way to improve performance, and undoubtedly for short-lived sporting events where there can be no time to recover from problems it will not work. However, in many life situations where the finish line is not in sight, we have to be able to move on from our problems; the confidence of knowing we have the tools and skills to recover from a setback will bring energy to every situation.

It is one of my traits, and not one that is loved by my current technical team, that I need to experience tough situations, as well as failure, to grow my confidence. The more problems I have successfully faced, the more confident I become in my own resilience and the harder I will push when racing. If I am going to drive the boat hard in gale-force winds, I want to have pushed it to extremes while training, to uncover any unforeseen weakness – to induce failure. But this takes time. It involves many hours on the water to find the limitations of what is possible, then more time on shore repairing and re-engineering so that a problem will not occur again. That way, together we have moved our limitations. The Vendée Globe race is on a four-year cycle mainly for that reason, but in 2020 time was a luxury we didn't have. Only securing funding five months before the start of the race meant we had less than two months of actual sailing to make those vital stress tests.

The technical team could be enhanced with extra freelance labour to work at a quicker pace during the final stages of our refit, but I could not magic any more sailing hours out of the ether. Any time we had to go afloat needed to be focused and productive. With the upgrades we had made to *Superbigou*'s sails, rigging, electronics and hardware, we needed to learn quickly what the new performance potential looked like. We had to sail the boat hard to learn how quickly it would perform in as many conditions as possible, and we mapped those values to build a new set of polars (a theoretical set of performance values for all weather conditions) to help me calculate the best route to sail when racing. We also needed to practise manoeuvres, calibrate the new instruments, test and practise the swapping over to back-up systems (such as switching autopilots or installing the emergency wind wand). I needed to practise sail changes with my new sails and work out the optimum times I could make those changes according to conditions. We needed to test watermakers, batteries, back-up satellite and computer systems, video calling, media file transfers, spare remote controls, new winches. In an ideal world we would have had years to build this confidence, but I considered myself lucky to have even got the kit on the boat in the first place. Prepared to accept that we might not be able to stress-test in the way I wanted to, I just needed to make the most of the time we had.

In the end I turned to Paul Larsen, who has been involved in many extreme feats of sailing, to help me with pushing the boat and learning about performance. Paul, with his naturally restless, inquisitive nature, is a person that will push hard and keep trying to make the most of everything on offer. Our days would start with a tight brief and list of objectives, then we would head out into whatever conditions we had available to us, repeatedly sailing 15-minute legs, generating a fan shape on the water, sailing on each tack, then changing the course by 10 degrees and doing it again. Pushing the boat as hard as we could, we would start out, then ramp up to max speed, at which point I would push 'record' on my navigation software and capture some data. Once we had sailed one fan, we would start again with a different sail configuration, or using ballast, daggerboard, or less keel. Noting each of the variables on the track so the data could be analysed, the plan was that I would end up with a 'how to sail fast' guide for the boat's new configuration. We would never have time to build a comprehensive set of polars, even with the long days on the water when we would head home only once the golden light of sunset reflected off the white Jurassic cliffs of the Dorset coast. We would simply have to do the best we could in the time we had, and I was grateful for that.

On other days I would go out with a crew and we would test equipment, coming back with long job lists that would need to be managed between sailing sessions. As the Vendée came closer, these training days were interrupted increasingly by media requests. As word spread that I would be racing, an increasing number of journalists wanted to come and experience life on board, including BBC Breakfast's Mike Bushell, who gamely came out for a training sail despite having no boating experience at all. Far from resenting these media days, which I know some of my fellow competitors do, I was always grateful and excited that the mainstream media was paying attention to our sport. If I can share the human side of what I do and tell the story of my competition in a relatable way, it will help make sailing more accessible as a sport. I made sure that any reporter interested enough to really find out what we do was made to feel welcome and valued.

The summer months flew by with kind conditions. It remained dry, so the technical team were able to work uninterrupted and our sailing days were long and pleasant. However, by the time we got to September there was one gaping hole in our preparations. As the wind had blown consistently below 20 knots, I had experienced no heavy-weather training. It was only later on that month, perilously close to the start of the race, that a series of gales blew down the English Channel. I headed out to push *Superbigou* hard and test everything on board under load. It was sensible to head out with a crew in these big breeze sessions to make quick sail changes and guard against escalation of small problems under the force of wind and waves. But even with these sessions under my belt, I still felt unprepared and unconfident – I still couldn't imagine what it would be like handling the boat alone under the pressure of a race in the fierce conditions of the Southern Ocean. I always headed out with crew, and without pressure; our collective strength made sail changes quick and efficient; and we sailed a course that gave us space and time to deliver training objectives. Finally, in a bid to see how I would handle the boat under pressure, we had to get creative, and so, on 26 September, I set out to break a single-handed world record – a circumnavigation of the Isle of Wight – just as my competitors were tapering their preparations in the desire to preserve their IMOCAs before the Vendée.

RACE BLOG, 26 SEPTEMBER 2020

...Superbigou *was smoking towards St Cats. Walls of water were washing over the deck at me ... At one time the cockpit was so full of water it went over the top of my boots. I was constantly picking up ropes, checking nav, trimming sails, getting waves in the face. I felt like I was at the other end of a tennis court with a faulty ball launcher firing at me unremittingly. But oh, my word, it was fun! ... I rounded corner number three over 45 minutes ahead of the record. Full on into Armageddon ... I spent half an hour struggling to make any headway at all. I put the third reef in and was sailing with tiny sails, but the time between each tack was so short I did struggle to complete any task. ... If leg two was a tennis ball launcher, leg four was a classroom bully, pushing me over every time I stood up ... 13 tacks later I crossed the finish line. I had gone from 45 minutes ahead of the record to half an hour behind. But I had finished, and I proved to myself that I am strong, I am capable, and something like this is within my grasp.*

(Never one to give up on what I've set out to do, I do now own that record – I went back in October 2022, in my new boat, and had another go.)

In addition to preparing the boat in the weeks and months preceding the race, I had to prepare my body and mind for the event. It is over 50 years since Robin Knox-Johnston loaded up his Bermudan ketch, *Suhaili*, with the standard fare of the yachtsmen of his day before undertaking the *Sunday Times* Golden Globe Race of 1968. Over 1,500 tins of corned beef, condensed milk, baked beans and other canned staples – sterilised in boiling water and numbered – were packed into every corner of his vessel. These days, unsurprisingly, the food on board is carefully controlled and balanced, as well as being freeze-dried to reduce volume and weight.

Having the right food on board is an essential part of a successful race, and the preparation and planning of each sailor's meals must be done months in advance. A lifelong pescatarian, I also try to avoid wheat in my diet, and cannot abide a meal that has even been near a mushroom – all of which makes options quite limited. I cannot take any sugary snacks on board: after the initial rush, they have a terrible effect on my energy levels. In the early days, when I was racing minis (6.5 metre-long pocket-rocket race boats), I used to live off Haribo sweets and huge bars of chocolate. I would wake after a short nap on the hard floor of the tiny, stripped-out boat, still in my foul weather gear and covered only by a blanket. The cold, damp air would have seeped into my blood and bones so that my joints were screaming with pain. I would grab a waterproof food bag, frantically foraging for something to make life feel a little better. If the first thing that came out was a family pack of sweets, I would rip it open and start eating. I had no idea if I was even satiated or not, I just kept shovelling the sugar in until it was gone. The reaction was immediate. I would bounce up, work hard, be on my A game, but the crash that followed in the next couple of hours was always brutal. Eventually, I came to realise that if I pushed myself beyond the natural point to refuel, I couldn't control my impulses, so it was better if sugary treats were never on the boat. Now when I'm desperately hungry, I am forced into making a proper hot meal or I eat a bag of dried fruit or nuts, which doesn't evoke the same mindless eating. Even on land I try to take this approach, having found out the hard way that only with consistent blood sugar levels can I successfully deal with a large workload and stressful situations. When out on a training run, I will take a banana or a small bag of nuts to eat along the way. When I did the Three Peaks Yacht Race (double-handed), our support crew would be waiting with little avocado and peanut butter sandwiches and cups of tea at our fuelling stations. I am not alone in this way of eating – Jasmin Paris, who shot into the news when she won an ultra-running race (beating both female and male competitors), cites eating sandwiches along the way.

I worked with a nutritionist before the race, and together we studied my land-based calorie intake and expenditure, then calculated what my daily calories should be. This was a hard task, as there is very little data to go on from other sailors, and few academic papers have been written on the subject. In addition, when it comes to other endurance sports or explorers encountering challenging environmental conditions for extended periods, the vast majority of available information only relates to men. We settled on 3,000 calories per day in the warmer climates, jumping to 4,000 in the cold. As it happens, this was a woeful miscalculation, and I would pay the price in the second half of the race.

The food was packed into 24-hour bags, and I had a rolling ten-day menu. My objective was to eat the contents of one bag each day. We had teamed with Aparito, the wearable med-tech company founded by my friend and fellow sailor Dr Elin Haf Davies, to record and validate some of the physical changes that my body would go through during the race. Each bag was logged, and anything I didn't eat each day was recorded in an app. We used a Garmin watch to calculate how much energy I was burning through activity.

My average day pack and consumption would look like this:

Freeze-dried main meals – 2 in warm weather, 3 in cold – 800 kcal each

2 pouches nut butter – providing protein and fat – 500 kcal each

Freeze-dried fruit – providing vitamins and fresh taste

1 tin oily fish every 7 days

In terms of fitness, sailing the IMOCA is a very physical experience, with heavy loads to manage in awkward positions (including 100kg sails), so I needed to ensure that I had a strong core and was using the right muscles to do the right job. During lockdown, as I couldn't visit the gym I built my own in the garage – nothing fancy, just some TRX kit, a bench and a few dumbbell weights. Just existing on the boat would be exhausting as it is constantly moving, so to walk around without holding on to anything means you need to be in command of your core and have good balance. To move from one end of the boat to the other below decks I would have to climb through the bulkheads – solid frames across the boat with small round holes cut in them for a person to crawl through – and as the boat would invariably throw me around, flexibility was important. I installed a 'coffee grinder' in the middle of my cockpit – a little like an upside-down bicycle that I operate with my arms – which would allow me to drive the big winches on either side of the boat to put the sails up and down. To be effective on this machine, I needed strong legs, a good body position, strong arms and a big lung capacity. With sailing, there's rarely a time when you're not putting your body under some sort of stress.

I have always enjoyed running as a second sport alongside my sailing: it is a great way to improve cardiac fitness and can be done at any time, anywhere in the world. In the days and weeks before the race, it also became my mental salvation. As well as the endorphins it releases, it is one of the few activities that allow me to take my mind to another place. When I run, it helps me gain perspective, have great ideas and clear my head, which often becomes overcrowded with the day to day. In the days the boat was on the dock, this outdoor exercise kept me motivated and stimulated, dragging me away from my computer into the natural light to interact with the elements, rain or shine.

During my time ashore I was supported by the awesome team at Davies Chiropractic, treated regularly by Linn Erixon Sahlström, herself an elite ultra-runner who understands the demands of endurance sport on a body. We built a programme to enable me to self-treat my injuries on the boat and worked on conditioning exercises and strength building to manage existing conditions, the echoes of injuries accumulated over a lifetime of sport and adventure.

SIGNING UP TO BE A LAB RAT

Monitoring the effects of extreme sport on female athletes

Dr Elin Haf Davies is a Welsh adventurer and the founder of Aparito, a med-tech company that provides solutions for management of long-term medical conditions. I had met Elin several years before; we became friends and subsequently raced together as part of the only all-female team to win the Three

Peaks Yacht Race, in 2016. Owing to the dearth of historic data relating to female endurance athletes, I asked Elin if she might like to help me record some data. She jumped at the chance, designing an app that could interact with a smartwatch to collect data during my race. In a subsequent interview, Elin said: 'There is very little research on the effects of extreme sport and adventures on female athletes and that's something we want to explore in more detail. We'll be tracking Pip as she travels around the globe, looking at the impact of intense physical exercise over a prolonged period of time.'

In order to do this, I wore a Garmin vívosmart 4, which tracked my sleep, calorie intake and heart rate. They wished to analyse how much of my time would be spent in the higher heart rate zone and how much at my resting heart rate. If my heart rate were to start increasing over a long period of time, it would mean that I was not recovering and repairing muscle as efficiently as I could be. (In the first week of the race they saw a higher heart rate for the first few days, probably as a result of all the nerves, but as I relaxed into the race I was back down to an average of 52.1 beats per minute. A mast climb – terror – caused the graph to jump all over the place.)

We would track my daily calorie intake through a food diary, with the aim of making sure I didn't fall into too much of a calorie deficit. My daily mood would also be monitored, and every three days I would have to complete a problem-solving test and numerical challenge. Elin explained: 'These tests are based on those neurologists use to assess patients for dementia, the concept being that sleep deprivation impacts how alert you are and how quickly you can think things through. We will not only measure the accuracy of Pip's answers, but also how long she takes to complete them, which will give us a real indication of how on her game she is.'

Much like the boat preparation, my physical training pre-race was time bound. With no previous research to fall back on, we could have no idea how my body would change or manage with the three months of sport that lay ahead. I knew I could have been in better shape before the race. I tried to build muscle and to raise my cardio fitness but there were only 24 hours in every day. I was stressed and tired, but I was there. There comes a point in every preparation where no more can be done. Time cannot be halted or created, and the best we can do is to use it wisely. When I'd turned up to the race village, we had three weeks left to finalise details on the boat; we had made an incredible job with the time that we had. But now no more could be done. I had to take the fruits of so many people's contributions over the last 18 months and use it to race around the world.

4

Pacing Myself

I have always been massively inspired by the thrill of the unknown, the concept of starting something with no idea what the outcome will be. It is both terrifying and exhilarating: I feel entirely exposed and yet completely liberated going toe-to-toe with personal frontiers. At the start of the Vendée Globe race, I had no idea either how it would end or what would unfold over the next three months. I believed I could finish the race well – there would be no point in starting if that hadn't been the case – but there could be no guarantee that I would finish at all.

I knew from the start of my campaign that I could not win the Vendée Globe race with the second oldest boat in the fleet and only one year of racing in the class, but in no way did that diminish my desire to compete. Over the course of the project, it was interesting to see other people's reactions to this information. The first question they would regularly ask, when discovering the project for the first time, was 'Can you win?' When I answered in the negative, there would be a pause. The brave ones might continue with, 'Why do it then?' Others would consign my project to a life experience 'bucket list' adventure rather than a sporting endeavour, which was more painful to me than being asked 'why?'

I had come to terms early in my career with the fact that without the right resources, my sporting performance would be capped, but that this would not diminish my sporting objectives. Before each race, I needed to clearly define what success looked like according to my own individual circumstances. This was never just about taking part, but always about driving forwards.

I would measure my success or failure against tailored objectives designed to stretch me in every way. Never was this more important than on the start line of the Vendée Globe, a race where, historically, only 55 per cent of competitors made it to the finish line.

On the start line I had four clear goals in my mind, one general, one for sporting performance, one personal, and one for business and legacy:

1 General: To finish the race and join the elite group of 74 sailors who had made this happen in the past.
2 Sporting performance: To finish the race in a time that would have put me in the top three finishers for the year *Superbigou* was built. Comparison to the year 2000 results.
3 Personal: To reach the end of the race knowing I had made the most of the opportunity I had created. To never back away from the option to sail harder or faster, no matter what my position in the fleet.
4 Business and legacy: To tell the best English-language story of the race, encourage followers to watch my progress, attract attention from the mainstream media, and give a good return to my sponsors.

I reminded myself of these goals as I drove through the deserted streets of Les Sables d'Olonnes on the morning of 8 November to start the race.

With France in lockdown, the start was very different from how I had imagined it over the previous 30 years. There were no crowds, no hugs, no family to send me off. I walked down the dock alone, having been in isolation for the previous days to avoid any last-minute risk of catching COVID. It was a lonely moment, but I remained grateful as we left the port that we were the ones who got to compete. Motoring down the canal that would normally be lined with hundreds of thousands of people, fans were instead hanging out of the windows of houses and flats, banging saucepans and cheering loudly, while the parade of boats was livestreamed to an international audience in their locked-down homes.

It took two hours for the whole fleet to leave the port and assemble close to the start line, by which time thick fog had descended across the course. I had a crew of five on board – Joff, Lou, Paul, Paddy and our photographer, Richard – to document the start. It was tense and gloomy; at times, the fog was so thick we couldn't see the top of the mast. There were 33 IMOCAs, with around 100 RIBs and other support boats in the same area, all milling around, some at high speeds. The risk of a collision in these circumstances was huge. The stress was writ large on both mine and Joff's faces. The race was due to be broadcast live on terrestrial television, as well as online, and over one million fans were tuned in and waiting. We just needed to get across that line and go.

After two hours of delay, the fog all at once started to lift, and our race committee wasted no time in sending us off. Notified by radio, we turned *Superbigou* towards the line, and before I knew it, my crew were scrambling to get off the boat, keen not to incur a penalty for me by remaining too long. The hugs were brief, and then the RIB was gone. I checked my timing, unfurled a big sail and headed for the line. The aerobatic arm of the French Air Force, the Patrouille de France, flew across the fleet, blazing red, white and blue trails behind them. I paused in the trimming of sails to take in the scene, while *Superbigou* charged towards the line. I was in the middle of the fleet with some great boats behind me; the sun was blazing, the sea sparkling blue. Two RIBs, full of team members and supporters, appeared alongside the boat, everyone cheering, smiling, laughing and crying. We had made it happen: this was our first success. Now all I had to do was sail around the world.

As I sailed away from the start line, and the other competitors shrank into small outlines on the horizon, the sheer magnitude of what lay ahead settled on me in a way it never had before. I had been so focused on getting to this point – banking experience, climbing the ranks, finding a boat, searching for a sponsor, starting many a journey over the last ten years not knowing how or where it would end, not least of which was the final leap of faith to make the Vendée Globe start line – that I'd never really considered what it would feel like to sail around the world, or how I would manage to remain competitive for weeks on end and through the Southern Ocean. I just knew I wanted to do it. There was, of course, a certitude in my heart and mind that I would finish the race, and that I could sail my boat competitively, but when I really tried to focus on what lay ahead of me, all my frames of reference ran out. The longest solo race in which I had ever competed was only 19 days. I had once been at sea alone for 48 days, but not in a racing environment. The furthest south I had ever sailed was to the Patagonian coast of Argentina. I had never experienced the Southern Ocean and, try as I might, I could not visualise what my time beyond these lived experiences would look like.

The vast expanse of time and ocean that lay ahead of me could not be put into a neat game plan. I could not predict my route, how the boat and I would perform, what weather might help or hinder progress, or even if some unforeseen and unavoidable event, such as a collision with a semi-submerged piece of sea junk, might end my race for good. It became clear to me that I needed to find a strategic way to pace myself both mentally and physically. I needed to cage the wild and unwieldy expanse of time that stretched ahead, because trying to dash directly to the finish would destroy me within weeks. My strategy needed to be smart, balancing the constant basic need to sail the boat faster than my competitors with the long-term goal of arriving at the finish. Push the boat too hard and I could risk damage that might end my race; push myself too hard and I could burn out after a couple of weeks. But equally, were I to choose a more conservative approach in order to preserve the boat, it would surely lead to fellow competitors leaping to a new weather system, and the expanding distance between us making it impossible to reach them again. I had to find a way of balancing my long- and short-term objectives and know when to push and when to rest, taking myself step by step to the finish line.

There is no fixed course to follow when you race around the world. There is a start line and a finish line, and a direction of travel. We are geographically bound by the land, and there is an ice limit that defines the furthest latitude south that competitors are allowed to sail. But within these confines, all sailors must plot their own best course, determined by the design and capability of their boat, their competitive goals, attitude to risk, and mental fortitude, as well as the technical problems they'll encounter on the way, and of course the weather. When we race round the world, we are not navigating around continental landmasses so much as around weather systems. We can view the weather as friend or foe – it can slingshot us forward or create an impenetrable barrier across the direct route to the finish, with mirror-flat seas or waves the size of tower blocks holding us back. Though the broad path chosen over the past 20 years is roughly similar, at a local level every skipper must make their own decisions, balancing individual objectives and obstacles with the knowledge and understanding of how their boat will perform in any given weather condition. A skipper who is risk averse, having to manage damage on board, or who is simply exhausted, may choose a slower route with smaller waves and less wind than their fully functioning, gung-ho opposite number. But unlike the fable of the hare and the tortoise, this elite-level world-class race cannot be won by a slow plod. In every edition of the Vendée Globe race, performance records have been broken; over time, as reliability of boats and designs have improved, so the intensity of competition has increased. Gone are the days when just getting to the finish of a round-the-world race was enough to secure a top ten position. With boats that are now capable of outrunning weather systems, and the current course record set at fewer than 75 days, there is no choice but to push. The trick is knowing when to back off. I needed a clear-cut way to manage these long- and short-term objectives, while balancing performance, risk and energy till the finish.

The added complication when navigating a path through the world's oceans is that a weather forecast is just what it says on the tin. It is a forecast, not a certainty, and though weather prediction models are astoundingly accurate and readily available even in the middle of an ocean, as navigators we base our decisions not only on the predicted weather outcomes but also on our own degrees of confidence in those weather models.

To pace myself well while racing, I must be aware of and assess continually the many risks that encroach on both performance and survival. It sounds dull, I know – the concept of risk assessment conjures up grids of red, orange and green boxes relating to slips, trips and falls around the workplace, not a plunge headlong through gale-force winds a thousand miles from land. But in my mind, risk is subjective; it cannot be pinned down to one quantifiable thing. The risks that I encountered racing around the world would change on a daily, sometimes hourly, basis. From an outsider's perspective, sailing around the world alone on a 60-foot yacht is fraught with risk, and I wouldn't disagree. But those known risks are the ones we acknowledge and mitigate before we're even afloat. In the previous chapter, I described how as a team we recognise and prepare for the worst that may happen, and equip the boat with tools, spares and safety kit to recover from most conceivable eventualities. And once afloat, I use a process of dynamic risk assessment to dictate the priorities and the pace at which I should work over long races.

Dynamic risk is not always obvious, but it is the first thing to consider when trying to divine the right pace to perform in any given moment. The risk could be the centre of a huge weather system barrelling across the ocean, it could be a small island in the middle of the ocean that I must navigate around, or a competitor gaining fast and breathing down my neck, or a rip in the mainsail that will only get bigger if I don't stop to repair it. Or maybe it might simply be that I am too tired to make good decisions or too weak to manage the boat and keep myself safe. Pushing the boat and myself hard would inevitably increase the risk of damage, yet not pushing hard would risk my falling short of performance objectives.

In late November, the Bay of Biscay can be as brutal a stretch of water as you will find anywhere in the world. Even now, with my Southern Ocean experience behind me, I can say categorically that the Bay of Biscay has served me up the worst sailing experiences of my life, including having been in a yacht that was turned upside down by a 12-metre wave during a hurricane force storm early in the 2000s. Known as the Golfe de Gascogne by the French, the Bay of Biscay is a relatively small body of water between France and Spain, opening out to 5,500km of open water to the west, where wind and waves can grow in size and power as they travel, untrammelled, from America. The continental shelf to the east, where the depth sharply decreases from 4km to 120 metres, causes the waves to ricochet like pinballs off the land. It is sea state, not wind strength, that makes conditions challenging. Any sailor who crosses the Bay of Biscay needs to keep a keen, experienced eye on the weather forecast. If you're trying to judge swell it isn't easy, because swell isn't directly linked to the conditions around you. The long, sloping waves that precede a depression will build up to around 5 metres high, and as the centre of the system approaches, the waves will be amplified by the wind, making them both bigger and steeper. Waves grow with time and distance, so by the time a deep weather system has made its way across the Atlantic it is not uncommon to find 9-metre waves at its centre. With the continental shelf in the mix, this sudden change in water depth can cause waves to break, so it is no wonder that skippers can experience a nausea-making and hairy roller-coaster of a ride or that the bay has been nicknamed the Valley of Death. Many a square-rigger of the past, designed to run downwind at speed, has been dashed to bits on a lee shore, having been boxed in to the bay and unable to run off before the wind to get out of trouble.

The usual weather patterns of late autumn in the North Atlantic are a procession of never-ending depressions, with aggressive, trailing weather fronts that start at Nova Scotia and fire themselves relentlessly across the Atlantic to arrive in the Bay of Biscay and western Irish shores. Nearly every race leaving Northern Europe in November will end up crossing a weather front in the Biscay during the first two or three days of competition. There are almost always boats in a Vendée Globe race that have to return, limping, to port after trouble in the bay. This rarely spells the end of their race – the rules allow for a ten-day window to return to port, repair the damage, and restart – as competitors are nothing if not tenacious. Nothing about the bay promises to make the start easy on us. It is not simply the weather and sea state we have to watch: the continental shelf is a favourite fishing spot for trawlers, and as you round Cape Finisterre the shipping lanes are busy with merchant vessels. In the wide open sea you can afford to take a nap, but here you have to be constantly watchful. It is even worse at the end of the race when both you and your boat are shadows of your former selves. Sleep deprived, at the end of your rope physically and mentally, you are at real risk of a collision.

On the second night of the race, the fleet sailed out to cross a cold front. This aggressive weather feature causes a continual strengthening of the wind and sea state, building to a crescendo of intense force, coupled with a sudden change in wind direction, resulting in breaking seas – and, often, breaking boats. Our first front did not disappoint, as if to affirm the power and brutality of the oceans we had chosen to take on. As we sailed into our second night afloat, the wind and sea state steadily built. It was ink-black, the sky totally covered in cloud so that not a star nor a slither of moonlight could cut through the darkness. This complete deprivation of vision beyond the halo of my head torch made the oncoming storm seem like a hidden monster. I could feel the power of the waves easily pushing the boat around, but I couldn't see them – neither their height nor shape – or tell at which point they would land. I could hear waves breaking, and detect the different levels of noise: a deep rumbling like an approaching juggernaut; breaking water, violent and painful like someone upending a drawer of glass from the top of the dishwasher on to a stone floor; the fizz and hiss of spume being blown off the deck of the boat and rigging, something that only happens in the strongest of winds, where the sound carries as much venom and menace as a hiss ever could. Every hour, the wind climbing, I pulled on my drysuit and lifejacket and headed on to the deck to reduce sail, until *Superbigou* was being propelled by tiny triangles of material, but the boat still felt overpowered. In my pre-Vendée training, I had only encountered a maximum wind strength of 35 knots. Though I had confidence in the boat, it would have been irresponsible to test it in higher winds – when in the open ocean, I would choose to avoid winds of over 35 knots, at which point racing strategy becomes more about damage limitation than racing hard. As we sailed closer to the front and the wind kept increasing, my head was full of horrific thoughts about sails ripping or waves swamping the boat. I sat in my drysuit down below, miserably watching the wind strength increase from 35 to 40, then 45 knots. The boat was slamming into the oncoming sea, each crash resonating through the tight carbon structure, sounding like it was about to split in two. I was constantly thrown into the air, landing back on the beanbag, the wind knocked out of my chest. Sleep was out of the question: I was cold, wet and anxious, just wanting it to be over. I knew I had to trust the boat was strong and well prepared, but just two nights in and I felt my race was on a knife edge. At its peak, in the black horror before dawn, the wind reached 50 knots, then at around 0700 hours the weather front finally passed overhead. The change was brutal, with a horrendous sea state; though the wind strength had mercifully dropped, the wind direction had changed by 90 degrees, meaning the course I now sailed with *Superbigou* was side-on to the still enormous waves.

Before the front, I had loaded all my spare sails into the bow to weight it against the might of the oncoming waves. Now the waves were to the side, this was making *Superbigou* slow and hard to handle.

It was the third day of our race; the pack was tight, and I was lying around 23rd position. I needed to maintain speed to stick with the fleet, which meant opening the forward hatch and winching all four 50+-kilo sails on deck, one by one, and moving them to the back of the boat. As I worked, the erratic motion of the boat constantly made me stumble and fall. I was deluged by great, slow-moving walls of water that were big enough to lift me off my feet as they crashed down on deck, and my open cockpit filled with water multiple times. The work never stopped. I had not slept for longer than ten minutes in the last 36 hours and had not eaten much in the last 24 hours; the adrenaline of the start and the stress of encountering this first front had killed my appetite and stopped me from sleeping. I struggled with energy, and as my muscles filled with lactic acid my work rate began to stop and start as my strength failed me. I knew that pausing to sleep or eat would be at the cost of boat speed. If I was not to fall behind, I had to retrim the boat for the new conditions. With my lack of experience racing in this fleet, I had planned to use a group of similar boats to help manage my pace at the start of the race. If I were to fall behind them, I would risk losing that opportunity. No matter how tired I felt, I must put up more sail, move all my sails from the front locker to outside on the back of the boat, and push on. I could slow down my rate of work to match my energy levels so long as I got the work done. I methodically went through my to-do list as I watched the sail slowly inch up the mast, one cycle of the winch at a time, promising myself tea and a rest when it was all over. But I would not stop until *Superbigou* was back up to course and speed again. At one point, a rogue wave caught me just as I was hauling a sail through the hatch. The weight I had just removed from the bow was instantly replaced by gallons of seawater, and I would have no choice but to go into the bow locker with a bucket and sponge to empty it out. After the bow was empty and the rest of the sails were moved, I performed a final check below decks to look for any damage from pounding through the front. In the back of the boat I discovered more water, and realised that the steering connections had worked loose from one rudder. I had no choice but to climb back through the black carbon tunnels, gather my tools and a bucket, and spend another hour sorting out the problem. It felt like my limbs were made of lead; my brain was foggy, and I was near to tears. *Would it ever stop?*

I have a name for that state you get to, when every dial in your body is on empty. I call it 'post-frontal fatigue'. Your muscles ache, you are damp and slightly chilled, your mind and body are out of fuel. The best remedy would be to spend a lazy day eating soup and reading a book by an open fire. Post-frontal fatigue is not a bad feeling – I quite like that depleted sense when you've done a lot of exercise – but for us skippers in the race there is no book reading or open fire. The thing about ocean racing is that time is not defined by the passage of the sun; it's mostly about the passage of weather. Our rest is not just based on our own needs, because we have to see to the needs of the giant machines we are driving, and even when we have slightly more stable conditions, what would be our downtime is taken up with maintenance tasks and troubleshooting to ensure that we make it cleanly through the next weather system.

I was both surprised and happy at this early position in the fleet. On paper I was ranked 32nd out of 33, according to the age of my boat and my experience in the fleet. The fleet was split between daggerboard boats like mine – which had flat boards that dropped through the hull into the water below to stop the boats slipping sideways through the water – and the foilers. This generation of boats had first been launched in the last Vendée Globe race in 2016; instead of daggerboards, they had wing-like structures protruding horizontally from the sides of their hulls, which would lift the boats clean out of the water, giving them performance potential as much as 8 knots faster than my older boat at certain wind angles. Now, just a couple of days into the race, I had *La Mie Câline*, a boat ranked much higher, on my tail. Having Arnaud Boissières (nicknamed Cali) breathing down my neck, with three previous successful Vendée Globe races under his belt, only added to the adrenaline-fuelled experience. And at the point when I decided I could afford to take a nap, I had just settled down to sleep when my AIS vessel proximity alarm went off. Behind me, *La Mie Câline* was on a collision course. I breathed a sigh of relief when he passed us, even though it had been exciting to battle it out with a foiler.

RACE BLOG, 12 NOVEMBER 2020

Morning! All good on Superbigou. *We are currently gliding along in 10 knots of wind, flat seas, and have spent the whole night fighting off* La Mie Câline, *which finally overtook me about 30 minutes ago … I expect to peel to the jib any minute now. I have a full jobs list of sewing and splicing to get through in the final post-front clear-up. I need to get some sleep, and eat more, or I will be stuck in the granny gear for the rest of the race.*

SLEEP – THE LONG AND THE SHORT OF IT

How I'm preparing to sail solo around the world with very little sleep...

As any offshore sailor would tell you (particularly solo sailors), sleeping during an ocean race takes on a completely different form to what we're used to on dry land.

When solo sailing, you can't have the luxury of a dedicated time to sleep. You sleep when and how you can. The top three questions I ask myself when I'm on the water are: Is the boat going in the right direction? Is the boat safe? Have I had enough sleep? I ask these questions at regular intervals every day. I will push myself through hours with very little sleep to keep the boat safe and performing, but I'm always looking for opportunities to bank sleep. I try to get the minimum for me to function, trying to get four hours of naps in a 24-hour period.

In terms of training, I've never been able to practise my offshore sleeping patterns when ashore. I learned to nap through trial and error during my first solo voyages. During these first trips I tried to learn the best times to sleep and the best lengths for me to sleep, and I learned that it's all about making sure you wake up in the right phase of the sleep cycle.

The first two weeks I spent alone at sea I kept a diary every time I tried to sleep, noting the time of day, how long I slept, and what I felt like when I woke up. I found that my body would naturally tell me what worked, and now I know that 0–40 minutes is about the right length for a short nap – if I wake up during that phase, I will feel refreshed. If I try to wake up between 40 minutes and 2 hours of sleep, it can be detrimental to my performance because I feel more tired, groggy and disorientated. Essentially, I try to stay in the light sleep phase of my sleep cycle and avoid dropping into deep sleep.

In a typical monophasic sleep cycle (sleeping for a single period in a 24-hour stretch), we spend hours transitioning between light sleep and deep sleep, then eventually move to REM sleep at the end of the night. When I have been offshore *for several weeks, I find that REM sleep (which is associated with re-energising the brain) can occur within minutes of falling asleep – I can cut to very vivid dreams within a ten-minute nap.*

HOW I SLEEP ON THE BOAT

I like to sleep sitting up, either in my navigation chair or on my beanbag, and do so for about 30 or 40 minutes at a time. Sometimes I will take my beanbag outside and sleep under the cuddy. I usually wake myself up naturally: it's just so subconscious. There are times when I might oversleep on the boat, but I have an alarm that vibrates against my collarbone, and several audible alarms too. Changes in how the boat is sailing will also wake me up – it could be a sudden change in motion, or a flap of the sails I wasn't expecting. It's amazing how naturally in tune you are with your environment when you're on water. As it's a busy, noisy environment, even a lack of noise might stir you from slumber ...

I know there are going to be moments during a Vendée Globe when it will feel impossible to get rest. When I'm in the Southern Ocean and get the big breeze and big waves I will be anxious and frightened at times. There will be a lot of adrenaline pumping through my body, stopping me from falling asleep, which can lead to a sleep deficit from which it is difficult to recover.

SLEEP TIPS

My advice for anyone attempting to sail solo or take part in an extreme sport is just to keep banking sleep whenever you can. You're always going to need more sleep, and you're never going to be at a stage where you're fully rested, so keep grabbing it at every opportunity.

Every one of us has different circadian rhythms, and most of my competitors will have worked at some point with a sleep specialist to understand their own particular profile and needs. The trick is to strike a balance between getting enough to function adequately and avoiding sleep inertia, which generally happens when a deep sleep cycle is interrupted. Think of how groggy and bewildered you feel when you're woken from a deep sleep. This sleep inertia can be a dangerous few minutes for sailors who need to be fully awake to deal with sudden crises.

Solo sailing never allows you the freedom to organise your day according to your 'flow states' – those times when you're feeling energetic and best able to function. In everyday life, most of us know to avoid doing cognitively demanding tasks when we're in an energy slump. We get to recognise when those slumps are likely to hit and avoid them when we make our plans. The natural troughs between those high-functioning, energetic bouts occur when the brain is undergoing its own recharge and repair. You might be familiar with the post-lunch slump and the second wind you get in the early evening. I do try to roll with my natural energy rhythms, but very often I simply have to push through the trough.

Even after the front had passed over – the waves slowly subsiding to calmer, flatter seas – I continued to drive myself hard. I was now out of the Biscay and making my way south; we were properly heading down the Atlantic and I wanted to make the most of every last breath of the dying wind to coast south as far as we could – similar to when you pedal hard downhill, hoping your momentum will propel you through the dip and take some of the sting out of the uphill section. When the wind died, mid-morning of 12 November, I decided to use the time to do some of the outstanding maintenance that had made its way to the job list over the last week. There was such a lot to remember – checks, routine tasks, media commitments – and I'd taken to writing notes to myself on the bulkhead in front of the computer station. Here, I could clearly see the last times I checked the keel and rudders (which needed to be done every two days). My job list was scrawled along the bottom, on a level with my beanbag, so that my eyes could focus on it the moment I woke from a nap.

In the early days of the race when I asked myself 'where is the risk?', I was more concerned with damage, and would mitigate this through keeping my boat in pristine condition and staying in contact with rather than racing ahead of my 'peer group' – the boats with similar designs and age of build against which I benchmarked my performance. I gave each task on board every ounce of my energy and was blissfully unaware of the erosive nature of the three months of sport that lay ahead; and perhaps now, with the benefit of hindsight, I would elevate exhaustion, muscle wastage and energy depletion in the ranking of dynamic risks and give my own self higher priority. But the fact remains: I finished the race, so whatever my naivety, the strategy worked.

RACE BLOG, 13 NOVEMBER 2020

It's got a lot warmer in the last 24 hours and it's finally time to change out of my thermals. So I took the time to have a shower in the cockpit, then change to my next set of clothes – marked 'warm weather' on their vacuum bag. Now that is exciting. I cleaned and sorted the living accommodation, then got out my rigging kit to do some work on the deck. Most notably to put a new cover on the tack line of the J3, which had chewed through in only five days of sailing. This is something I clearly need to watch. I had also noticed in my post-front inspection that the tie-back elastics on the second set of spreaders had broken. It had been niggling at me as it didn't seem right to just ignore this one week into the race. I hate climbing the rig at sea, it is utterly terrifying!

By 13 November, there had already been upset in the fleet. Strong frontrunner Jérémie Beyou had damaged his sails and rigging during the front and had been forced to head back to port, thus destroying his chances of a win. The front of the fleet was already 365 miles ahead of my position, but I had found a pack to sail with, which offered a level of comfort during the days. It helped gauge a good starting pace, similar to a mass-participation marathon when competitors are started in waves according to their expected finishing time, and this dictated a benchmark from which I could improve. Having held pace with my pack for a number of days, I saw my first opportunity to push ahead. If I were to take the calculated risk of jumping on the back of tropical depression Theta, I could use the stronger winds to get me south. The majority of the fleet had chosen a course to the west, avoiding the strongest winds and biggest seas, the smoother path potentially preserving their boats for the long run. Didac Costa and I had both seen our opportunity to get south to the Canaries by getting closer to the centre of the depression, then gybing back out again. In this instance, when I asked myself 'Where is the risk?', the answer was not clear cut. To sail close to the centre of this tropical storm was not in itself a huge risk: I was in control of the boat, I could choose to bail out at any time and head west to join the pack. The greater risk would have lain in wasting the opportunity. After all, the boat was designed for this type of sailing, and these levels of wind and waves would become the norm later on in the Southern Ocean. I would have to push myself hard, yes, and bigger conditions naturally meant less rest and more stress, but this was a RACE.

It was a lot of fun being neck and neck with Didac again after having been competitors nearly a decade before in the Mini Transat of 2011, when he had been sailing *Kingfisher*, the boat Ellen MacArthur famously sailed in her Vendée Globe race. On the weather chart, Theta was a tight red circle of strong winds and big waves ahead of me. It made me anxious just to look at the chart. In reality, the sky was a greyed-out mass of thick cloud and the sea state flecked with white-crested waves. I could feel the energy building in the wind and sea around the boat. A quick look at the race tracker confirmed that only Didac and I had made this choice, and I briefly wondered if I had made a wrong call to choose performance over safety this early in the race. But the sea around me looked familiar; I had sailed in gale-force winds hundreds of times before and in much smaller boats. I felt in control: at any time, I could head back west to calmer seas. The boat speed increased as *Superbigou* started to surf the waves, harnessing the power of nature then forging forwards. As the waves built, *Superbigou* surged ahead. At times its bow would be lifted into the air by a wave of 5 metres or more; for a moment the bow would just hang in thin air, before an explosion of water crashed over the deck. The boat was straining under the increased wind strengths, but unlike the merciless crashing into oncoming seas of our first weather front, this time we powered forwards on each breaking crest. I thought back to the heavy-weather training during my race preparation: everything felt as it should be. This was what I was out here to do.

When the barometer had fallen as much as I dared let it, I gybed back west to stay out of the strongest winds and was immediately gratified to see that both Didac and I had pulled ahead on the race tracker. The risk of losing an opportunity to advance had outweighed a fear of damaging the boat; I had learned from the experience and set myself new benchmarks to work against, a process I would continue throughout the race.

5

TACKLING UNCERTAINTY

As we flew into the second week of the race, I had set a pace I was desperate to keep up. At the beginning of the race, I had laid down performance benchmarks against other skippers with older non-foiling boats, and those on their first Vendée Globe. Didac was my closest frame of reference, in a boat the same age as mine, although on his second Vendée. If I could stay close to or ahead of him, I would be pleased. There was a pack of 2007-generation boats, much more modern in design, which I marked as a high-performance target, and these were already some 250 miles behind me. I was riding higher than I had dared to imagine. There had been more post-start problems across the fleet: in total, three boats, including two of the brand-new foilers, had had to head back to Les Sables d'Olonnes for repairs. Kojiro Shiraishi, the Japanese solo-racing veteran, had also suffered damage, having ripped his mainsail in half when the autopilot failed and crash-gybed his boat. But the whole fleet was racing now, and by 15 November, with four damaged foilers behind me, I was lying 21st out of 33. Sailing the boat was pure joy. I felt genuinely free, as if the lid had come off a huge cage and there was nothing to restrict me.

Working a big boat hard on the open ocean is an experience that involves every one of your senses. It forces you to be present in every second; it engages you at every level. The work is physical, the loads are high, the boat constantly demanding. In my day to day, I was lifting, dragging, pulling, winding – often bracing with one hand, while the other arm, backed up by the rest of my bodyweight, was left to do the hard work. Just standing on a constantly moving surface used energy. My brain and body had to make continual micro-adjustments to keep me standing and keep whatever my attention was on in focus. Every time conditions on the ocean changed, I had to react with a corresponding alteration in the trim of the boat. These changes can involve hours of physical effort.

SAILS AND HOW TO SURVIVE THEM

I carried eight sails around the world. Three of them were in constant use: the mainsail, J2 and J3 were permanently hoisted, but there were a further three of the eight that I could fly from the bowsprit (the stocky frame that extends beyond the bow of the boat). These were my downwind sails, bigger and more powerful than the J2 and J3, each of which was designed to perform in specific conditions. Part of my success would come of knowing which sail to use when, so that I could get the best performance out of the boat, and these sail changes were the hardest work I had to do. They can take between 45 minutes and an hour, and during that time I would have to work relentlessly. First, I would select my new sail from the pile stacked on the back of the boat, then I would take the straps off the stack, pull the 70-kilo sopping-wet bag out from under the others and drag it to the front of the boat. The sails weighed the same amount as I did, and I was having to lift and drag them at awkward angles on a moving surface. On one occasion early on in the race, I put out my lower back trying to lift a sail bag. I went to stand up, and a stabbing pain shot down my back and legs. The breath went out of me. I couldn't straighten up. Every time I tried, I got dizzy, and struggled to breathe through the pain. I managed to do the ties back on the stack, and then, lying on my belly, used my arms to pull myself along the deck, slithering into the cockpit and headfirst down the steps to the cabin. The pain was so intense I was crying – not because I felt sad, but because it was my body's natural reaction to the trauma. I took the strongest painkillers I had on board and waited for them to take effect before going out and trying again. For a further three days after that, every movement took intense focus and self-talk. I had to remind myself that it was just a pulled muscle and moving was good for it. Every time I had to grind the winches or move kit around the deck, I would mentally lock on to the pain in my back. Far from ignoring it, I would focus on it, feel its heat, acknowledge its presence – but I refused to let it stop me. I had great medical support during my race from our incredible team medic, Lou, but also from my badass chiropractors, Linn and Shelley. I trusted their advice, so when they said, 'It's only pain. You can work through it', I knew it must be so.

Back to my sail changes: after I had moved the new sail to the bow of the boat, dragging it along the deck and tying it in place, the original sail would need to be furled. This involved rolling the sail on to its cable at the front of the boat, like a perpendicular blind. I would do this from the cockpit, hunched over a winch, winding the handle in the top round and round. For every three turns of the winch, I would get one turn on the sail. It took me between 250 and 300 turns to furl the sail, depending on the wind strength. In stronger winds I needed a lower gear, so more turns were required. This would take around five to eight minutes, during which I would be at max heart rate, sweating hard under my many layers, breathing rapidly, lactic acid burning through my muscles. At night, I would need to pause every now and again to throw the spotlight of a high-powered torch on to the sail and check progress. I cannot count the number of times I felt crushed by the sight of an almost complete sail still flapping in the dark, despite what seemed like an age of winding. Once it was tightly furled, I would need to take it down. Unlike most boats on the course, I had to hoist and drop all my sails from the mast, rather than from the cockpit. It was one of the many challenges of racing an old boat and added an extra level of effort and risk to my manoeuvres. Dropping the sail was all about timing: I had to work with the boat's rolling to ensure the sail fell on the deck and not in the water (otherwise I would have to battle against the weight of the sail and the force of water flowing over it to get it back on board). With each wave, the sail would swing wildly out over the water, then slam back into the boat, briefly coming to rest against the forestay. At that point, I would drop the halyard as quickly as possible, arresting it just as the outward swing started again. Once safely on deck, the old sail could be detached, and I'd check meticulously that each of the control lines was securely fastened to the deck or part of the boat's structure while it was not in use. No matter how quick the change, leaving any rope unattended on the deck could risk it being washed overboard by a rogue wave or the movement of the boat, leading to a whole chain reaction of extra work and strife. There can never be any shortcuts handling a big boat alone, no matter how tempting. The risk is too great. We must always stick to the process. I'd then drag the old sail back to the side deck, like a huge, thick snake, pulling it just enough out of the way so as to avoid confusion. The new sail would then be plugged in to the control lines, and I would walk back to the cockpit to pull the tack line on, go forward to the mast and wind the halyard up, with two to three minutes more grinding. Finally, the sail could be unfurled, sheeted on, and then manipulated into the shape that would bring best speed. This final action took just as much effort as the initial furling, heart rate up and breathing hard. Once the boat was again sailing fast, I could bag up the old sail. Wrapped around the cable, it is stiff and unyielding; it does not want to bend. And yet I must tame it into neat lengths and tuck it into the bag, which I'd tie as tight as possible to reduce bulk and stop water ingress. Often, I would be performing this job while being hosed with freezing water as *Superbigou* took off down a wave. It was the one job on the boat I resented – such a seemingly simple task, but the sails fought me every step of the way.

But the physical work was not just to be found in large actions. At the smallest level, I needed to focus on the adjustment of the sheets that control the shape power of the sails. A full crew will have one person dedicated to each sail, watching it for hours on end, rope in hand, easing centimetres at a time, then pulling back in. These tiny adjustments translate to extra speed or maintained momentum; they can make less than 0.1

of a knot's difference to a boat's speed, yet races can be won or lost by seconds. In my 2022 Route du Rhum transatlantic race, I finished 77 seconds behind the 11th-placed boat. Over a course of over 3,500 miles, how many 0.1-knot adjustments would have made up that place? It matters.

Sailing an older-generation boat meant that even the tiny adjustments of sail trimming required substantially more effort than that experienced by the majority of my competitors. In the year 2000, when *Superbigou* was designed and built, covered cockpits to protect sailors from the elements were not yet considered an important part of an ocean race yacht. Through the following years, you can see this philosophy changing: boats in 2004 were fitted with small, covered cuddies under which skippers could take shelter; then the front half of the cockpit was covered; later, roofs were retrofitted and extended; until, finally, the 2020 generation of boats had fully enclosed cockpits. From the dry comfort of these, my competitors could look out, adjust sails, and sit in natural light in safety and warmth. There were three skippers in the race who didn't have this luxury: me, Alexia Barrier (who was sailing *4myplanet*, the only boat older than mine, built in 1999) and Didac Costa. Of the three, *Superbigou* offered the least shelter, with only a small extension of the coach roof overhanging the cabin hatch to stop water pouring over the top of the boat and straight inside the cabin. The extension was just wide enough for me to sit under it with my arms tucked by my sides, and I had two PVC awning-type flaps that rolled down to protect me from the water. Didac and I joked often during the race that there should be two classes in the rankings: those with roofs and those without.

For those of us without enclosed cockpits, making any adjustment to sails in all but the most benign conditions meant fully kitting up in foul weather gear, including tops with rubber dry seals at the neck and wrists. In hot weather I would have to choose between going on deck in my T-shirt, accepting that I would be drenched to the skin by the time I had finished, or putting on my dry top and sweating almost as much underneath.

For us, the extra effort required to get on deck and ease that sail and gain 0.1 of a knot could easily have created a barrier to performance – after all, I would only need to pull the sail back in again in another half hour. But at the beginning of the race I had made a promise to myself that I would never give up an opportunity to perform, no matter how much my inner thoughts might be convincing me it did not matter. Sometimes it would take a moment of straight self-talking to get me off the cabin floor and into my dry top, but I always reminded myself how hard I had worked to get where I was. I thought of my journey, of the people – friends and complete strangers – who had donated time and money to get me to the start line. I owed it to them as much as to myself to give my best performance. I was carrying a part of them all with me, and this could be my only opportunity to race at this level. These thoughts always got me on to the deck.

I was gratified to see hard work reflected in results, during the first week of the race. My body ached a lot, but not with the obtrusive, miserable pain of an injury. It was more satisfying than that: the kind of ache I have felt after completing a long run or spending the whole day on my feet walking up a mountain. I felt there was a tangible connection between the aching and my performance. I loved the raw potential that lay ahead of me, I loved the fact that my hard work had paid dividends, and yes, I was 'sticking it' to all those who had so readily written me off because I was not like them. No one knows what any person is genuinely capable of until that person is given the occasion to show it. And I had only just begun.

Life on board had settled for a short while, and I was relishing the routine and stability, busy with maintenance and trimming the boat. We were making rapid miles to the south and had passed the latitude of the Canary Islands. The temperature was rising; my first set of thermals had come off and were packed away in ziplock bags, with the hope they would finally be washed in another three months' time when I was back on shore. I was a little alarmed at the number of technical problems I had already encountered: I had broken part of my mainsheet system; the tower supporting my satellite antennas had come completely unstuck and was letting water into the back of the boat; I'd managed to burn a hole in the water cooling tank on my engine; and the hydrogenerators were vibrating an abnormal amount. All of which were causing concern. From my standpoint, no one else in the fleet seemed to be doing this level of maintenance; I didn't have the bandwidth, literally or metaphorically, to look at the social media from other teams, and all the chat on our skippers' WhatsApp group had been of a positive nature. I was desperately worried my technical problems would hamper my performance. I messaged Joff Brown about my concerns.

Text message conversation with Joff, 15 November 2020

Joff: *It's more like a 3-month endurance maintenance project than a race isn't it. Did I remember to tell you that?*

Pip: *I was just coming to terms with the 1 day's sailing to 2 days' maintenance regime ... And genuinely wondering if anyone else is on it. They all seem to be doing posts with perfect sailing and great snacks ... no one else seems to be rocking the Sika gun.*

Joff: *No, they are, I can assure you. Depends how they communicate it. Most don't say much. But there are cracked fuel tanks, loads of pilot issues, hook problems, sail problems, split tin of sardines, broken structure.*

The split tin of sardines was on board with my fellow Brit and role model, Sam Davies. It sounds trivial, but I could imagine how disgusting and annoying the smell and the oil seeping all over everything must be, difficult to clean up with limited resources on board, making everything slippery. I would happily keep my wobbly radar tower over that.

This was the first indication I'd had that I was telling my story differently. While other sailors were tight-lipped about the problems they were having, I was openly sharing my concerns and how I overcame them. It seemed completely natural to me that I should – after all, no one was expecting this race to be anything but a challenge, and from a human-interest perspective, overcoming the difficulties was going to engage more people long term than months of social media posts saying how great the sailing was. I had set out with the objective of telling the best Vendée Globe story, and that had to be warts and all. It was very different to the overwhelming majority of communication that came off boats in the past. There is a view that sharing the bad stuff demonstrates weakness; if you show less than perfection, it might have negative connotations for both sailor and sponsor. Furthermore, some teams believe it is better to let your competitors think everything is perfect on board, so that they can establish a psychological edge. In my opinion, watching a fellow competitor break, then repair or build a secondary system to trim their mainsail, all the while maintaining their position in the fleet, shows great strength. Only imagine what this person would be capable of on those days they are trouble free.

It was not until after the race was over that I came to learn what an impact my honest and open communication had made on some of my followers. While I was battling it out with nature, the rest of the world was in COVID lockdown, confined to home, feeling powerless against the pandemic that raged through each of their countries. So many people faced pain and trauma during our COVID times, and I still meet people regularly who tell me how watching me overcome challenges and push myself hard day by day had helped them to face their own battles at home. It is genuinely humbling to hear these stories. I was exactly where I wanted to be, feeling freer than I ever had, becoming the person I had always wanted to be, while others were restrained and suffering. I knew I was lucky at the time, but hearing individual narratives after the race really brought it home.

I am still a great believer in telling it straight. Even now, as my team nudges into the top tier of ocean racing, I will not allow the veneer of perfection to descend on our story. Too many times in modern life we are only allowed to view the airbrushed version. But life is messy; success never comes without mistakes and mishaps. These bumps in the road do not represent failure, they are the times when we learn and grow. They are the tools with which we become better human beings.

On 16 November, I heard news that *CORUM L'Epargne* had dismasted. Just 12 days into the race, Nico Troussel had lost it all. The years of hard work and development, all gone in a moment. It was news that sent a wave of nausea through me.

I could not imagine how he felt, and of all the things that might happen to me, I feared a dismasting the most. I was still sporting the 20-year-old mast the boat had been built with. We had ultrasounded it, of course, and changed all the cables that held it up, but without doubt it was the chink in my armour. The thoughts swarmed into my head: should I slow down or back off? Was I pushing too hard? Could that have been me? I had been happily pushing myself up the fleet. It didn't feel extreme, but maybe it was too much. These thoughts continued to hound me for the rest of the race, but in this instance they were short-lived, as the weather took control of my narrative and created a different reason to be concerned.

On the evening of 16 November, I ran straight into a wind hole. I had to cross an area of high pressure, a vacuum that had been created between the might of tropical storm Theta sucking wind towards its centre to the north of me and the global momentum of the trade winds to the south. During the morning, *Superbigou* was jogging along with vigour, making great progress to the south, but by the evening I was becalmed in less than 5 knots of wind. The sails hung listlessly, the boat completely stalled in the water. The psychological pain of being becalmed is always immense. It brings out my inner toddler. I feel wronged, frustrated, angry, tearful at my total inability to move forwards. Entirely alone on the ocean, from horizon to horizon, I imagine that I am the only one in the fleet to succumb to this punishment. And while I am being held back, my competitors are making steady progress towards the finish.

RACE BLOG, 16 NOVEMBER 2020

At midnight the wind shut off and for the last six hours I have been slopping around in hell. There is always a temptation to change sails, change tacks, hand-steer, trim this and that in the desperate attempt to get moving. All this might gain me a couple of miles in the general scheme of things but exhaust me at the same time, so I have had to learn to think big picture in these circumstances: what is the best thing for me to do? And

> *quite often it is to chill out, to keep the boat going on pilot in roughly the right direction, yet to move the weight around the boat to maximise any movement we have but after that to rest, wait for change and be ready to act when it happens.*
>
> *Meanwhile, my mind is mercilessly hounding me ... am I the only one to be in a hole? Is all that work I did to break away going to go down the drain? Did I miss something in the navigation that put me here? If I can't sleep I listen to audiobooks, anything to keep my mind under wraps. This is just one moment in time on a long, long race and I need to take it and move on.*
>
> *It's also been good to spend time outside, there is no moon at the moment and with the calm seas, the night is an utterly seamless 360 of black silk, punctuated only by the brightest of stars. It's incredible.*
>
> *Today I am hoping the breeze will fill in properly and I might get the first whiff of the trade winds south. It's only been a week, but it does seem like this has been a long journey south.*

Over my years of solo racing, I've had to develop the ability to 'zoom out'. The mental technique has served me well whenever I feel that cage of negativity close in on me. It involves taking time to think about where I am. It is almost as if I am looking down from above at me and my boat. Looking at where we are, how far I've sailed, where I am in the fleet, and then reminding myself that *I* am the skipper on this boat. *I* have made this happen and am still making this happen. Me – little old me. Just a normal person with big ambitions. Even now when I think about the Vendée Globe race and I imagine looking down on myself, it makes me smile and gives me strength, and it helps me remember who I can be. With this visualisation, I remind myself that not only am I moving through the ocean, but I am moving through time as well. This difficult period is just that – a moment in time – and things will change. Just as I can work to sail my boat faster through the ocean, so positive actions can help me move faster through the difficult times. This encourages me to lift my head and do one positive thing: listen to music, make a cup of tea, make one step out of my negative headspace and start on the road to fighting back. The occasions when this was not enough, I held fast to the certain fact that the difficult times would not last forever. I coaxed myself through each motion and each hour, often saying out loud, 'This will get better, this will end'. And it always did.

Sure enough, the wind returned, and before long *Superbigou* was heading south with a purposeful stride. All was well. I'd taken a deep breath and split with Didac, my Spanish running mate of the last few days, to gain some miles to the west in the hope of finding some stronger winds. Feeling the need for power, I set my biggest spinnaker, an impressive sail of 400 square metres (which I call Big Bertha), but after a couple of hours it had already reached its max wind limit of 20 knots – way quicker than I was expecting. I only intended to head west during the daylight hours, and having the big kite up was definitely allowing me to sail a better course. I was greedy to bank this strategic gain, but deeply concerned that I might not be able to wrestle Bertha to the ground if the wind increased further. My competitive nature forced me on; I knew this big sail was making a difference and I was excited by overtaking more boats. My wind speed limit of 20 knots breezed past, up to 22, then 23 knots. I had never managed this sail alone in that strength of wind, but I was not willing to take 45 minutes out of my progress and take the sail down when we were making gains.

After six hours of agonising internal debate, I saw 25 knots on my wind instruments, and finally admitted it was time to get Big Bertha out of the sky. This is one of those manoeuvres that can go so badly wrong, and it is when wrestling this spinnaker that I feel my most ineffectual as a human being. The forces acting on the spinnaker are immense, and whether it wants to fly or to fall in the water, one 73kg woman is not going to stand in this sail's way. Performing these drops is all about having a plan, good preparation, and making sure you understand everything that could go wrong.

It took me an hour and a half from end to end to get Bertha down and replace it with the smaller downwind Code Zero. During the process I was dragged across the deck, got a rope wrapped around my rudder, and had adrenaline coursing through my body. Once the sail was sorted, I gybed back and flew south through the night towards the equator.

RACE BLOG, 17 NOVEMBER 2020

All being well, tomorrow will be a great sailing day with very little human interaction required, which means a bow to stern boat check and some time to get messy with epoxy trying to rebuild my engine water cooling sub tank.
Happy days...

The move to the west paid off, and as I sped south towards the equator in stronger winds I made sure to remember that less than 36 hours ago I had been feeling becalmed and helpless. I banked that memory for the future, when I could remind myself that change will always come.

6

Battling the Doldrums

The English are renowned for their tendency to talk about the weather whenever they meet, to the extent that foreigners often find the habit a bit eccentric. Sailors, however, take the subject to another level, where it becomes wholly consuming – and for good reason. During the Vendée, global weather patterns very much dictate the course, as they have done since men first attempted to cross an ocean. The earth is striped from pole to pole with areas of high and low pressure, between which the wind flows in much the same way as water moves downhill until it finds a stable level. At around 30 degrees latitude, in the northern and southern hemispheres, areas of high pressure tend to establish themselves, with corresponding low-pressure areas found at 60 degrees latitude and around the equator. The high-pressure areas produce stable, windless conditions, with clear, cloudless skies, while the low-pressure areas are wilder and less predictable. At 60 degrees, I knew to expect fast-moving, whirling systems that would barrel across the oceans, the warm, moist air creating huge amounts of energy in the form of clouds, rain and strong winds. At the equator, the doldrums were likely to prove equally unstable, but instead of a gale-force beating, we were likely to encounter a different kind of torture altogether.

Throughout the course of the Vendée, we would be picking our way through these large-scale weather features. Broadly speaking, the wind is stronger towards the centre of a low-pressure system and weaker at the centre of a high. The wind behaves like water whirling around a plughole, the high-pressure centres pushing it outwards while the low-pressure centres suck it in to fill the void. Our course had us first of all negotiating the petulant missiles of the northern hemisphere low-pressure systems in late autumn, then we skirted the Azores high, keeping a safe distance from its windless centre before being slingshot into the trade winds that blow steadily from east to west in the bottom third of the North Atlantic. Once through these trades, we would have to cross the doldrums, pop out into the South Atlantic trades, then dodge around the St Helena high, before a final slingshot into the Southern Ocean. The Southern Ocean leg of the race is the longest. Once there, we would be sitting in the direct path of the low-pressure systems that barrel relentlessly and unhampered around the earth's surface. My competitors and I would have to spend six weeks in these conditions, trying to both ride and avoid the constant gales that would come at us. The course would involve rounding three capes – The Cape of Good Hope, Cape Leeuwin and Cape Horn – before we could once again head north up the Atlantic.

Each weather feature would entail a different strategy and mode of sailing, and as I proceeded through the course I ticked off each weather phase once it was complete. By 19 November I had moved through three of them, and my final days heading south in the trade winds had been a particular joy. I'd been pushing hard, loving the sailing in steady winds and sunshine, the endless blue, beautiful ocean stretched out ahead of me. Being diligent in these conditions was easy: the warmth and light of the sun filled me with positive energy; I couldn't stop myself from smiling because there was nowhere else on the planet I would rather be and nothing else I would rather be doing. There is an incredible energy that fills me when I am sailing well, when every part of the boat feels like it is working correctly because of all the expertise and experience that has gone into designing, building and maintaining every aspect of it. The power of the wind on the sails transfers itself through mast and rigging to the hull of the boat, which, because of its weight and shape and the diligence of preparation, is able to slip through the water at ever increasing speeds. In this happy state I am always aware that every part of the boat is making a difference: the autopilot is being fed data from wind instruments, compass, speedo and rudder sensors so that it can steer a smooth, fast course; the winches are holding loads of over 5 tonnes, enabling me – a small human being – to make micro-adjustments. All around me I can feel the energy of the ocean, the wind and the waves, and this energy transfers through the boat into speed. The boat feels alive – buzzing, vibrating – and at the centre of it all I am the lone human conducting an orchestra of the skill and knowledge that put this boat together and allows it to perform. The energy is immense and addictive. I always want to go back to the ocean to feel it again.

The relative stability of the trade winds had allowed me to maintain my lead on my original 'marks' and jump forward to establish a new peloton. For several days I had been riding in a group of four with Didac, Manuel Cousin – a French sailor in a non-foiling 2007 boat – and Cali in his foiler. By now, the feeling of surprise at being this far forward so early in the race had worn off. I accepted that I belonged in this position and was gunning to reach further forward in the pack. The potential was tantalising. But the course was taking me away from these heady conditions towards the doldrums, where a sailor's fortunes could be crushed in a matter of days.

The doldrums are a zone of about 600 nautical miles stretching across the equator. The area is so famous that an expression was coined off the back of it to describe a mouldy feeling of depression that it's hard to pull oneself out of. What most people don't realise is that the doldrums aren't purely a zone of calm under a leaden sky, like something out of Samuel Taylor Coleridge's *Rime of the Ancient Mariner* where the ship's crew was doomed to perish 'a painted ship upon a painted ocean'.

In Bernard Moitessier's poetic account of his round-the-world solo race, *The Long Way*, his description of the doldrums is eerily memorable: '*I feel empty, like this sea without sun, without fish, without birds, dead as a doornail despite the goddamned swell that tosses the boat ... I have to pull myself together and hang on, trim the sails twenty times an hour, move out of the doldrums at all costs, before I get completely fed up with everything.*'

On 20 November, day 14 of the race, the front half of the fleet had sailed straight through the doldrums, with little to no disruption to pace, and I couldn't help wondering if my fate would be quite so good. My pack was still 550 miles north of the equator, and the forecast showed that the route they had taken with a solid path of breeze to the south was disappearing. There was no obvious alternative game plan, and I knew that there were many miles to be gained or lost in negotiating this tricky area.

While the sailing at this point was pure, clean and fast, the future hung uncertain for *Superbigou* and me. I pushed south, trying to keep the speeds as high as possible and hoping with all my might that the passage through the doldrums might stay open. It was good close racing, and I could feel the pressure from Didac and Manu and it kept us all fast. It was so hot and airless down below without ventilation that I spent as much time as I could on deck. At night, under a beautiful star-strewn sky, unblemished by other light, I felt the cool air against my skin. My feet were constantly awash with the waves that rolled down the deck and into the cockpit.

In the morning, before it got too hot, I would work on maintenance and inspections, looking for problems before they happened, crawling around the inside of the boat with my head torch, a knife and some spanners. It was almost pleasing to find something wrong – a nut a bit loose, a bit of chafe – because it was something I could put right: a problem averted. I felt that I had a modicum of control, and that felt good even though I knew that ahead of me lay the dreaded doldrums where I might feel a singular lack of control.

I waited and watched the forecast unfold.

The closer we got to the equator, the more it felt as if the air in my small cabin was slowly turning solid. I slept twice through my alarms; each time I woke I felt like I had been drugged: my body heavy, brain slow. Everything was an effort, and although at this stage *Superbigou* was still making good progress, I knew that things could change rapidly. This is an area on the course where so much can be won or lost.

Then, like that fluttering of nerves before an exam, a bouncy kind of motion crept in as the breeze started to ease off a bit. Overnight, my average wind speed dropped from 17 to 14 knots, and with this drop in intensity came a sort of lolloping across the waves. I knew that the slight dip in wind speed would undoubtedly herald a sail change, so Big Bertha was once again hoisted, maximising sail area to keep up momentum south in the dying breeze. As each forecast came in, I could see a gaping wind hole opening on the charts ahead of me. There was no route around it: I would have to sail through. Blind hope suggested that if I was quick, I might dash across the area before it got too wide. My sole focus was to get south with as much momentum as possible, and if I was going fast enough I could propel myself and *Superbigou* through. But hope does not bring the wind, and by 21 November the express route to the southern hemisphere closed.

The doldrums is not just a place of no wind, it is also punctuated by huge thermal clouds, which build up due to evaporation during the extreme heat of the day. These clouds release energy in the later afternoon and overnight, in the form of torrential rain, electric storms, and aggressive wind squalls that come from completely random directions. During the day you can see the clouds and try to sail around them, but in the pitch black of night they must be tracked by radar, and even then may sneak up undetected. The arrival of clouds can herald drastic changes to conditions, requiring quick sail changes, that send the boat haring off in the wrong direction. Then, stopping just as quickly as they arrived, they leave a sailor floundering for hours in a deluge of rain. My first cloud must have been blown over from a landmass somewhere, as the air smelt sweet – of flowers and foliage. Ahead of it, a whole heap of insects landed on my boat, little bugs, a dragonfly, and a tiny baby bird with webbed feet that tried to nestle into the spinnaker while I was putting it away. I tried to pick up the bird and relocate it to the cockpit, but it flew off and I never saw it again.

As I watched the wind direction change and increase rapidly, I knew I had to wrestle Big Bertha out of the sky as soon as I could. As I set things up for this drop, the wind direction changed, forcing me to run due west instead of south, and it started to rain. Bertha was compliant: I got her down with only a moderate fight, shoved her through the forehatch, then went to grab my downwind zero as a replacement. All the while the rain chucked it down, soaking through my shorts and T-shirt, making it hard to see as the light from my head torch reflected back at me from every huge raindrop. The zero went up, the wind changed again, and now we were sailing upwind and fiercely, still in the wrong direction with the wrong sail. It was completely disorientating in the total black of the night. Only the colourful letters on my instruments gave me any clue in which direction I was sailing; I could have been heading anywhere.

The upwind sailing felt like it was there to stay, and I was acutely aware I had my whole sail wardrobe stacked on the back of the boat. I started to drag them out one by one, pulling up against gravity to the windward deck, then dragging them along to the forward hatch. Halfway through this procedure, and still in the rain, the wind shifted by 90 degrees – effectively, the wind had tacked but the boat had not. I was left with the keel and sails on the wrong side while I hung on to a sail bag to stop it from sliding over the side. In these situations, there is a little part of me that wants to shout at the sky, 'Oh come on! Really! Just back off!' (I have done this in the past, but can report that nothing changed ... but it does make you feel a bit better.)

Bit by bit, I put the boat straight again, keel on the right side, sails trimmed, ropes tidied, engaging that same low gear I had used after the front to slog away at the jobs and get things done. *Superbigou* had always been a difficult boat to sail tidy. All the ropes come to two places, one on each side of the cockpit – exactly the place water rushes over when a big wave comes down the deck. It is a squeeze to get all the ropes in, and you can be sure if there is a job to be done then the rope you need will be at the bottom of the pack. By now I had been at it for two and a half hours, seemingly just moving sail after sail, pulling one rope then letting the same one off, constantly getting set up, then having it all thrown up in the air again. With every change in wind strength and direction, I had to look at the instruments and say to myself, 'What is the fastest route south?' Then change everything again.

After a relentless night of activity, it calmed down and I was left with weak northerlies in the early hours of the morning. It was once again the right conditions to have Bertha back up again, but I couldn't risk getting into trouble in a squall and I needed desperately to get some rest after my night-long cloud-messing ordeal.

I realised that I could have another two days of this ahead. The most recent forecast suggested that this area of doldrums might stretch a further 160 miles. With a pace of only 5 knots – in light airs, then capricious squalls – I would need to steel myself. Over and above the frenzied activity a squall will bring, being becalmed is the worst sort of sailing. Frustrating, soul-destroying. And the thwack of the mainsail, followed by a jolt as it violently flops from side to side in swell and no wind ... well, that is enough to try anybody's sanity.

RACE BLOG, 21 NOVEMBER 2020

OK folks, in the spirit of total honesty I am putting my hand up and confessing to being grumpy. Yes ... it's true; Little Miss Sunshine over here is in a stinker of a mood. I'm done with the doldrums. Totally and utterly done with being thrown around by sloppy inconsistent waves, listening to sails flogging, blocks banging, the pilot struggling to work out which way it is supposed to be going. I'm done with being alternately drenched in sweat then drenched in downpours. I'm done with changing sails only to have to change them back 2 minutes later. I'm done with endless trips up and down from the engine room to drop the keel, then raise it, then drop it, then raise it. And most of all I am done with every time I put my head down the boat starts going slow or the wind changes direction and I have to get back up again. OK ... I'm done!

The reality is I have not slept enough, drunk enough or eaten enough in the last 48 hours and that is manifesting itself in the form of swearing at inanimate objects, a lack of patience, feeling sorry for myself, being close to tears when an unexpected wave spilt my cup of tea this morning, and once ... only once ... a full-on belly roar at a cloud to 'just get lost and go and mess someone else's life up for a change' (this language has been adapted to protect the innocent).

For the last two days there has been no stability, so my energy and my willpower have been slowly eroded until I am standing in the cockpit screaming at the sky.

I know this is a temporary state so it's bearable. In fact, just writing this now has made me feel better already. It's allowed me to zoom out of my tiny little world and rationalise that it will all seem better after food, drink and a kip. There is hope after all, coming over the horizon in the form of some nasty little waves that my bow slaps into, making the whole boat shudder. Something has created these waves that are marching towards me with no mercy. Judging by the direction of them, it must be the south-east trade winds. So we can't be too far off now.

I guess I am also grumpy because I care. I have put so much effort into the last week of sailing. It was unexpected to be so far forward in the fleet, and I feel all of the miles made I fought for, and it would be such a wrench to lose them because I got stuck under a windless cloud in the doldrums for half a day. So, I carry on fighting for every mile, safe in the knowledge that when I pop out the other side of this equatorial hell, my world will seem a better place, so that cheerful, positive inner me can be back with a vengeance.

Managing these short-term hold-ups has always been a challenge for me throughout my sailing career. In this race it was hard not to compare my progress with others on the course, measuring my performance when stuck in a wind hole against their speed and progress. But there was little point in measuring on-the-water performance against boats that are hundreds of miles away in completely different conditions. The same could be said of many situations in life: we constantly compare what we do with others who are in totally different positions.

While competing in the Vendée Globe race, I had the added challenge of having to assess progress against a finish line that was thousands of miles and months of time away. I was never going to move towards that end goal at a linear rate, so I needed to find a way to make it hurt less whenever I was held up by either the weather or some other problem. This meant setting realistic short-term goals to provide me with punchy yet achievable objectives that were relevant to my own personal position on the racetrack.

I could benchmark progress against boats that were close to my position, but I had to be driven by my own circumstances and not let the perceived progress of the rest of the fleet get in my head. In reality, I already had a method to manage this, a structured approach that had evolved while I learned to manage the variable data surrounding weather forecasting. I just needed to adapt this way of thinking so that the same practical and mental approach could be applied to all aspects of my race.

Weather forecasting has become increasingly reliable with the advent of supercomputers that are able not only to take in real-time data from around the world's surface, but also to analyse multiple years of weather patterns and phenomena to accurately predict how strong and in which direction the wind will blow. Of course, weather forecasting is so much more than just the wind, but for me on the ocean there is nothing more important. With access to all manner of weather information through our on-board satellite communication systems, we must first work out which weather sources to trust, how frequently to look at them, and how to validate their accuracy, before taking the predictions of wind strength and direction and plugging the data into our navigational software in order to calculate the best route forwards. At my fingertips I had 12 different wind forecast models available to me, as well as eight wave and current models. I had synoptic charts showing the position and progression of individual weather features, and satellite imagery to get a real-time view of clouds. I had to choose which sources of information were valid and reliable for wherever I was on the globe and how often I should update. It would be really easy for a sailor to be sucked in to all-day navigation – and for a full crew ocean race, this is indeed a full-time role. For the solo skippers of the huge ULTIM-class trimarans, for example, a dedicated team of meteorologists work in shifts on the shore to manage this aspect of their racing. IMOCA skippers, on the other hand, must navigate entirely alone, all external help or discussions about the weather are forbidden, and we must balance this immensely taxing job with everything else on board. After all, you could plot the fastest route in the world, but if you are not able to keep the boat sailing at its polar-predicted speeds it will be worth absolutely nothing.

On a day-to-day level, the forecasts are impressively accurate. However, the further out on the timeline a forecast goes, the less accurate it will be. As it is hard to predict any long-term course or performance, I use a five-day rule when it comes to making reliable decisions. Although I am looking at the evolving weather picture up to two weeks away, I structure my progress with a 24-hour goal, a 48-hour goal, and then the five-day benchmark. The latter will guide my immediate best path, while the 24- and 48-hour goals stretch and cajole me into action. I routinely download new files every day, sometimes twice a day if there is instability, and I amend objectives with new information. This structured action helps me to manage the crushing disappointment that invariably comes with any measurement against my overall goal.

I have also adapted this technique to everyday life ashore when managing long-term or complex projects. It is common wisdom to break big tasks down into manageable sizes, but embracing the concept that short-term goals are continuous and should be adapted to match changing circumstances has also served me well. Just as I adapt my racing line to avoid areas with no wind or storms, so I have learned to respond with agility when building my business, so that I can change emphasis or strategy according to conditions.

7

RUNNING ON SHORT LITTLE LEGS

On Friday 27 November, after only three weeks at sea, British solo sailor Alex Thomson, one of the most experienced and best-funded skippers in the race, collided with detritus in the water. He was below deck when there was an enormous bang. *Hugo Boss* broached violently, and when Alex went on deck to inspect the damage, he quickly saw that one of his rudder blades was broken, a large piece of fishing gear jammed into the cracks. Now, without a working steering system, all he could do was roll the sails away.

When I heard the news, I was yet again chilled. A second competitor had been dealt a blow by fate, demonstrating there is no rhyme or reason to the bad luck that can happen during a race such as this. No matter your standing in the world's sailing ranking, these unforeseen, unavoidable accidents can happen to anyone. In an interview he gave to *Yachting World* after the disaster, Alex didn't try to preserve a brave front – he was absolutely gutted, his hopes and dreams smashed to pieces: 'I'm normally a very positive person but if I'm honest right now I feel pretty broken. For the best part of 20 years this race has been my goal ... I have the boat of my dreams ... I've given my life to this sport and it's a very difficult pill to swallow.'

I couldn't help but feel unnerved, and I'm sure every one of the other competitors experienced a similar pang of empathy and unease. How can you not cast an eye over your boat and wonder how you would fare in similar circumstances? In my struggles to get to the line, I had been forced to prepare in just five months of the four-year cycle; I had an old boat and no experience of what lay ahead. Surely I was at more risk than the others? I asked myself, would I be able to change a damaged rudder if I had to? Would I make it to the end of the race without some freak collision over which I had no control? When I first heard the news of Alex, I had thought that he'd be on his way again after making repairs, but he retired from the race after he'd sailed his boat – flat – to Cape Town, with just one rudder.

Meanwhile, *Superbigou* was anything but flat. We were now in a drag race to the south of Brazil with the small peloton that had formed over the previous week. Breaking out of the doldrums had given me my freedom back, and for a brief moment on 25 November I had pulled ahead of my whole pack, lying in 20th place and leading the others into the strengthening South Atlantic trade winds.

RACE BLOG, 24 NOVEMBER 2020

With the breath of Cali, Didac and Manuel hot on the back of my neck, I feel like I am being hunted. I am trying hard to stay ahead, but slowly Cali and Manu are taking the miles out of me and my 20-year-old boat, which is doing so, so well, but there are no more gears left – we have reached warp speed. The wind is between 13 and 18 knots, which means to keep Superbigou *on pace I need to regularly trim the sails to power up and depower the mainsail. This has not been helped by one of the U bolts holding a mainsheet block on to the traveller ripping out last night, so now I have a jury-rigged mainsheet system until I can make a proper repair.*

At this point in the race, I was to feel acutely the penalty of sailing an older boat. In the relatively flat water and stable breeze of the trades, this part of the course was a 2,000-mile drag race with the wind on the beam, and it was all about straight line speed. We have learned so much about yacht design, weather patterns and the strategic benefits of different hull shapes over the last 20 years of ocean racing. My boat was state of the art in the year 2000, with its slim hull, round coach roof and single daggerboard in front of the keel. In the years after its build, boats moved to twin daggerboards set on either side of the mast, which improved righting moment when reaching with the wind on the beam. Then the width of the hull (also called the beam) was increased, which gave more stability, making boats more powerful. Next, daggerboards were angled outboard, again to lift the boat, which increased power. Then more width, and after that, the addition of small foils in 2016. These wings, which projected out of the side of the boat, acted like aeroplane wings: when water flowed over them they would lift the hull of the boat upwards, with the ability to hold half the weight of the boat, allowing it to skim over the waves rather than through them. Finally, in 2020, we had big foils, designed to lift the entire weight of the boat. These new generation IMOCAs, of which *Hugo Boss* was one, were capable of flying clean above the ocean's surface in the trade wind conditions that I was currently battling. The speed differential between my old *Superbigou* and the front of the fleet was at times as much as 10 knots, meaning they could be stretching away from me at a rate of 240 miles a day. It was impossible to think I could compete on that level, and I wasn't. Meanwhile, the pack around me started to show their strengths: Cali was in a foiling boat, Manu, a year 2007 design, and although Didac's *One Planet One Ocean* was built in the same year as mine, its design was ahead of its time, with twin daggerboards, and he had adapted it before his Vendée Globe race in 2016 to make it more competitive. No matter how hard I tried, the rot was setting in.

On 28 November, Paul Larsen gave a summary of my more recent progress:

'It's been incredible to watch. The fleet has broken into a few groups, and Pip has managed to make the jump across in the North Atlantic, turning a few miles of separation from her "pack" into something now approaching 700 miles, which is amazing. Pip has now joined around four boats, and she has managed to keep pressure on them because of the light downwind conditions that have suited Superbigou. South of the equator, the beam-reaching conditions meant that the newer, more powerful boats around her put the pedal to the floor to break away from her, and Pip doesn't have a lot in

her arsenal to beat that. You could see her losing miles, and it was frustrating to watch, but in the trade winds and those conditions there's only so much she can do with the boat she has. She's had a great race so far, and she'll have plenty of opportunities to show her strengths.'

It was always going to happen, but it was a bitter pill to swallow – I was immensely proud of having stuck it out in front for so long. We were now on a three-day fetch down the Brazilian coast, wind angle between 55 and 70 degrees, sailing in a straight line. As there were basically no tactics on this leg other than to sail fast, the three other members of our gang of four slowly overtook me and extended their lead. I knew that I had to resign myself to this part of the race, but I couldn't give up trying to chase them. Sadly, determination can only get you so far. For the next week, at least, I would need to recalibrate my objectives, ignore the competition, and stay focused on making my race as fast as I could, until the next phase opened another door.

Once again, I had to refer to my initial objectives. I knew my boat could not possibly win this race, but how was I going to balance my nature as a competitive person and yet be happy with that state of affairs? There were probably only ten skippers who realistically could hope to win the race, yet every one of us was in it to perform and would have created our own benchmarks. We all knew we were bound to encounter setbacks during the race, which might move our goals further from reach – like Jérémie Beyou, who, tipped to win, had those hopes removed from his grasp within the first days of the race. My goal had been to outperform the boat and to always push hard when there was opportunity. Even if I fell behind my current peloton, I could stay true to that.

Once again, I needed to reflect on the nature of the race we were undertaking and learn to measure performance against my previous personal best. I would make mistakes or encounter problems that pushed me back down the rankings, but over a race that would take three months to run, I had multiple opportunities to recover and fight back. Every failure or slip-up must be viewed as a step towards getting it right next time – this sport is all about learning through trial and error. Just as I had clawed my way past plenty of individual targets before the race even began – reaching crowdfunding targets; chartering a boat; finding a sponsor; getting through the qualifying races – at each stage there would be a new goal to reach for, a new group of skippers to tough it out against. Over such a long race, the goals changed continuously.

My new objective at this stage was simply to try to keep as close to the others as I could. If they were averaging 1.5 knots faster than my average speed, I calculated that over the next three days I would lose 108 miles to them – a recoverable distance. I couldn't let the fact that they were pulling away from me in ever increasing increments lower my morale to the extent that I stopped trying. The feeling of pushing against an immovable force will halt any sane person in their tracks. The fact was that I would still be in with a chance of catching up again, so I needed to keep sailing as fast as I could.

RACE BLOG, 25 NOVEMBER 2020

I am using this information all the time to keep pushing Superbigou *forwards, to make sure I am not wasting even a tiny 0.1 of a knot of speed. My days and nights are spent in the cockpit, gazing at the numbers on my instruments, monitoring course, wind angle, boat speed, then checking my rudder angles, the heel angle, and how well I am doing against my polars. Any time I feel the boat speed drop, I am trying to understand why. If I am under-performing against my polars, I tweak, trim, steer up or down a couple of degrees, fine-tuning to get my speed back up again. Always wondering if I could be faster. When I have consistently outperformed my polars, I adjust them. I am, after all, still learning how to make this boat go fast, and I need to bank this knowledge so that we keep developing together.*

It was relentless work, taking a huge amount of focus, but I loved the open-endedness of this kind of challenge. There was no one to say you could not do better: all you had to do was try. Sometimes what I tried made the boat go slower, then I knew not to try it again. I was in my own little bubble; I couldn't see my opposition, so I had to drive myself. I put on one of my many playlists, felt the music, felt the boat, and became absorbed in the numbers and the ocean. Whenever I felt we were going well, I would take a nap on my beanbag, positioned carefully so that when I opened my eyes I was looking directly up at my instruments.

One of the incredible traits of human beings is our ability to adapt to new circumstances. It is not always easy, and I know that some people struggle with change, but the truth is we can and do adapt throughout our lives: it is what makes us strong and successful in any sphere. During this week of trade wind sailing, I had to adapt to 'life on the lean'. *Superbigou* was heeled permanently at an angle of 25 degrees or more, while I adjusted the power to keep the toe rail just clear of the water. Twenty-five degrees doesn't sound much, but imagine tipping your whole house up at that angle and living like that for days. Every time you want to walk from one end of the kitchen to the other, you either have to lean into the hill and push hard to get uphill or grab hold of the kitchen counters to try and control your descent to the downhill side. Every task you perform – cooking, maintenance, trimming sails or walking around the boat doing daily checks – you have to fight gravity. If you are sitting, you must be wedged; if standing, you must permanently lean into the heel with your legs and knees flexing as you crash over waves. Every implement needs to be either attached to you or placed somewhere it can't fall. Nothing left unattended will stay where you put it.

I was sure that the force of gravity only increased as the days got hotter. Doing anything at all required a plan. At one point I went to get a new packet of wet wipes from my stack of bags stored in a windward cubbyhole. It wasn't easy to find the bag I wanted, and I had nothing to hold on to, so I kept falling backwards while rummaging, and dislodged bags fell on top of me. In the end, it was easier to clear a space and get into the locker with the bags. That way at least, I couldn't fall out, and I wasn't straining every muscle to keep in position while I looked.

MAKING A MEAL OF IT

As an exercise in forethought and contingency planning, take the basic job of making a meal. First, I would need to fill my Jetboil stove with water, which involved removing the aluminium canister from the top of the stove and taking it to my water tank, then filling with just the right amount of water for conditions. Too much would spill over the top of the container and put the flame out; not enough would mean having to repeat the process to finish preparing the meal. The water canister was plugged on to the top of the Jetboil, which was supported on a gimbled mount at the side of the cabin. The gimble allowed the stove to rock with the motion of the boat, compensating for the angle of heel, to keep the water level in the canister flat. At times, the motion of the boat might cause the water to jump out of the stove, which meant I had to remain on standby while the water boiled. I would grab my chosen freeze-dried meal and rip the top of the packet open. Unable to do it with one hand, I'd either need to be sitting on the floor or braced, leaning into the side of the cabin with my body ready to roll with the motion like a human gimble. Once the bag was open, I had to fish around inside to pull out the dehydration pouch of silica granules. Ideally, I would place the rubbish directly in the bin, but with no structure to grab hold of in the centre of my living area, moving around the cabin could be hard work. There were handles on the roof of the cabin, but when the boat was heeling over hard, I couldn't reach them without jumping. At times I would find myself swinging in mid-air, having taken hold of a handle just before the boat was hit by a gust. I would have two choices: hang on in the hope the boat would come upright again or let go in a controlled fall. I was always covered in bruises and quite often had pockets full of rubbish that had never made it to the bin.

Back to my dinner. While the water was boiling, I would reseal the packet. If I failed to do this, the contents would spill when I stumbled or if the boat went over a particularly large wave. I remember once being bounced over a huge wave with a bag of open food in my hand. I went up, the food escaped from the packet and went up with me. Gravity threw me back to the cabin floor a little sooner than the food, and I looked up to see a whole Mexican quinoa supper raining down over me. The only way to get clean was to stand in the full force of a wave, which turned my foulies and hair into cold, tomatoey goo. Pouring boiling water into the food bag was hazardous even with the gentlest of motions. I know of two fellow sailors who have had to be med-evacuated off their boats, having poured scalding water over their bare legs. As a general rule, I always wear my foul weather trousers and closed shoes when making a hot meal or drink. Even if it is too miserably hot to face putting trousers on, I never go near the Jetboil in bare feet or with open shoes. Countless times I have spilled boiling water over my hands, but happily never enough to cause injury. I now use a silicon glove when it is really rough, though the loss of dexterity can create different problems. Life on the lean takes patience and planning, as it will always find your weakness and exploit it.

Just existing on a heeling boat for days on end was physically exhausting, but this stretch of the course, down the Brazilian coast, would also challenge me mentally with the horrendous analysis-paralysis of 'crossover hell'. I carried a selection of seven headsails on *Superbigou*, each with a specific range in which it would provide best possible performance – the right combination of wind angle and wind speed. The crossover is the point at which one sail becomes more efficient than another, and it is normally reached through a change in either wind angle or wind speed. For days, the wind remained on the cusp of a crossover, and trying to stay true to my race goals, I set about changing back and forward between sails at a totally unsustainable rate, losing miles to my competitors and exhausting myself physically and emotionally.

RACE BLOG, 26 NOVEMBER 2020

Right now, and for the last four hours, I have been relentlessly sailing first on one side then the other of my crossover between my J2 and the upwind Code Zero. I was here a couple of nights ago and was quick to make the decision to go big and change up to the zero. A few hours later I had lost ground to windward, was struggling to make an acceptable course with the bigger sail, and had to change back. Two changes end to end cost me an hour of time and a fair few miles on the racetrack. It's not a decision to rush into, that's for sure.

Chastened by my previous experience and with the wind constantly tempting me, I tried to be more cautious: I desperately wanted to use the bigger sail, but it seemed as if every time I made the decision to do so, I'd go on deck and loosen off the ties where the bag was stacked, then the wind angle would change and I knew it would be the wrong decision. So I'd leave it, trim the jib a little, and descend below to stare at the wind graphs for another 15 minutes. Sometimes it was clear the jib was the right sail to use, but at others *Superbigou* would fall badly off a wave, grind to what felt like a halt, and inside me it felt like nails down a blackboard. Mortified at not getting the big sail up, I'd go back on deck and the same thing would happen all over again. I was acutely aware of the penalty in time, miles and energy I would have to pay if I made a sail change and then had to change back. But there was always a nagging voice in the back of my head telling me that I was missing out on an opportunity, that not taking action would mean less speed.

Trapped in this mindset, I badly needed to raise my head and take a proper look at the bigger picture. What was it I wanted to achieve over the next few days? Both *La Mie Câline* and *Groupe Setin* – both more modern boats than mine – had gone for the speed option. If I were to 'crack off' and follow them, I would just be running on my short little legs and not only losing ground but losing height too. Knowing I wouldn't have been able to keep up with them, I decided to sail my own course in my boat. It was good to remind myself that we were all unique, with differing design attributes, and were powerful at different times. So far, *Superbigou* and I had been punching above our weight, and I needed to stay grounded and remember that the boat I was sailing had its limits, no matter how much I pushed and cajoled it. Every part of me wanted to put up a big sail and push hard, but this was the time to sail smart.

All very sane and logical, but it didn't change the fact that I hated the thought of losing contact with my little group. It was definitely time to focus my nervous energy on something positive. As I was overdue some deck checks, I gave myself a job list to get through. I told myself I wasn't allowed to look at the numbers again until I'd done my chores. But of course I couldn't resist sneaking a glance now and again, and would always find myself staring at those numbers as if the answer to life lay behind those multicoloured displays.

Every sailor knows, intellectually, that nothing ever stays the same out on the ocean: conditions eventually change, and then the whole picture looks different. Sometimes, though, it's hard to feel that truth – when you are tensed up, nerves jangling, trapped in a cage of anxiety and restlessness (with a dash of thwarted ambition in the mix). And on this occasion it was no different, and though I tried to shift my mental state, it only really budged once the conditions altered enough to allow me to power *Superbigou* up, after days of kicking and thrashing, to shoot off through the night. I hardly needed to lift a finger, just set it up and the autopilot did the rest. Just a change in wind direction of 10 degrees had taken the handbrake off and made all the difference.

In this more relaxed and empowered frame of mind – and with the beauty of a moonlit night – I was able to take a breath and feel thankful.

8

FEEDING THE SPIRIT

One of the questions I am most commonly asked about my 2020 race around the world and my sport in general is: 'Don't you get lonely?' And I always answer with the same words. 'There is a huge difference between loneliness and being alone.'

I am not sure that I was born as an individual who is happy to be alone. I come from a noisy large family, with three siblings and only six years between us in age from youngest to oldest. While I was used to having people around me throughout my childhood, I think that relative to some I am an introvert. Never comfortable competing with others for attention, I am terrified of walking into a room where I know no one. So I avoid those situations, sometimes at great cost to myself and my goals. But I love, more than anything, cooking a huge meal and filling my house with the sounds of friends and family – chatting, eating, laughing people – and knowing that I have brought them together. I don't ever want to be the centre of attention, but I like to be among happy people. Did I take up solo sailing because I wanted to be alone, or have I become comfortable with being alone because I solo sail? I think it is the latter.

When I race across oceans in my IMOCA, I have chosen to be alone. This is the discipline in which I have sought to excel for the past 15 years of my life, and everything is as it should be. If I longed for other people to be with me, I would be seeking to take part in a different sport. To race alone around the world, I must leave my home, friends, family and colleagues and spend three months on my own. It cannot be any other way. But when the final team member gets off my boat before the start of a race, I feel genuinely liberated. Yes, there is always an enormous pressure to perform, and a gnawing in the pit of my stomach, but I am exactly where I want to be, with no one holding me back. I have the freedom and the opportunity to achieve my potential at every start line and every second of every race thereafter. I don't feel lonely, because I know that the people I leave behind are still part of who I am; they support me, care about me, follow my races and want me to succeed – all the while living their own lives and facing their own challenges. I don't want or expect to be the centre of anyone's thoughts while I am at sea, but I know that if I need anyone to say a kind word, I can call or text them and they will respond. Loneliness is quite a different feeling. You can be the centre of attention or in a room full of people and feel that aching chasm.

I have had to learn to be alone at sea, to develop strategies to cope with a whole range of potentially destructive human emotions, some of which I outline in the chapters of this book. Perhaps one of the hardest aspects of competing alone for months on end is finding the energy to keep going without the interaction of other human beings. How often in life do we rely on other people to pick us up when we are low? A reassuring nod, a warm hug, a call of encouragement from the sidelines?

From the moment a well-cared-for child enters the world, they are given the motivation from their carers to develop and grow. It starts with encouragement to learn basic skills – smiling, talking, walking – in the family setting. Schools, clubs, sports teams and friendship groups soon add to that potential for nurture, where the words and actions of other people continue to encourage us to accomplish new things. Later in life, we transition to becoming the motivators ourselves, with our own families or in the workplace. But how many of us have ever been in a situation where that energy from positive reinforcement is simply not available for months on end?

We feed our bodies with food and water to maintain our physical energy levels. Part of my job when I am at sea is to keep eating, to regularly perform a 'self-scan' so that I can understand what my body needs to keep moving on physically. This could be food, water, sleep or, in some cases, medical attention. Here, the equation is simple – energy in must equal energy out – and we can feel the effects if this is not the case. Emotional energy, however, is a different thing. It's not tangible and can't be measured, and yet a deficit has the power to floor us in much the same way as not eating would. Without emotional energy, our ability to deal with problems, to dig deep and push ourselves through fear or stress, to believe in our ability to find the next level of performance, gradually erodes.

In my years alone on the water, I have needed to find ways in which to feed my spirit, and in doing so recharge my emotional batteries. In the early days I had no access to satcom, whether I was racing in classes where they were forbidden or in a race where I didn't have the budget to pay the exorbitant airtime tariffs. I learned instead to find energy from my surroundings, and that skill has stuck with me, both on and off the water, to this day.

On 29 November, in my Vendée Globe race, my writing positively throbs with this energy that I had absorbed from a starlit night:

RACE BLOG, 29 NOVEMBER 2020

When there is no other light pollution, the moon is an incredible source of light. It lights the deck, the sails; its path across the sea glitters silver, everything is bathed in its light; there is no need for torches, the world is lit up in monochrome. It was still cloudy, so I could see a few stars. The moon would disappear behind a cloud, not doing a very good job of hiding as its light burned through the cloud edges, making them look like they were full of energy and about to explode. The world would go dark for a few minutes then burst into light again as the cloud moved on. As Superbigou's bow broke through the waves, the water coming down the deck looked like molten silver. Just being on deck and experiencing these colours and sensations was a privilege.

And so I sat, and dozed a bit, while Superbigou delivered me south, and for the first time in days had a cup of tea, which I realised that I'd really missed ... I was pleased the night has been a good one, I feel more rested ... The route down

---

to the south is looking far from simple, and every day I have watched with interest the tracks of the front of the fleet, still battling high pressure when they expected to be riding the lows ... Meanwhile, I am thankful to be out here in this beautiful ocean. Sure, we have to deal with some intense and difficult situations in the ocean, but we also get to see nature in its most unadulterated form. The ocean is a stunningly beautiful place, and I know I am lucky to see it in this way.

As a sailor, I get to visit places on this planet that few other human beings will ever see. When we race across the world's oceans, we are immersed in the most natural of environments. We are eyewitnesses to nature at its purest, untouched by man (except the intrusion of our boats cutting through the water), and it is magnificent.

When sailing at night in the middle of an ocean, the stars can be so bright that even before the moon has risen it is possible to see the deck and ropes clearly by starlight alone. When the light of the moon cuts through the spray from the bow, in just the right way, I have seen a 'moonbow' – a magical rainbow of whites and greys, a completely different spectrum of light from that which we experience with the sun. At night-time in many parts of the ocean we see phosphorescence, a type of bioluminescence where plankton in the water emit light when they are disrupted by the movement of the water. I have sailed through fields of phosphorescence where the pattern the breaking waves make on the surface of the sea looks like a shining chessboard. When the boat sails through patches of these plankton, it leaves twinkling contrails where the rudders cut through the ocean. But perhaps the most spectacular sight of all is that of dolphins amid the phosphorescence, which look like silver torpedoes under the water, their sparkling trails criss-crossing each other and the boat's trajectory. At night when there is little light and the boat is going fast, it can be impossible to tell where the sea ends and the sky begins – it feels as if you are sailing out into the universe.

Out there in the ocean, I am blessed that I can see the night sky as generations before me would have seen it. Cosmologist Roberto Trotta talks of a starscape 'steadily retiring under the advance of lampposts, searchlights, digital billboards, and solar-powered fairy lights in gardens', and Bernard Moitessier, the celebrated skipper, wrote of his dread of returning to so-called civilisation where 'if a businessman could put out the stars to make his billboards look better at night, he might just do it'. In the 50 years or more since he wrote those words, light pollution has continued its relentless progress, and we now know so much more about the damage and confusion it wreaks on the planet's precious wildlife.

It is not only the night-time that brings such episodes of intense spiritual sustenance. Sailing fast in dazzling sunshine on a bright blue ocean is the most joyous experience, and it is during the day that I have had the most incredible encounters with living creatures, always humbling, each of which makes me intensely aware that I am invading their habitat. Dolphins are the happiness creators of the world. I have never met a person that does not crack a smile when dolphins appear, and most sailors I know, regardless of their miles on the ocean, will still rush on deck to watch them. They are incredible creatures. When I am becalmed or sailing slowly, I can hear them chatting from many miles away. Through the thin carbon hull of the boat, I will pick up the squeaks and clicks well before the pod appears. When they do show up they are curious and athletic, trying to keep pace with the boat, diving under the bow and stern, leaping out of the water next to the foils. At times it is clear that the adults with calves are giving lessons to their offspring on how to interact with the boat. Twice, while sailing smaller, slower boats, I have had the most incredible experience with dolphins, once off the northern coast of Spain and the other off Argentina. On both occasions, I had hung over the bow of the boat and trailed my hand in the water, all the while speaking or singing to one particular dolphin, which was engaged and interested for over an hour at a time so that eventually I was able to touch its back. Both times the dolphin clearly saw me, never went far from the boat, came back to where I was hanging over the bow and rolled over to look at me. They evidently wanted to know as much about me as I did them. The intelligence and curiosity of these creatures is hugely humbling.

In the Southern Ocean, I got to see my first albatross. Though I've seen them multiple times on wildlife programmes, nothing does justice to the scale of these birds in real life. Adult birds have an average wingspan of over 3 metres, and they can weigh as much as 11 kilos. An albatross's body is like the enormous fuselage of a cargo plane – it looks too big to fly and yet it glides effortlessly just above the surface of the ocean, barely flapping its wings, always watchful. The Southern Ocean itself matches the might and strength of these birds: they belong here; they were built for this world. They follow the boat, getting so close that at times you can see into one black eye. At night they are lit up by the moon or dart in and out of the light I have created around my boat. I have that feeling of trespassing in their world.

In the Vendée Globe of 1996, French sailor Catherine Chabaud was accompanied on part of her Southern Ocean stretch by a tame albatross, which she named 'Bernard' after her hero Moitessier. In the mind-bending weeks of solitude, she half believed that the bird was a reincarnation of the great sailor. In his book about that disaster-ridden race, *Godforsaken Sea*, Derek Lundy writes: 'She was brought to the great questions about life that only solitude allows a person to truly contemplate ... Chabaud's experience confirmed what everyone believed about the Vendée Globe: it was far more than a harsh, manly bash around the world in the roaring forties. It was a spiritual journey.'

I, too, learned to take energy from my beautiful interactions with the natural world. It is not enough to just see these wonders of nature: I try to feel them, to open myself up and imprint inside myself everything I am experiencing in those incredible moments. I take energy from the good times and use it to recharge and reframe my emotional state for when things are tough. When I recall these moments, it's like a three-dimensional memory, rather than a flat image. I have learned a way to absorb my own feelings, as well as to remember what I see, both emotionally and physically. That way, when I evoke those positive memories, they come with a flood of endorphins and good energy. I have found that in order to harness the power of such incredible recollections, I must give myself the time to properly 'record' them. In the same way that a ten-second selfie filmed quickly on your phone can never really share the brilliance of a sunset, so memories need attention to record for future use and enjoyment. It is all about allowing myself enough time to be in the moment.

The mental techniques I developed to aid my performance in solo sailing have been self-taught, but when I read around the subject, I discovered that they follow a common methodology, which seems to come in and out of fashion. I think I taught myself to be immersed in the moment because I grew up in a generation before the internet or text-messaging services were an everyday thing. When I first started sailing as a young adult, I travelled a lot. In my 20th year, I was working on private charter boats in the Caribbean and then took a job as delivery crew on a boat that sailed from Trinidad through the Panama Canal, across the Pacific, all the way to New Zealand. None of my friends from school knew anything about sailing; most of them thought I was absolutely crazy to have run off and got a job on a boat, as they moved forwards with university or started jobs after school. We kept in touch by letter – an airmail lightweight sheet of paper that would be covered in tiny words and hand-drawn pictures to maximise communication, then folded into three, sealed and posted. It would arrive around two weeks after I had posted it, by which time I would, inevitably, be somewhere else. I wanted to share my experiences with my friends, to really try to explain what I was seeing and feeling to people who never had and probably never would have that same opportunity. By wanting to convey what I saw with the right depth and emotion, I needed to stop and properly engage with what I was feeling. This is 'being in the moment' in our modern vernacular, and over time I have learned not just to record this to replay for others but to feel the good moments more deeply myself, to bank them so as to get me through the tough times.

(As an aside, I still try to communicate a more holistic picture of my life on board to a wide audience, including those who know nothing about sailing. I always think of my friends from school.

Though I don't write letters now, and the comms I deliver off the boat are to an audience of people I do not know personally, when I have the time I try to share a wider perspective than the selfie video of me talking about my day. This does take time and energy, and arguably it is diverting energy away from my racing objectives, but it does remind me to be in the moment and to share the power of those moments with others.)

In the early days of sailing alone, I did miss the presence of another human being during the good times. It's a normal human reaction to want to turn to someone and let them know you are happy and enjoying life. When we see something incredible, or we experience an emotion, we are fairly hardwired to describe it out loud, to express directly what we are feeling and to solicit a response that will amplify or acknowledge that emotion. But through my years of recording the moments for later, I think I have really learned to appreciate the extra intensity in experiencing something incredible alone. When I am alone in the moment there are no interruptions, I am not subject to other people's assessment of the situation, nor am I asked to agree with emotions I might not feel. I get to decide and decipher, to experience how the world interacts with me alone, and I find that a very powerful thing. We live in a society that expects us all to be in the constant company of others. Our social norms lean us towards feeling sorry for lone holidaymakers or diners, or someone sitting in a cinema on their own. Some people might even be made to feel selfish or ashamed by onlookers critical of the way they have chosen to do things on their own. But I would like to advocate for the power of occasionally being alone through choice: to walk up a hill and watch the sunset, to listen to music and let it wash right through you, and to be alone with positive thoughts.

My second energy builder is music, which is also one of the greatest loves in my life. I cannot imagine a world without it; good music has the most incredible energy, which can turn my mood around in seconds. I have an eclectic taste that spans from the big Indie sound of the late 80s and early 90s, when I hit my stride as a teenager, to the timeless, powerful voice of Aretha Franklin, and taking in a good dollop of techno and electronica on the way. I take music with me wherever I go, using it to tie myself to the people I care about and to change my mood when I need a pick-me-up. Before each race, I will create playlists of my favourite tracks, and my friends and family do the same in order to share them with me. When I need a pick-me-up, I put in headphones or use my portable speaker to change the mood. A playlist created by a friend at home will remind me of them and the times we have spent together. It is a bond between us that makes me remember a good friendship and how it makes me feel. There are some tracks that I could listen to over and over again because the artists are so talented or passionate, or just loud. I remember concerts and festivals I have been to, or where and when I bought a record as a teenager. In that moment, the song makes me think of my journey through life and how I got to be here in the middle of the ocean. Because I have always enjoyed listening to music while I am sailing, I have started to map my own experiences through a soundtrack. Some tracks will evoke magical moments from other races, other boats, and campaigns. Whatever your musical taste, I firmly believe the right music has the power to change a mood in seconds. It can absorb and energise a person, and will enhance a memory. The next time you need an emotional pick-me-up, give it a go.

RACE BLOG, 21 DECEMBER 2020

This morning is an Aretha morning – she's been blasting out in my cabin and on deck and I have been singing along like a strangled cat, but she doesn't seem to mind. I've had an incredible couple of days' run, Superbigou *has been on fire and has made a great job of sneaking along to the south of my competition and gaining some miles. I've been pushing hard, driven on my best tunes, and I think it's impossible not to put your heart and soul into your work when backed up by Aretha. ... maybe 'Respect' is the right song for the morning ... although 'Chain of Fools' is a little way down the playlist too.*

And a month later:

> ### RACE BLOG, 21 JANUARY 2021
>
> *For the first time in many many weeks yesterday I hand-steered Superbigou and it was magnificent. I took a cup of tea, some great sounds (Daft Punk and Muse) and sat on deck steering my way through the shifts and the waves for five hours, until night had fallen and my neck and back were tired and a big ugly cloud rolled over the top of us and stole all of the wind.*

Though the bulk of my time is spent alone with my own thoughts, I have a team on land who are always ready to support should I need their help. In the next chapter, we explore race communication: what is allowed, how we do it, and who the people are that I turn to when I can no longer manage alone.

9

Using Two Heads – Communication

Extract from interview with Joff Brown, technical director

'When boats are in the dock, it's my favourite place for them to be because you can do anything, fix anything. But suddenly, when they go out to sea, the only things they've got with them are what you've put on them.

'You advise as much as possible, but it's frustrating for us on the shore as there's only so much you can do to help. Skippers like Pip are incredibly capable people, though. In my experience they never really panic on the phone if something goes wrong, and they stay quite calm. Ultimately, the technical team's job is to speak to them, speak to suppliers, and try to give them the support they need.'

During the Golden Globe solo non-stop round-the-world race of 1968 – the famous disaster-riven precursor to the Vendée Globe series – communication was a patchy affair. The radios they used back then could only be used on a short-range frequency close to another ship or shore, so when the skippers were mid-ocean, no one back home knew where they were or even if they were alive. Bernard Moitessier became renowned for his slingshot skills – he would catapult a bag of letters to a passing ship. (Even now, some Moitessier fans leave a slingshot on his grave when they visit to pay homage to the great sailor.)

Communication in modern races is a completely different affair. Satellite communication first became available to sailors in the 1980s, with basic text messages being sent from yacht to shore, charged by the 32 characters. The system was expensive, and connections could be hit and miss, but no longer relied on third parties to forward information. Since the start of the Vendée Globe race, in 1989, every edition has seen a leap in both satellite coverage and the capabilities of each network. First voice calls, then comprehensive email and internet availability, and now, with more coverage than ever, the quality and speed of a satellite internet connection is good enough for me to give live video interviews on national television. Now that Elon Musk has entered the arena with his Starlink satellite communication network, I am able to get better broadband speeds at sea than via some terrestrial services, but only when my antenna has a clear view of the sky and is not covered in water, a requirement that in itself is problematic. In the last edition of the race, competitors had to carry two separate satellite communication systems and to have one of them online at all times so the race committee could always reach them. I chose to leave my iridium system always switched on, and carried a boat smartphone with number known only to my team, the race committee and my inner sanctum of friends and family. This phone was always connected to WhatsApp, and my team often joke that it was easier to get hold of me in the Southern Ocean than it sometimes is when I am at home in the UK.

Interestingly, the attitude to having communication with shore varies with skippers. Some like the feeling of being alone on the waves, on their own floating island, without the distraction of messages and land-based responsibilities. They rather resent having to get in touch with shore at all. Moitessier became so attuned to the solitude of life on board that his writing increasingly began to sound like that of a Buddhist monk. The very thought of being part of the hubbub that would greet his vessel on return to Portsmouth and the need to conduct interviews with the media horrified him to the extent that he gave up what was sure to be a first-place position in the Golden Globe race and sailed another halfway around the globe to Tahiti in order to avoid going home. In the modern race, we can have no such indulgences. Communication is vital. It's not just part of the safety and race management protocol, but it's how we keep audiences engaged and generate interest and viewing figures for race and team sponsors.

I am not a person who particularly needs to chat. I love language, especially the written word, and I enjoy hearing other people's talk or ramblings. But if I don't have to speak for a whole day it's fine with me.

On a boat, I am entirely happy in my own company. Because I have had to drag myself through the ranks of solo sailing on low-budget campaigns, I have never had satellite communications readily available to me. The equipment is expensive to buy, and the call plans in the past were always exorbitant, with voice calls as much as £5 per minute, and data costing thousands of pounds per gigabyte. In my history of racing, I have never had spare budget to spend on satcom. All funds have gone into the basics, such as buying sails or safety kit. When satellite phones have been a requirement, I borrowed or rented mobile systems, bought the minimum packages, and guarded airtime fiercely. This naturally had a huge impact on performance potential, but it was all that was available to me at the time. In those days, I never had the option of 'phoning a friend' if I had a technical problem, was feeling low or scared, or just needed to hear a human voice. So being in communication constantly with the shore, and having a dedicated team to support me, was a completely new experience when I set out on the Vendée Globe race, and far from needing to adapt to a lack of contact, I had to develop a whole new discipline in order to communicate effectively.

Joff, our technical director, is a Vendée Globe veteran. Having worked with five skippers before me, he already had a picture in his head of how we should and would communicate over the three months of the race. I trusted him beyond doubt, but we still did not know each other that well at the start. He had no idea what I would be like afloat, how hard I would push, how observant and diligent I would be around the boat, or how I would communicate with him. But to his huge credit, he never tried to force me into the same communication style or regime as his previous skippers. In the final days building up to the race, I asked him, 'At what point do you want me to get in touch with you? What do you want to know about? How bad does it need to be to warrant getting you involved?'

He answered, 'Well, everything really. Just don't cry on the phone to me. I don't do crying. If you need to cry, ring someone else.'

This made me laugh, but it also made me think. Firstly, I couldn't imagine ever wasting valuable satellite airtime minutes blubbing down the phone. Secondly, I could see how inefficient voice communication could be when discussing technical problems, especially when a person might be feeling emotional or if the satellite connection was of poor quality. And thirdly, I had never considered that voice calls would be part of my Vendée Globe world. I knew of plenty of other skippers, both now and in the past, who spent considerable time speaking daily to their teams and friends, but I couldn't envisage my wanting to do that. With the exception of live and recorded media interviews, I would communicate almost exclusively via text messages during my race.

We exclusively used the WhatsApp messenger service for our comms, and established a routine of daily check-ins with the team for welfare, technical and communication purposes. These were timetabled according to the changing time zones, and shore-based rotas were scheduled a week in advance. The race committee were in regular contact as well, in order to health-check the fleet and build a picture of how the race was developing. They and my team relied on me to tell the truth about the situation on board. From a risk management point of view, it was better for the committee to know that I'd had a problem and fixed it than for it to escalate. Quite often there was little time to convey information, either because the satellite signal was weak or something happened on the boat that required immediate attention. We needed focused and efficient exchanges.

The Vendée Globe race rules are strict when it comes to what is and isn't allowed to be discussed. No skipper can receive performance-enhancing advice while racing. This includes any conversations about the weather, weather routing, raw weather files, help with trimming the boat, information about fellow competitors other than that freely available on the internet, advice on tactics, and anything else that might give the sailor an edge. We are allowed to discuss and receive help diagnosing and fixing technical problems, but no physical help in fixing them.

Hence a sailor can have a Zoom call with a technician to help them find and fix a wiring fault in the autopilot, but they cannot discuss which autopilot settings might make the boat sail at a better course to the waves. This element of the race is hard to police; it is practically impossible to prevent boats from receiving covert outside assistance. Personally, I could never understand a mindset that would allow a sailor to step outside these rules, and for this reason have always been tight about giving my boat phone number to anyone outside the team. Joff, the only person with whom I communicate daily, would never cross that line, and doesn't allow conversations to stray into a grey area. He will ask me what conditions are like if he needs to understand a situation, but would never give me his opinion on speed, performance, or the weather in general, and I would never ask. With other sailing friends who had my on-board number, I had to be super clear from the outset to make sure they understood the rules. Paul, in particular, messaged me regularly with encouragement. I know his mind is permanently curious about how to make boats go fast, and I could tell that sometimes he was holding back, wanting to ask questions but remaining cautious to protect my integrity. If ever the text message thread felt like it was straying towards the grey, either one of us would cut it off. 'Let's talk about that when I'm back' or 'a discussion for the pub' would put an end to it. Hand on heart, I can comfortably say I have only crossed the 'outside assistance line' once during my racing years, wholly inadvertently and in no way boosting my performance. It happened in 2010, when, together with co-skipper Phil Stubbs, I was in the final three days of the two-handed Round Britain and Ireland Race, which we would eventually go on to win. We had sailed a furious race, starting in Plymouth, which took us around the west coast of Ireland, the top of Shetland, and down the North Sea. Having gained a lead of over a day on our closest competitors, we turned the corner at Dover into an English Channel with no wind. The next 300 miles were excruciating. We moved forward on sea breezes and tidal currents, then were forced to anchor when the wind dropped at night and the tide turned against us. All the while the boats behind us headed down the North Sea, steadily catching us up. Within 50 miles of the finish, our lead was down to 20 miles, and things were fraught. We had no satellite systems on board, but were able to receive a standard GSM phone signal if close to land. It was dawn when we were forced to anchor at Start Point. Stuck in a wind hold with the tide rushing past us back to the east, my phone locked on to a signal and rang. It was my mum. When I'm racing, she always looks at the race tracker on waking, while my dad goes off to make the tea. Before I could even say a word, she started: 'You need to go offshore, they're coming in fast behind you. You need to go out!' And there it was. I had unwittingly received routing information from a lady in her seventies drinking tea in bed. To be fair, it was nothing we didn't already know or could see for ourselves, and there was nothing we could do about it anyway. But I wasn't very polite to my mum. Upset at the prospect of losing our hard-won lead, I was also a little put out by being told what to do by my mother. This hasn't stopped her tracking all my races. Now in her eighties, she is actually pretty good at using weather overlays to interpret conditions and work out different routing options, but she now very much knows this can be for her eyes and ears only.

Race control watch the skippers' trackers 24 hours a day. Any unexpected course changes or drops in speed raise a flag, and if a skipper doesn't check in to explain a drastic change in performance, the race committee will try to call them or contact their shore team for information. Any actions I intended to take that might put me at increased risk – such as a need to climb the mast or go over the side of the boat to check damage or make repairs, or if I was ill and needed to administer first aid to myself – required me to report to my team, and the race doctor when relevant. It was my job to report progress and confirm that everything was OK as events progressed. Failure to communicate, either through my not answering or failing to make a scheduled call, would be considered an escalation of the situation. Should a crisis occur for any skipper, communication might be widened to include other competitors within close geographical range, maritime rescue services, family, and the media.

Whenever I have a problem on board, it is vital for me to be precise and concise in my verbal and written communications.

Writing takes on the style of a telegram, where all warm and cuddly politenesses are eliminated. On shore, one might start an email with 'I'd be really grateful if you could ...' and finish one with 'Good luck, I'll be thinking of you', but I have schooled myself to be a lot more abrupt. Every social frill tends to be stripped out of my communications, and the same goes for those of my team. Later in the race, when Kevin Escoffier got into trouble (more on that in the next chapter), he sent a WhatsApp message to his team: 'I am sinking. This is not a joke. MAYDAY' – and I rather think that if the same had happened to me, I wouldn't have needed to include the 'joke' part of the message, because my team are used to my being a stickler for the baldest of comms. (The trouble comes when I'm on land again and bring these same habits to my emails and texts there – a style that can come over as rather rude...) Though I chose to communicate mostly in text messages during my race, I adapted the same style rules for any voice calls not media related. Whenever I had to problem solve with one of the team, the exchange had to be clear and precise.

Before making a call or sending a text message, I always establish in my mind the best person with whom to make contact. I ask myself: who is an expert with this piece of kit or type of repair? Who understands the limitations of working alone on a moving boat? Who knows what tools I have on board? If I need to speak with more than one person, their responses must be co-ordinated in order to avoid any of us going over the same ground more than once or giving conflicting instructions.

If I do need to make a phone call, I like to 'preload' information before making the call, often adding videos and photos. I will set out what I have already tried, and my own hypothesis for a solution. I lay out expected response times from the team, which take into account the rate at which a problem is escalating, current weather, other immediate issues in my own environment, business hours to get hold of experts in different places around the world, and daylight hours if this is important to my work. Once initial contact has been made, the team creates a schedule of comms to help manage a quick solution and ensure I do not miss a call. I have now taken to running team meetings in the same way, establishing at the start why we are all here, making sure everyone has the necessary information beforehand and realistic expectations of what will be discussed.

It was only after the race, while watching an interview with Joff, that I came to understand how stressful it was to be the crew on shore. For the whole time I was racing, he was never out of phone range, with the exception of one ferry journey across the Channel when I was approaching the finish. His phone was never on silent, and he checked the tracker every three hours, even through the night. The stress of waiting for something bad to happen was immense, and we all knew it would happen. You can't race around the world without breaking something. What we never knew was how bad it would turn out to be and whether we would be able to sort it as a team.

I am a ridiculously self-sufficient person, sometimes to a fault. Historically, I have not wanted or needed other people to help me with my problems, because I made my way through my sailing career at a time when women were not considered able or capable. If ever I asked a man how to fix something, I would risk ridicule or being pushed out of the way, unable to watch and learn, and certainly never trusted again. Most of the skills I have learned that enable me to race offshore have been self-taught – electronics, engineering, boatbuilding, sail repair – using manuals, or by trial and error, taking things apart. (In the days before YouTube, self-learning was a lot harder.) Joff was different from the men I worked with in the early days. I trusted that he would never patronise me; he respected and understood my level of aptitude for practical repairs, and I knew he would always give me the best advice.

The thing I struggle with the most while I am racing is the thought that what I do creates stress or upset for other people. This wish not to do so naturally holds me back from sharing my problems on the boat. In the context of technical problems during the Vendée Globe race, this approach would have been neither professional nor competitive. In the final months leading up to the race, I had to get into the mindset that we were now a team, albeit a tiny one. In Joff, I had managed to secure one of the most experienced and successful technical directors in Vendée race history. It would be crazy to keep him at arm's length. Yes, I still felt guilty when I texted any of my team in the middle of the night with a problem. But I learned to understand that we had all signed up to compete in ocean racing at international level, and that meant we were all competing 24/7. It is what we do.

Soon, Joff and I were exchanging between one and six messages a day. Most work was routine, but during the second week of my race I started to develop problems with my hydrogenerators (machines that convert the boat's movement through the water into electrical current that can charge the batteries). I had two 'hydrogens' mounted on the back of the boat, one on each side, so when it was heeling over I could always have one in the water. The units looked like outboard engines with legs, attached to which were propellers. The faster the boat goes, the quicker a propeller turns and the more power is generated. During the second week of the race, the hydros had started to vibrate violently at speed, then to break propeller blades. Quite soon, I realised that I'd been getting through one a day for the past three days.

Power generation is critical to both safety and performance for any boat that sails for extended periods offshore. When racing hard, an IMOCA uses electricity to drive the autopilot, to process and display all manner of data, to fix a position and navigate, to maintain communication systems, to keep a lookout using radar and VHF radio, as well as running lights and water pumps, charging torches, and keeping computers and tablets running. On average, *Superbigou* would be drawing 13 amps at 12 volts continuously – more if conditions were fruity and the autopilot had to work hard.

We store power in a bank of batteries that need to be charged regularly. Failure to do so can lead to the end of the race, as well as a sailor being stuck in the middle of the ocean with no means of communication. Having to hand-steer the boat and rely on the traditional methods of navigation, using estimated speed and a compass bearing to find a safe way to shore, would be a tough end to any race.

We had three available means to generate power on *Superbigou*. Firstly, there were solar panels, which provided a small, base level of charging but only worked during the day and when they were not shaded by the mainsail. The solar panels didn't need sun, but they did need light, so on the dim grey days in the Southern Ocean, they would not be able to provide much power. Secondly, we had an alternator, driven by the engine. The engine gearbox had been sealed, so that the engine could be run in neutral without generating forward propulsion. A super-efficient way to generate power, but reliant on having enough fuel – and as fuel is heavy, the more you carry, the more it will slow the boat down. We chose to take 220 litres, which filled both of our permanent tanks. We expected to use around 10 litres during pre-race manoeuvres and when motoring out to the start line. Taking that into account, I would have around 134 hours of charging available for a race of 100 days, which, at the necessary four hours a day, would only cover one-third of the race. Hence the installation of my two workhorses, the hydrogenerators. The drag of these units would slow the boat down a tiny amount, and they would only generate power efficiently if I was sailing at over 12 knots, but they were excellent. Having the three systems – engine, solar, hydro – covered all bases: the solar panels would soak up about a quarter of my charging needs, and the alternator could be used (sparingly) whenever I was sailing too slowly for the hydrogens or if conditions were too difficult to lower them safely.

At first, we were not concerned when I started to break the hydrogenerator blades. It was one of the problems Joff had foreseen, and I had four full spare sets on board. But when it kept happening, sometimes twice a day, it became alarming. We exchanged multiple messages about what might be causing the problem, and engaged with the manufacturer to work through solutions. The units were not happy; they seemed to be experiencing a lot of vibration, and this in turn was breaking blades. The whole thing came to a head as dawn broke on 29 November, when I discovered the bottom of the starboard hydrogenator had fallen off. Not only were there no blades, but we had no propeller either. I sent Joff the following message, with a picture of the hydrogen missing the bottom half:

Hi Joff are you up?
Solved the hydrogen blade problem... (picture attached)
Fuck

The hydrogens were our workhorses and we had lost one. To make matters worse, my engine wasn't a reliable power source: I had melted a hole in the plastic water cooling tank attached to it and had been struggling to effect a repair for the past three days. Nothing would stick to the greasy surface of the tank; each time I ran the engine to try a new repair, it would result in water being sprayed over the engine compartment.

Throughout the rest of that day, Joff and I exchanged 193 text messages. We needed to create a plan to keep the boat powered. With just 60 per cent left in my battery bank, the first thing was to reduce power consumption in order to buy as much time as we could. I duly turned off any equipment that was second order, such as phone chargers, duplicate data screens and the radar. Joff and I agreed we would not put my spare hydrogen to work until we understood why the first one had fallen apart, just in case it happened again.

We decided to divide and conquer. I took control of the water tank repair while Joff worked with the manufacturer on the shore to find a solution for my hydros. He came back with a solution to the extreme vibration that had caused the problems: I'd need to overlaminate the other unit, bonding it together with epoxy and carbon cloth on the outside, so its parts could not separate as they had with the first unit. The plan he sent was detailed, with an itemised list of materials that I'd need, from gloves and paper overalls to rollers, thinners, syringes, brushes and different weights of cloth. For each item, he told me in which of the colour-coded bags I'd find it and how much I'd need. Before I started – as if it were some giant treasure hunt – I assembled all the items. I then followed Joff's written instructions and sketched diagrams to the letter, laying down a plastic sheet on the cabin floor, cutting out shapes of carbon cloth, wetting them with epoxy resin, covering the carbon with another plastic sheet, then using a roller to ensure the even spread of epoxy. I transported the carbon shapes to the back of the boat, where I put them in place. The end result was not pretty, and I don't think a career in boatbuilding is ever going to come my way, but together we saved my race, and the hydro continued to chuck out power for a further 75 days.

RACE BLOG, 30 NOVEMBER 2020

Today in the last of the sunshine I am going to laminate the bottom of my remaining hydrogen on to the top part ... All I need to do is execute this on the back of a moving boat. It's mission critical, I'd better do a good job.

When it was time to move the unit, once again Joff provided detailed instructions on what to do. The hydrogenerators, mounted on to plates hanging off the transom of the boat, were suspended over the water. I would have to reach through the guardrails and project my whole torso outside the boat in order to access the screws and wires. I would be doing the work upside down, back to front, and over the water. Not to mention the fact that I was still sailing as fast as possible to hold my place in the fleet. But none of this bothered me half as much as the implications of dropping either the whole unit or a vital part of it in the water while I made the change.

In moments like these, an intense concentration falls over me. Anything could happen around me and I would not miss a beat. My world shrinks to the tiniest of movements: a turn of a screwdriver, the pulling of a pin. At times it can be painful, contorting your body into unnatural shapes or leaning against hard objects to gain access. Quite often, limbs will go dead and pain will grow from bits sticking into my flesh, but there is no one there to hold a screwdriver or bear the weight of a unit for me. One false move, and I could lose all my power generation. *Don't move a wrong muscle, don't lose focus for one second, this must be successful.*

I had to tack the unit (move it from one side to the other) about 15 times during the rest of the race, sometimes in freezing temperatures. During those moments, I had to manipulate the small fastenings, my gloveless hands becoming numb in minutes; at other times, the motion of the boat would knock me off my feet. It never got easier, but the stress wore off once I became confident that I had enough diesel to see me to the finish line.

I was glad my hydrogenator problems had happened while still in the Atlantic – the ocean was, after all, familiar territory. I had raced and sailed those waters in one form or another since the age of 19, having made around 20 crossings of the Atlantic in the intervening years. I was keenly aware that soon we'd be entering a whole new environment, and as our peloton in the race would shortly jump on the back of a nice little weather front, we'd be carried east and south towards the famed Southern Ocean. We were lining up to make the most out of the breeze – the boys ahead, me running along behind, refusing to be left out as I hung on to their coat-tails. I was nervous and excited at the same time. We were heading to the most remote ocean in the world, a mystical place that people always speak of with awe, and I was going there in a 60-foot race boat all by myself.

10

MANAGING ANXIETY

RACE BLOG, 4 MARCH 2020

Inside the life raft, my fellow survivors' faces are garishly lit up by a flash of lightning before it goes back to pitch black. The wind noise is so loud we have to shout at each other to be heard, even though there are eight of us crammed into an area of less than 10m². The canopy over our heads is battered by waves and rain, and when a wave breaks over the top of us the canopy is depressed against the back of our heads. We can feel the cold weight of the water and then the wave floods its way in through the door and the lookout post, despite our efforts to close them securely.

There are eight of us sitting in a circle, facing inwards. Our legs are piled on top of each other in the centre; we are sitting in water up to our hips, soaked to the skin; all of the raft's equipment floats around us. Even the smallest task requires the movement of several people; the raft wobbles. We are constantly trying to bail out the water but more keeps flooding in. Waves toss the raft around; it feels unstable, soft and flexible, not like a safe haven against the sea. We are vulnerable; we will have to work to survive...

Thankfully, this ordeal will end before too long. The blackout blinds will be lifted, the wave machine turned off, the soundtrack will come to an end, and once again I will see the friendly, positive faces of the RNLI volunteer crew with whom I've shared the last half an hour in such close quarters.

In my role as a Helly Hansen ambassador, I had been invited to join a Royal National Lifeboat Institution crew personal survival training course. The experience made me realise, not for the first time, what an extraordinary and selfless act these brave men and women volunteers of the RNLI perform every time they put on their yellow foulies and set out to sea. It also made me realise that I had no real idea what it might feel like if the unthinkable happened and I found myself at sea in a life raft on my own, a thousand miles from land, where it would be too far for a ship or aircraft from shore to reach me. If that situation were to materialise, there was one thing for certain: I'd be wholly reliant on the other racers to save me.

On 30 November at 1345 (UTC), my fellow competitor Kevin Escoffier's boat, *PRB*, was charging headlong towards the Southern Ocean at a speed of 27 knots, some 840 miles south-west of Cape Town. He was standing in third place, with Jean Le Cam 25 miles behind. Here, in the Roaring Forties, everything was going well. He was prepared for strong winds and a worsening sea state, with his J2 up and two reefs in the main. All was as it should be ... until suddenly it wasn't. Without any warning at all, his IMOCA snapped in two. It only took four seconds for it to fold in on itself, its bow pointing skywards at 90 degrees, stern underwater. In Kevin's first reflex action, he sent the three-line WhatsApp message to his team: 'I am sinking. This is not a joke. MAYDAY.' This unorthodox choice to send an initial distress via a personal messaging service went completely against all conventional training, yet this communication greatly enhanced the speed at which the subsequent rescue was launched. When Kevin set off his EPIRB (the Emergency Position Indicating Radio Beacon – the world-acknowledged standard for indicating distress), there could be no doubt he was in trouble. Everything afterwards happened so quickly that he only had time to make a couple more split-second decisions. The first was to get into his survival suit; the second was to not dive down and snatch his grab bag with satellite phone and VHF, as it was already deep underwater inside the cabin beneath the cockpit floor. Kevin reports looking down below and seeing solid walls of green water flooding through the forward bulkhead openings and into the cabin. It would have been impossible to fight against the pressure and speed of this water ingress: the bag was lost. Instead, he grabbed his second bag, which contained food and water. As it turned out, it was one good habit that ultimately saved Kevin's life (these habitual actions very often do) – he always kept a personal safety beacon tucked in the trouser pocket of his wet weather gear.

Back at race headquarters, the organisers received a call from MRCC to say they'd received an EPIRB alert from Kevin's vessel. This was not a good sign – it meant that he'd neither the time nor the means to communicate. A call from Kevin's team who'd received the WhatsApp message confirmed the worst, and the organisers swiftly confirmed that the tracker on the boat wasn't working due to lack of power. Moving into gear, they alerted all of us competitors and Jean Le Cam, who was in the best position to attempt a rescue.

As Kevin was trying to decide whether it was best to stay on deck or get into his life raft, the decision was made for him when he was washed overboard. His life raft didn't inflate on its own, so in the perilous 3-metre waves he followed the training we have all often repeated throughout our sailing careers: he found the painter, braced himself against the life raft's solid canister exterior, pulled hard to inflate the life raft, then clambered aboard. Two hours later, Jean Le Cam arrived at *PRB*'s last known location. He picked up an alert on his radar that indicated that Kevin's personal beacon was transmitting. An horrendous nine hours then ensued, with Le Cam initially seeing Kevin's raft, only to lose visual contact once he'd turned his boat to pick him up. Criss-crossing again and again, Le Cam finally collapsed with fatigue. He had lost all idea of his position by now, and dark was falling. Soon, three other competitors had joined the search – Boris Herrmann, Yannick Bestaven and Sébastien Simon – but it was Le Cam who eventually spotted the life raft once more and rescued a thankful Kevin.

A few days later, Paul Larson was interviewed about the rescue:

'What happened to Kevin Escoffier was unbelievable – such a catastrophic failure that escalated so quickly to his being washed off the deck beside the life raft. We have seen things happen like this before in previous races, like the incident with Yann Eliès in 2008. [While working on deck, Yann was thrown

across the boat by a wave and in landing fractured his femur, which led to him being incapacitated in complete and extreme pain, unable to manage the boat or give himself the required medical attention. In this instance, two fellow competitors were tasked to stand by Eliès' boat while the Australian navy launched a medical evacuation team to take him off.] It just brings it home that every little decision you make can escalate so quickly. I listened to how Kevin dealt with everything this week, such as his decision to always carry a personal locator beacon, and it's simple: little decisions, like having a knife in your pocket and charging your head torch, matter. Kevin was fortunate to have boats so close to him and Jean Le Cam nearby, who is such an experienced seaman, and he was able to come alongside and pick him up from the life raft without the extra complication of foils. Kevin is hugely experienced, too, and comes from a big sailing family, so if there was ever a guy that could ride out the time in a life raft it is him. But it has been a sobering experience for everyone. I'm sure everyone moved all the safety stuff closer to them this week.

'Three other boats ahead of Pip have now been knocked out of the race. Each one by hitting objects in the water with a different appendage: keel, rudder and foil. Such incidents can be very random. At least her boat is less exposed to this, as it is very clean and simple under the water. We're very aware it's a reality, and fingers remain crossed.'

In the same interview, our technical director, Joff Brown, commented:

'When things happen to other skippers it is natural for us all to be concerned, but Pip is on a very different boat, which hasn't changed in terms of its safety and build for over 20 years. All of the boats are different, so everyone will have their own safety strategy in place, and we all plan for a number of different scenarios. After the incident in 2008 that Paul referred to, a lot of the rules were tightened up, including things like having safety gear near the main hatch, moving everything within a

metre and a half. It's a bit like in F1 racing: you learn from incidents, there are briefings from people who share their experiences, and we changed a few things following the briefing this year, like putting a clip on the EPIRB beacon as opposed to rope, so you don't have to tie a knot.'

My team and I were quick to allay any fears that might be rising at news of Kevin's sinking among both our building fan base and my close family and friends. Everything we said was true: we had all already considered the serious implications of managing an emergency alone at sea, as had the race organisers. Every boat had been required to pass rigorous design and build criteria, which were then remeasured every four years to ensure they still complied with the ever-developing rules. Far from being flimsy on-the-edge speed sailors, our boats were built to withstand the harshest of conditions. They were regularly surveyed to inform of weakness in the carbon structure; every four years keels would need to be demounted, the bulb pulled off the strut, and the whole thing surveyed before rebuilding. Our righting moment, which is a measure of the boat's inbuilt ability to come back up to upright if knocked over by a big wave or a gust of wind, was set at a minimum value, and every four years each boat had to be tipped over to 90 degrees by lifting the keel bulb out of the water with a crane so that this value could be measured. In times gone by the boats would be flipped upside down, without the mast and with the skippers inside, from where they would have to prove that, using the keel and water ballast, they could get the boat the right way up again. Happily, thanks to advanced computer modelling, this is no longer a requirement as it caused more problems than it solved. Instead, at our 90-degree tests, the Class measurer takes key data that can be fed into a computer model that calculates a boat's ability to self-right from upside down. The fact that nearly every modern IMOCA is able to survive high-speed collisions with underwater objects, dismastings, and other race-ending damage, and still make it to the shore, is a testament to the strength of these boats. But when you are pushing the limits of design, there will be freak failures – and *PRB* was one of those. When this happens, we must fall back on our survival training.

All competitors in the Vendée Globe race do survival training and we take it very seriously. A testament to how good this training is was the fact that Kevin, even though his boat broke up really quickly, managed to get into a life raft in his immersion suit, set off his EPIRB, and he was found. The important thing is to keep your training current and put into action all those small, practical things that will make a difference. We must keep everything serviced, and we constantly think about how quickly we can perform certain actions: for example, launching a life raft and getting our grab bag.

In the build-up to the Vendée Globe race, all competitors were invited to a feedback session with Louis Duc, a French Class40 sailor who has now joined us in the IMOCA fleet, who on his return from the TJV race in 2019 had lost his boat, which was rolled over by a massive wave as he approached the Azores. Louis went through everything that happened, in minute detail; he talked about mistakes he'd made and the things that he'd learned. One of the key pieces of advice that both Joff and I took away from the session was Louis' recommendation that a grab bag is best designed as a rucksack. He described how difficult it was to carry his grab bag (the waterproof bag loaded with survival essentials not already in the life raft) once his boat was flooded with water. He had needed his arms to guide his way as he swam through the small hatches to get out. After the session, the backpack was an adaption we immediately made – and indeed it would become mandatory in the following issue of IMOCA class rules.

Since Kevin's sinking, Class IMOCA have made a review of the life raft specifications. Already, every competitor is required to have two life rafts on board (in most cruising or racing boats there will be only one). One must be stowed below deck and is launched by pushing it out of a hatch in the back of the boat; the other is on deck and either self-launches in the event of a sinking or can be pushed over the side by the skipper. Using learnings from the 2020 race, the class has bolstered the life raft specification so that it is suitable to our own particular circumstances. These leaps forward in equipment specification are one thing, but it is very often the small strategies and the ingraining of habits that ultimately prove most useful in an emergency situation. Luck has very little to do with it: training has always been my armour, as well as the methodical preparations we make in the months and years prior to a big race.

It was inevitable after such a catastrophic failure that I and my team would start to consider our own 'what ifs'. At times like this, the hubbub of communication can bring with it negatives as well as positives: the concerned, unsettled messages from friends and family, the requests for media interviews, as well as the unfolding minute-by-minute news. Even after Kevin had been rescued and confirmed safe, there was little to no information about what had actually happened. Other boats had been hitting detritus in the sea: could his accident have been the extreme result of a collision? That was our greatest fear, as there is no way you can prepare for a freak event like that. It was a risk we all shared. My blog post the day after the rescue reads a little like a statement for the media, but it reflected how hard I was trying to keep a lid on speculation that might cause concern among my family and friends – and indeed my sponsors.

RACE BLOG, 1 DECEMBER 2020

I have had many messages overnight from friends and family, wishing me to stay safe, and with underlying worry and concern. It has been a horrific few hours for everyone, and something like this certainly brings this risk that we have chosen to take into sharp reality. I won't say that I am not shaken, but every time I have crossed an ocean I have implicitly understood I am stepping out of the safety net of quick rescue, and so this is a risk I am familiar with. Superbigou is a strong boat, and we have spent a lot of time and effort preparing her for the worst conditions. I have great satellite comms on board to help me monitor the weather and to keep me in touch with my shore team and the race committee. I have trained and trained to keep myself safe and well on the ocean and to preserve my life should things go wrong. I love this sport because it pushes us to the limits as human beings. None of us go into this wanting or expecting to end up in a life raft, but should that happen we are ready for it.

> *The fact that we are racing actually brings some security to this situation. Kevin's rescue is testament to this, and I look at the pack around me in this part of the South Atlantic and I know they will be there for me and I for them should we need it. The only thing left to say is I will look after myself,* Superbigou *will look after me, and this morning I have nothing but respect and thanks for Jean Le Cam, Jacques Caraës (race director), Boris Herrmann, Yannick Bestaven and Sébastian Simon, all of whom worked tirelessly to rescue Kevin.*

So how do you manage the anxiety of the existential threats posed by racing a powerful boat around the world on your own? Firstly, I have acknowledged that I could die during the Vendée Globe race or at any other time while solo sailing. If I were to fall over the side in the Southern Ocean, regardless of the safety equipment I was carrying in my pocket it would be highly unlikely that a fellow competitor would be close enough to rescue me before I died of hypothermia. I know this all too well from having sat for three years on the Casualty Review Panel hosted by the British Maritime and Coastguard Agency, which had pulled together a group of experts from various maritime bodies. We had the grim task of reviewing and analysing every vessel-based fatality in UK waters the previous year, in a bid to understand both the mechanism of death and whether any piece of safety equipment could have changed the outcome. The most interesting and sobering view came from Professor Mike Tipton, the UK's leading expert in cold water immersion: even with a lifejacket to keep them floating, a person left for as little as 30 minutes in water below 10°C (50°F) will ultimately lose consciousness through hypothermia. A stark fact, which I seldom talk about with other people. However, the knowledge that this would happen were I to fall over the side comes with a certain power. It means that I am innately more aware of and careful in situations that could cause this to happen. I do everything possible to protect myself from going over the side, which already places me a step removed from any fatal end to my story. Others might imagine that the risk of my falling is a lot higher, because they don't know or understand the steps I always take to protect myself – how I have adapted to manage being on the deck safely. So much is in my control, and each time I go on deck I risk assess and take appropriate precautions. For me this is normal, everyday behaviour, like the routine we go through every time we cross a road. In this way, I am not anxious about it.

There are of course many other fates that could befall me and my boat as we race across an ocean, events that would be completely out of my control, such as hitting underwater objects. On 2 December, *Arkéa Paprec,* a 2020 generation foiler, hit a UFO (unidentified floating object), which ripped one of the foil cases open and ended the race for Seb Simon. Shortly after that, in the same 24-hour period, British Vendée veteran Samantha Davies also hit a UFO in her big foiler, *Initiatives-Coeur.* The impact threw her across the cabin, breaking one of her ribs and damaging the keel. After making repairs in Cape Town, an action that disqualified her, she opted to go on to finish the course so that she could continue raising money for the charity her sponsors had chosen to support. For every 'like' on her social media pages, her sponsors had offered to make a donation to a charity that provides life-saving heart operations to children in developing nations. If she had cut her race short, the campaign would have had reduced exposure. Continuing, though disqualified, meant that Samantha's circumnavigation would save as many lives as possible. She was another person who had mapped out multiple definitions of success.

On 6 December, Didac and I were sailing west to pass some 500 miles south of the Cape of Good Hope. He was 100 miles ahead of me, and I was hanging hard to his coat-tails, when he messaged to say he had hit something in the water. He and the boat were fine, but he warned me that I should be careful. It was hard to quash my own building anxiety. So many other competitors had hit underwater objects and I feared it would be my turn next. I had been sailing *Superbigou* hard in an effort to make up the miles I had lost in the trade winds. Cali in his foiling boat had leapt a huge 575 miles ahead, and Manu had gained 316 miles. Once we were sailing more downwind angles, I had been pleased to see that our relative speeds were closer; at times, when I really pushed, I had gained miles on both Didac and Manu. With my foot to the floor, *Superbigou* had been doing 18 knots, shaking and shuddering as the energy came through the hull. But my exhilaration at knowing that I was coming back at them vanished all of a sudden when I received that news from Didac, my closest competitor. The fact that he had suffered a collision made me sick to my stomach. I wasn't frightened of sinking, but I was terrified of being put out of the race.

I messaged Joff to ask his opinion on whether there would be a significant difference between hitting an object at 15 knots or at 10, in a bid to rationalise whether I should slow down or not. I actually wanted him to say no – which would have been a green light to continue sailing fast. His answer was vague and expected: the slower the impact, the less the damage – of course – but he couldn't put an absolute figure on it.

I think it is fair to say that I was plagued by feelings of anxiety most days when I sailed through the Southern Ocean. I was pushing the boat hard, often setting new PBs, holding sails in more and more wind with each depression that came over. At these speeds, even if I'd had the forward-facing camera systems some of my competitors were using, there would be little or no opportunity to react to a semi-submerged object in my path. It would be a *fait accompli*. The development of safety systems is marching on even as I write this: the two major manufacturers of navigational software have recently added a hazard reporting button to their programmes, so that sailors all over the world will be able to report in real time their collisions, near misses, and sightings of marine life or sea junk. The time stamp and location can then be sent to a central server to be downloaded by other sailors navigating in that area. We trialled the system in my last major transatlantic race, and it will be fully up and running by the 2024 Vendée Globe.

But none of this was available to me during my race, and sometimes the fear of something going wrong would grip me so hard that I would be paralysed for hours at a time. Rooted to the spot, wearing full sailing kit, standing by the hatch staring at the instruments, looking for any indication that something was wrong, my brain would be constantly working over the what ifs, my stomach clenched in a tight knot. At those times it was hard to eat or even drink; my mind would be host to all manner of wild thoughts roaming round inside my head and tormenting me. Though I was not outright frightened very often during my race, the slow and continuous creeping feeling that something was about to go wrong did often plague me.

But we cannot live like this and hope to perform. Being scared of the unknown and the uncontrollable is a normal thing, but if left unmanaged it will send a person to a dark place from where escape can be difficult. I developed a method to manage this stress every time it reared its ugly head. At the end of the day, it all comes down to trust. I had not entered the Vendée Globe race as a 'wet behind the ears' novice. I had over 200,000 miles of sailing experience already under my belt and 25 years working as a professional in the industry. I had chosen a boat that, although old, was incredibly strong. *Superbigou* had already made it around the world four times; it had been surveyed, measured, and passed as Vendée-capable by the governing body for the sport. In Joff I had employed one of the most experienced technical directors in Vendée Globe history, who had an unblemished record of his boats finishing the race. I trusted his opinion, his decisions and his methods of preparation. I knew that if the boat hadn't been up to the job, he would neither have wanted to be a part of the campaign nor would he have endorsed my entry to the race. The boat was built to withstand impact; I had the necessary safety equipment and training should the worst happen. My fellow competitors were out here with me and ready to respond. Worrying about a potential underwater collision wouldn't make the risk any less, so I had to pack up that worry in a metaphorical box, seal the lid, and trust in our preparations.

Think of it like this. When we get into our cars, we trust that we will not be involved in a road traffic accident. Those of us who are more concerned may choose to buy a car based on its safety features – its ability to keep us and our passengers safe should the worst happen. But if we are constantly made anxious by the thought of being involved in an accident, it is unlikely that we would take to the roads at all. Yes, collisions can and do happen. But, as with many risks in life, I had to put the potential for such an accident into perspective and then choose to accept the risk or not. If I were to allow the anxiety to build and affect the way in which I was sailing the boat, I would no longer be competing seriously. And in that case, what would be the point of entering the race at all?

◄ Under full sail, *Superbigou* carried close to 400 square metres of cloth. That is enough to cover three tennis courts. All to be managed by one tiny human being.
© Richard Langdon

▼ My volunteer shore crew at the start of the Transat Jacques Vabres. Though a little ramshackle in appearance, we were one of the biggest teams in the race and everyone worked tirelessly and cheerfully to prepare *Superbigou* to race across the Atlantic. We finished the race, and in doing so completed my Vendée Globe qualification.

▲ Paul Larsen became a mentor and inspiration from the moment I met him and we raced together in the Fastnet 2019. He taught me to never settle, that it was not crazy to push for what many considered an impossible goal, and to make the absolute most of everything I had. He is pretty good at celebrating, too.

▼ The mural which overlooked the race village in Les Sables d'Olonnes. It felt strange seeing my image blended with those of my sailing heroes. © Helena Darvelid

▲ Being lonely and being alone are two very different feelings. Walking down the dock to my boat without my friends or family to support me at the start of the race, was a feeling of extreme isolation and loneliness. In contrast, I was completely happy being alone for the following three months of racing. © Richard Langdon

▲ In Lou Adams and Joff Brown, I found two people I could trust and rely on, who gave me an enormous capacity to perform. © Clark Creative

▼ My entire life was contained in this small section of the boat. All tools and spares were stacked in the area behind the steps under the cockpit, I sat in my chair to work at the PC, I slept on a beanbag or just on the floor.

▶ Moving sails around the boat was an incredibly physical exercise. When wet, the bags could weigh more than I did. I was constantly working against gravity and the motion of the boat.

▼ Maintenance and repairs were part of daily life during the race. Whenever possible, I tried to carry out work without impeding the boat's performance. This often meant working in odd places, clipped on while *Superbigou* screamed along.

◀ Climbing a 30-metre mast, alone, while your boat is sailing in the middle of the ocean is a terrifying prospect to any skipper. I had to dig deep and employ a rigorous methodology of self talk to give me the courage to leave the deck.

▶ Zooming out to take in moments of joy became an important ritual for recharging my emotional energy and maintaining a positive perspective throughout the race.

▼ Any encouter with nature is both magical and humbling. These hour glass dolphins came to visit me during a moment of calm in the South Atlantic. Seeing any living creature on the ocean reminds me I am trespassing in their environment.

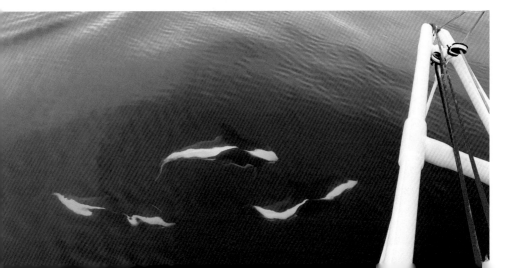

▲ Sailing an older boat, with no protection over the cockpit, meant kitting up and battling the elements every time I stepped on deck. Just to ease a sail 5cm, I would need to dress in full foul weather gear.

◄ I only hand steered *Superbigou* twice during the whole race. The rest of the time, the autopilot took the strain.

▼ The energy I felt from sailing *Superbigou* fast through the Southern Ocean was a complete revelation. Far from being afraid, I was excited and stimulated by how fast we could actually go.

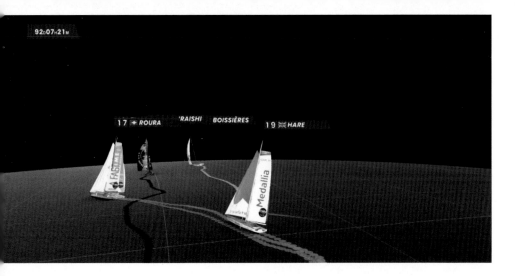

▲ With less than one week to go, I was still chasing Stéphane and Alan hard. I never stopped believing I could catch them. I finished less than six hours behind Stéphane after 95 days of racing. © Vendeeglobe.org

▶ A Portuguese man o' war washed onto my boat in a storm off the coast of Uruguay. I had no idea just how much trouble this small organism would cause me.

▼ Arriving at the finish line, I was riven with the stress of the final 12 hours at sea. For the last three months, I had known exactly what to do each day. Now, in the public eye, I wasn't sure how to behave. I missed the presence of my family and friends. © Richard Langdon

▲ The Vendée Globe race of 2020 was unequivocally the best three months of my life. I got to be the person I had always dreamed I could be. I stepped up to the challenges, became stronger than I imagined possible, made the most of every opportunity and never stopped believing I could do better. © Richard Langdon

▶ My boat for the 2024 Vendée Globe is a completely different beast. When extended, the large foils lift the 9-tonne boat clear of water so it actually flies. © Mark Lloyd

11

STEPPING INTO THE UNKNOWN

RACE BLOG, 2 DECEMBER 2020

As we smoke along in front of our first Southern low-pressure system, my mind is doing cartwheels and my stomach is in knots thinking of all of the things that could go wrong on a boat hurtling through the darkness with waves crashing over the deck and one sole occupant left to clean up the mess.

When I set off on the Vendée Globe race I was, in part, stepping into the unknown. I knew there would be times when I'd have to learn on the job, and occasions where I would get it wrong. I couldn't wear my habitual cloak of self-imposed isolation any longer. My commitment to share the real story before and during the race, combined with the fact that the race was being broadcast in real time, through race trackers and daily shows, to over two billion people across the globe, meant that my successes and failures would be a public affair. Pundits would share their analysis, and our stories and strategies would be aired, commented on, and critiqued across millions of social media accounts. I wouldn't be able to hide my mistakes; I'd need to own them and be proud of my learning journey. My confidence would need to be nurtured as carefully as a rare plant, for I knew it would be a fragile thing when faced with the harsh environment of the Southern Ocean – and that of the internet.

Confidence is an essential part of achieving high performance in every walk of life. It is the knowledge that we can make good decisions, that we are physically capable of taking on a demanding task, that we are skilled enough mentally, physically and emotionally to deal with adversity. A lack of confidence can undermine us at the most critical of moments, whether it's your voice cracking as you deliver the first sentence of a presentation or not hitting a rock with enough pace to clear it when learning to ride a bike off-road. Not everyone achieves confidence in the same way. For some, it appears to come easily: they trust themselves to perform with little or no preparation, and are able to banish any doubts that might hold them back. For others, like me, it is a hard-won characteristic, built over time and fragile in the early stages.

I approach building my confidence in the same way I approach physical fitness. I learn a skill, then practise, train, repeat, increasing the load gently, spending hours alone pushing forwards, demonstrating to myself I can both perform and recover when things don't go to plan. Only then can I take it to the next level. I like to hone my skills in isolation, having learned the basics from a book or a coach. I am careful, making my mistakes in private, reaching out for support only when I can't replicate a task or method. I calculate my own steps of progression, making sure they stretch me just the right amount, avoiding small steps that waste time and those too large, which only damage my progress. I used the same methodology when I learned solo sail changes as I did in public speaking, both of which have the power to terrify me at times. My desire to go away and practise in private is born of climbing a career ladder in sailing where I was constantly being told that I would never be able to achieve my goals as a sailor. I didn't want the mistakes I made while learning to be used as evidence to thwart my ambitions. I only ever put myself on show when I was ready. And, to some extent, that is still the case – or it was until I embarked on the Vendée, where I had to get used to being in the spotlight.

One of the strangest things I have discovered through my years of sailing is that the skills I learned through bitter experience – bad luck, getting it wrong, or a total misunderstanding of risk – are the very lessons that have given me the most confidence. And with those tough experiences under my belt, I have learned to repair all manner of equipment, to manoeuvre boats away from near catastrophe, to believe in my immediate environment over a weather forecast, and to never let other people's opinions ride roughshod over my own learned experience.

But how do you call on confidence when you are about to step into the unknown? The largest part of the race is sailed in the Southern Ocean, or as the French call it, *Le Grand Sud*, or 'the Big South'. Technically, it starts at the latitude of 60 degrees south and stretches to Antarctica. It is the unbroken body of water that circles the globe below the capes of each continent, and it encompasses the waters south of the Atlantic, Indian and Pacific Oceans, becoming one fast-moving, enormous oceanic fetch. The Southern Ocean is the only place on the planet where a continental landmass doesn't disturb the great expanse of water. In the same way that pilots flying between Britain and the US will choose a route, where possible, that passes over Greenland and through the Arctic Circle, so we sailors must take into account the curvature of the Earth's surface to find the shortest route for circumnavigation: as close to the poles as we can get. To visualise this concept, imagine a globe suspended so the North Pole is at the top and the South Pole is at the bottom. If you were to take a piece of string and run it around the centre of that globe, that circumference at the equator would measure the longest distance around the world. Now take the string and move your route close to either one of the poles. The further away from the equator you get, the shorter the distance to circumnavigate. In the Vendée Globe, that is your strategy: get into the Southern Ocean as far south as weather or rules will allow, loop round the top of Antarctica, then get home.

Our race course was simple – we must pass south of three capes on three continents: Good Hope (Africa), Leeuwin (Australia) and Horn (South America). The route to the south was governed by an ice limit, a safety rule set by the race committee, who used expert analysis from meteorologists and glaciologists as well as satellite monitoring of the ice around Antarctica. This line, which defined a latitude below which we could not drop, is set to keep sailors out of areas where the risk of encountering floating ice fragments is high. The smaller pieces, known as growlers, are of particular danger to sailors. Seventy-five per cent of a growler can lie submerged and is difficult to see or detect with technology, especially in rough sea states. Any collision with even a small piece of ice, while travelling at speed in a carbon-hulled race yacht, could have catastrophic consequences. In 2017, a slab of ice the

119

size of the US state of Delaware broke free from the Larsen C shelf on the Antarctic peninsula. It took just under four years for that giant iceberg to melt, and during our race, in late December 2020, what remained of it lay just to the south of South Georgia, according to satellite images. As a result, our ice limit kept us a minimum of 400 miles to the north and west of South Georgia. As the movement of ice was monitored at all times, the ice limit could be adjusted ahead of the lead boat, to take into account any new information. This happened six times over the course of the race.

Extract from interview with Paul and Joff, 4 December:

Paul: *'The Southern Ocean is a place that's spoken about with awe. It feels like the sailing equivalent of going to space. It's also been the playing field for some of the great legends of sailing, and now it's Pip's turn to go down and write her story on it.*
'... Down there feels different. You are thousands of miles from land in the middle of nowhere; it's that remoteness that starts to strike you. When you're watching the albatross fly around, they don't have a friendly gaze ... they look back at you like they're wondering what you're doing there, like you don't belong ... Going into something like the Vendée Globe, you're not looking for an easy passage. You're in the bear cage and you want to tease it, you want to come round that horn and feel like you saw it and you survived to tell the stories. You don't go there for flat seas.'

Joff: *'This week we ran through over 30 jobs and a checklist of things that need to get done to make sure everything is covered before the conditions change. Pip was experiencing 25 degrees earlier this week, and the end of this week it will drop to below 10 degrees.*
'The challenges in the Southern Ocean have changed a bit. Previously, it was the snow on deck and icebergs, but with the ice limit, that has now disappeared and made it tactically harder. We'll now see them gybing along that line, as they can't sail in a straight line and carry on south any more, and that makes manoeuvres more constrained. It's physically harder, too.'

Paul: '*Once Pip is down south, it will be more challenging for her as her boat's more exposed. Many of the boats have indoor/outdoor living capabilities, so you don't have to get into full survival gear each time you're on deck, which makes life easier. Pip doesn't have that luxury. That said, it's something she will live with, and Pip won't be sitting down below letting the boat sort itself out, as she's way too competitive for that.*'

The Southern Ocean was new territory for me. I had never sailed in those waters, which had such a fierce reputation for power and brutality. The only stories I had ever heard about it were fraught with drama and violence, and featured hardcore sailor protagonists. You never come across a yarn that starts, 'It was a nice day in the Southern Ocean'. I have consumed, mouth open, media stories that detail what it is like to exist in this icy wilderness where the energy of Mother Earth cannot be contained. I have seen pictures and videos of huge waves, wild winds, snow on deck, and sailors struggling to stand against the onslaught of frozen water. I have watched the faces of The Volvo Ocean Race (renamed The Ocean Race in 2019) crew members or Vendée Globe skippers age with every line of longitude crossed. I knew that the waves in the Southern Ocean could easily build to over 9 metres (the height of a three-storey house) in gale-force winds (the same weather systems would create 5- or 6-metre waves in my North Atlantic backyard). The largest wave ever recorded in the Southern Ocean was 26.4 metres: nearly the height of my IMOCA mast. The distance from land added to the menace of this section of the course: not only would we be over a thousand miles from shore-based rescue assets, at times, but we would also be separated by brutal weather systems that could block the way for days or weeks. After capsizing in the Southern Ocean leg of the 1996 Vendée Globe, British sailor Tony Bullimore had to survive for four days inside the upturned hull of his yacht before rescuers could get to him. Yes, there was good reason to be scared.

In analysing my own skills prior to the race, I identified my Southern Ocean knowledge gap and realised I had to fill it. At the very least, I needed a first-hand account of what to expect, and ideally some coaching in strategy and tactics when managing the persistent low-pressure systems in that part of the world. It was hard to justify the time to train myself when there were still so many tangible tasks to achieve, but I managed to find a day in September 2020 when I could get together with the renowned ocean navigator Wouter Verbraak. My object was to try and download as much of his brain as possible in a form I could apply to my own race. Wouter had experience as a dedicated navigator in fully crewed round-the-world races as well as having competed in the double-handed version of the Vendée Globe – the Barcelona World Race – on board an IMOCA. Not only did he know how to take on the Southern Ocean competitively, but he could also relate to the challenge of circumnavigating alone on a 60-foot beast. On that day in September, we did a tour of the world, talking about weather patterns, common race strategies, sources of weather, and what I might expect along the way. When it came to the south, the main strategy was clear: there would be a succession of low-pressure systems, travelling from west to east around the globe, and the best way to make progress was to place *Superbigou* in the path of these depressions. At their approach, I could use the strong winds and flat water ahead of each system's cold front. If I stayed well ahead, hopefully I'd be able to gun it, foot to the floor, and make as many miles east as I could before the system caught me up. Then the cold front would overtake, and – as we experienced in the North Atlantic when leaving the Bay of Biscay – the sea behind it would be a messy, breaking maelstrom, through which I would need to slow down, manage the boat, then gather myself together for the next system. The trick would be to position the boat well ahead of the front; generally speaking, the further south one goes, the stronger the wind, leading to more speed, but also more risk. The theory of the strategy was blissfully uncomplicated, and it did turn out that the weather in the Southern Ocean was a lot simpler to understand than the equivalent mess of fronts and troughs that are generally served up in the North Atlantic.

But knowing the theory is one thing, putting it into practice is another. And being confident enough to make bold decisions, to trust the theory and put learnings into a practice that allows you to take calculated risks, is quite a different thing altogether. My race strategy thus far had been based on a long history of navigating the Atlantic. Leaving Les Sables d'Olonne, bound for the equator, I was embarking on my 19th transatlantic voyage. I had a huge bank of experiences, good and bad, to fall back on. Now we were into new territory, and on 2 December I saw the first low-pressure system of the south creep up behind me. I now needed to race through the stages of learning in a real-time competition. I knew that falling off the back of a low-pressure system early could lead to a gap hundreds of miles long opening up between me and my fellow competitors.

RACE BLOG, 2 DECEMBER 2020

Yesterday morning the wind started to build, so in the last of the sunshine I prepared the boat for some hard sailing. It was beautiful, flat seas, blue skies, building breeze. I was busy working, but took every moment I could to sit and enjoy what I now think was the last of the sun. By mid-afternoon the wind was mid-twenties and Superbigou *was starting to move with some pace. Late afternoon, we hit 30 knots of wind speed and I changed down from my Code Zero to the J2, still flying, now getting very wet. As the night fell* Superbigou *was at full throttle. Averaging 17 knots, regularly surfing at 21 or 22. It's a bouncy ride, though the sea is still relatively flat; there is a constant roar of water past the hull and in the rigging. The cockpit is permanently full of water as waves crash over the bow and surge down the deck. Now I am fully jealous of the covered cockpits of my competitors. When I go on deck to check trim or do a job, it is in a drysuit and I am in the thick of every one of those waves.*

My first Southern Ocean depression arrived and left all too quickly. It had been, incredibly, just like the one Wouter had drawn for me with a felt-tip pen on a piece of blank paper. I had hoped to write up the notes from my one-day weather session into a meaningful road book to guide me around the planet. Instead, fighting time, I ended up laminating those scrawlings and taking them with me in the hope the hastily drawn pictures would jog my memory enough to recall the basics.

The joy of executing a clear strategy on that first weather front was immense. It felt like a huge step. I had not only seen the system coming, but had managed to position the boat, get the right sails up, and push hard ahead of the cold front. I was absolutely riven through by stress; I had no idea how hard I could or should push *Superbigou* ahead of the front; I knew the further I pushed, the more miles I would gain. But where was the red line beyond which my race might end? I had taken some comfort in my positioning to the south, having maintained a similar line to the peloton of boats that had formed ahead of me, all of whom had raced in the Vendée at least once before. I pushed as much as I dared, deliberating hard, as the wind increased, over when I should change down to smaller sails. Slowly down and earlier than my competitors would be double the penalty, as they would not only continue at a faster speed, but also bank more time riding the flat water ahead of the front. But they were more experienced, in faster, newer boats, and between our four-hourly tracker updates, where I might be able to glean a change in course or speed, I could have no idea how hard they might be pushing. I rode the front for as long as my conscience would allow, then changed down to my small headsail when the stress got too much. It was my first depression, and the first time I had put a new skill into practice, and I needed to remember that confidence could be both built and crushed. In short, I must push myself at the right level.

When I checked the updated positions on 3 December, it was writ large that I had backed off too early. Cali had gained over 200 miles on my position in 24 hours, whereas I was making slow progress behind the front, struggling at a speed of 11 knots in messy seas. He was still forging forwards at 18 knots, hanging on ahead of the front, banking those gains. It was crushing to see, but I needed to accept that this was just step one of my process. The boat and I had survived well with what we had done; we easily had more in the tank. I knew what it felt like, I knew I had backed off early, and I could see the consequences. My confidence in knowledge and execution had grown, and next time I would just push harder. And there would be a next time.

12

Tightening Focus

Race Blog, 6 December 2020

The temperature has really dropped in the last 48 hours. I am now wearing a hat and gloves all of the time and have two layers on under my foulies. One of the significant blows from losing a hydrogen [hydrogenator] is the fact that all of my diesel now must be reserved for power generation. I have a diesel heater on board, which I had planned to use sparingly, but as my Southern Ocean comfort, when things got really bad and I needed a morale boost. No more dreaming of blown hot air for me, it is only going to get colder and I need to manage this with my clothing alone. I'm thankful at least that I did not skimp when it came to warm kit. I invested in merino wool underwear and thermals, I have multiple mid-layers of varying types and the absolute rock-bottom position is a full-on woolly bear onesie, which though bulky fits under my drysuit and I have been warned will just make me too hot to sail. I think there will be days when I look forward to putting that theory to the test.

There were many reasons to fear my passage through the Southern Ocean and how it might once and for all expose me as not quite the individual I aspired to be. As we sailed south and east, the temperature would drop, the volatile weather systems would keep coming, and we'd be sailing further away from land-based rescue services. I had managed one South Atlantic depression, but there would be many more to come. At this point, the speed differential between me and Didac in our 20+-year-old non-foiling boats and the pack of foilers we had been with for the last four weeks seemed too high to bridge. The modern boats had pulled away from us by some 400 miles, and we were left in a pack of two, facing a stretch of over 12,000 nautical miles. I remember making a video during that first week in December, standing on the deck of the boat and pointing my camera out into the ocean on either side – 600 miles to the north was South Africa, 700 miles to the south was Antarctica, and ahead of me there was nothing.

The vastness of the ocean hangs heavy on the human mind. I had managed my first month of progress down the Atlantic by breaking my journey into phases related to my transition through the weather. Each phase of the Atlantic had taken five or six days, and after completing one, I would move quickly on to the next. The Southern Ocean would be different, I knew that. It would be six or seven weeks of the toughest sailing of my life, accompanied by the kind of oppressive grey cloud cover that hangs heavy over even the brightest of temperaments, so consistent and opaque that it was impossible to tell what time of day it was. There would be week-long stretches in the south where I would never see the sun.

On those days the damp and cold worked its way through every item of clothing into the core of my body, making it feel like I would never be warm again. Working on deck was the greatest physical and mental challenge. The water temperature was around 6 degrees, and when a wave washed over my exposed face or hands it would shock me instantly, followed by the raw, slapped skin kind of pain that comes when cold water is blown off your skin by an even colder wind. Just trimming sails – that minute-long action of looking at a sail shape, then gently easing a rope 5 centimetres – became a battle against the elements. To look forwards through the oncoming waves involved lifting my face into a shower of needles, the hard, icy spray driving straight into my eyeballs, so that my eyelids would automatically close. My hands would be numb within seconds of coming on deck, yet I needed dexterity to make micro-adjustments to a rope that supported 3 tonnes of load. Allowing the rope to slip out of control would risk entrapment of my own fingers and crushing injuries. If I were to allow the sail to slip completely, so that it flapped wildly, it could rip itself to pieces. I couldn't even bear the thought that I'd have to spend ten minutes of hard physical labour to wind the sail back in again.

Sail changes required me to be on deck for 45 minutes to an hour at a time. I would dress with fewer layers in anticipation of the rise in body temperature caused by my dragging 70-kilo sails around the deck and hoisting them to the top of the mast, but doing so felt utterly counterintuitive. Initially, the cold would stiffen my joints; my back would tighten like a rigid board, refusing to roll with the boat, threatening pain and incapacity at the slightest wrong move. I would try to warm up before going on deck; I'd hold on to the cabin steps, doing squats while being thrown from side to side by the motion of the boat. I knew that once I was working hard, I would be sweating inside my foul weather gear. But even then, kneeling with my body tucked into the frame on the bow of the boat, head hanging down as I attached a new sail, the oncoming waves would rear up ahead of *Superbigou* as we charged along, and, periodically, a giant funnel of water would rise, hover over me – as it does in that famous Japanese print, *The Great Wave off Kanagawa* – then envelop my head and body. The effect was horrific, the pressure of the water solid, heavy. It would find its way through any chink in my waterproof armour. If the collar or cuff of a mid-layer jacket was poking slightly through the rubber of a neck or wrist seal, the icy Southern Ocean water would flood in. The short-term consequences were painful – ice-cream headache and stinging skin – but the long-term consequences of wet clothing made me want to cry at times. I had limited clothing with me – two changes of mid-layers, four base layers and one new pair of socks per week for my six weeks in the south. If one set became wet, it would never properly dry in the sub-10-degree, humid atmosphere down below. I'd hang wet clothing above the engine whenever I used it to charge the batteries (which might be as little as once every four days when the boat was sailing fast). In extremis, I would lay super-wet things directly on top of the heat exchanger, which gave them a crusty finish, permeated with the odour of diesel and exhaust fumes. Even when things did dry, they were never the same to wear: the residue of salt water made the clothing stiff and itchy. I guarded dry clothes as if they were precious gems; once I had to hold back the sobs when a fresh pair of socks I had removed from their ziplock bag and placed momentarily on the back of my navigation chair slipped off into a puddle of water.

But it wasn't just being on deck that became challenging in Southern Ocean conditions. The inside of the boat became a cold, dank dungeon. The carbon structure of *Superbigou* provided scant insulation from the surrounding water temperatures. Being an older boat, it has a sandwich construction, with the hull formed by two layers of carbon, separated by an aluminium honeycomb – or 'closed cell' – foam layer. I was separated from the ocean by as little as 4 centimetres, which meant the hull of the boat was the same temperature as the water around it. Every surface was covered in a slick of water, as the moisture in my breath and from cooking settled and condensed. In more modern boats, including my current IMOCA, parts of the hull are 'monolithic' – they are made of a solid carbon plate with no sandwich construction – which reduces the insulation even further.

Trying to make repairs in this environment was difficult. I would have to squeeze my body into tight spaces, pressing myself against the cold hull. My limbs would go numb, hands seizing up. Tools went rusty within days if not dried off with a kitchen towel and sprayed with lubricant after every use; sticky tape, which acted as an extra pair of hands to hold things in place while I carried out repairs, was rendered ineffectual: the temperature made the glue less tacky and the surfaces it would normally adhere to were resistant due to the sheen of moisture.

Yes, everything in the south became a challenge. The energy around me was different, and it was clear I would need to adapt my style and perspective to make it through and maintain performance. I had already seen the importance of being prepared and holding my nerve ahead of an oncoming depression, and I'd been witness to the consequences of backing off too soon, but the change in environmental conditions produced an extra level of mental challenge that would only erode performance if it wasn't managed with conviction. The overwhelming urge of a cold, wet body and tired brain to find excuses not to go on deck, change sails or carry out routine checks and maintenance was huge. I had to keep pressure on myself at the right time and in the right way to make a good leg. But there was no routine to settle into: I would be required to change tempo often, adapting my rate and style of work to the weather, and maintain my motivation by reminding myself always of who I wanted to be – and that was a person who let no opportunity pass them by. Details mattered.

I have already mentioned the technique I used to help gain perspective on difficult times, the notion of zooming out through space and time, to positively acknowledge the length and breadth of both my progression through the race and my journey to the start line. But in the intensely pressured days of the Southern Ocean, I needed to rely on exactly the opposite perspective to break through the discomfort and exhaustion. When pushing myself hard through the cold and dark, my entire focus shrank to the size of the boat. In those conditions, it was all about details. I needed to check religiously that all the lines in the cockpit were still tucked into their bags, as they could quickly get free to clog cockpit drains or go over the side, where they might wrap themselves around rudders or the hydrogen. I needed to watch wind speed and direction constantly to ensure I made sail changes at the optimum times, setting alarms to alert me to changes around the boat, never allowing myself to sleep for more than 40 minutes at a time. In these circumstances, life is small; there is no time or space to lift your head above it all, to take a breather, to think about future or past. There is only the minute-by-minute present. In this state, I don't think much about my competitors, just about my boat and my performance.

I feed off pride when times are tough. When my inner thoughts challenge me not to go on deck and make a micro-adjustment, because it 'really won't make that much difference', or if they tell me there is no need to make the half-hour, painful crawl through the boat to check what 'that noise' is, I force myself out from under my blanket to do it anyway. I love the person I am on my return. I feel proud of the fact I took the hard option, and make sure to make a mental note of it. No one made me do it, and no one will bear witness to the fact that I did it. But in that one small motion, I am aware that I have made a small stride towards becoming the person I want to be. It feels good, and I acknowledge my strength.

RACE BLOG, 19 DECEMBER 2020

I know that this is only going to get tougher – bigger seas, more intense periods of fast sailing – and I wonder how wet everything will eventually be by the time I come back up the Atlantic. This is still early days. There is much more water to come. I've got a good routine going, but it requires a lot of self-discipline, which is easy to neglect when you are tired. Many people have asked me what I am most looking forward to when I get to the finish, and I've got other things to add to that small list now ... being dry, wearing dry clothes, having dry hair, and most of all dry socks.

And then everything will change again. Once a front has blown through, the winds back off, there is small respite in the sea state, and the tempo alters. As life suddenly isn't so physical, I can allow myself to zoom back out and take a long look at the world ahead. I find that I need these changes in focus for creativity and productivity. Too much close focus and, while it can be essential in the short term, you end up making poor decisions, as well as cruelly enhancing any negative mindset when faced with obstacles and disappointment. When you come out of these intense spells, free once more to un-focus your mind, you liberate it to look into the past, present and future, where it draws from memories and recombines different ideas. According to Dr Srini Pillay, who has conducted research into the unfocused mind and its power, in this mode you're much more likely to imagine creative solutions or predict what might happen in the future. Rhythmic, repetitive activities (think knitting, or mowing the lawn) can bring the brain into this relaxed but engaged zone. Though knitting was a pastime of sailors of old, it is never going to make my list of things to do at sea, but I find the same comforting rhythm when servicing winches or doing rope work. I put music on and let my hands work through these well-practised tasks on autopilot, then my brain, without my having to consciously prompt it, will find solutions.

During a long endurance race like the Vendée, it is easy to name and assess the physical limitations that a person will encounter. We cannot stay awake indefinitely, we need to eat and drink to perform. The body will tell us, quite succinctly, whenever we approach our physical red lines; we just have to listen to it and learn the language of warning signs. Mental energy is harder to understand, but as with our physical selves, our mental capacity is not infinite. In the same way that as we run up a steep hill our legs will fill with lactic acid and each step will become slower and harder, so attributes such as motivation and resilience are slowly eroded with every new challenge we face. I find that after intense periods of concentration, I need to allow my mind recovery time. On land, I achieve this through non-competitive sport – biking, swimming, wing foiling – just for the fun of it. This way, I allow my body to go through the repetitive motions I have already learned, and my brain can enjoy the endorphins produced by physical activity and being in the outdoors. During my race, I found this same pleasure when I performed regular, easy tasks. On maintenance days, fuelled all day by tea – a real treat, as I never got the chance to drink enough of the stuff – I'd work my way through the boat, fixing the little niggles that had developed. The work would take me into the transom with the steering quadrants, out on to the end of the boom to fix a reefing line jammer, to the cockpit to service winches, or into the keel box to change over a keel line. They were full, gratifying days, which allowed my brain to expand and relax from the pressure of what had gone before. In one blog, after a day of routine work, I noted that 'I had the rest of the world in my mind'. And it felt good.

13

ENGAGING BRAIN BEFORE MUSCLE

One of the things I am most proud of is that I am engaged in one of the few competitive sports on the planet where men and women compete on equal terms. When I am alone on the ocean I am judged as a sailor, critiqued on my performance alone; the ocean does not discriminate when it deals out problems to the fleet. I love this equality more than anything; it is incredibly liberating, and I have fought hard to be given the opportunity to be measured on my performance alone, good or bad. It is not without irony that I acknowledge this equal status exists only on the water, and it helps that I am at the height of my career.

There will always be media interest in a woman battling it out in a male-dominated world. French sailing legend Isabelle Autissier, who provided my teenage inspiration to dream big, explained to Derek Lundy (for his book *Godforsaken Sea*) that before the BOC Challenge of 1990–91, where she had been the sole female competitor, she had been asked repeatedly how she'd be able to handle such heavy sails, etc. She didn't feel that these questions were particularly relevant to her: 'I just did it because I wanted to do it, and that's all. Of course, I knew I was the only woman, but I didn't care about that. Everyone else cared a lot more than me.' In some ways, the attention was as unfair for the male competitors as it was for her. When a woman has done well she is put on a pedestal, and that is only another form of condescension. Autissier explained, 'First of all, you are not taken seriously because you are a woman. People thought, "She's a woman. She's not as good as the men, so she'll be at the back of the fleet." But then, when you prove you can do it – that you can win – it's the opposite. I dislike that very much. The race is difficult for everyone, for me and for the guys. We all have to deal with the same difficulties.' I could not echo these sentiments more, and demonstrated this in 2020 when I tried, and failed, to attain a World Sailing Speed Record. I was offered the female record instead, and turned it down. Part of my understanding of equality is the right to be judged on equal terms, and that includes when I miss the mark.

The boats we race in the Vendée Globe demand, undeniably, physical prowess. The sails weigh as much as another human being, the winch loads can go up to 7 or 8 tonnes. The biggest sail I have to manage alone is close to 400 square metres, big enough to cover two singles tennis courts. So how can we, as women, line up against our bigger, stronger male counterparts? The answer is firstly in the power of these boats, which is so immense that physical aptitude is only one of the skills we need to succeed. In all but the lightest of winds, the boats cannot be 'muscled' around. Every sailor needs to employ clever techniques, using winches and blocks (pulleys) to manage high loads; we use autopilots to drive the boats; we adapt our own cockpits and interiors to suit our physical levels. Yes, strength and fitness are important, but we all adapt our methodologies and techniques when managing the physical elements of sailing to suit our own abilities. This not only creates an arena where men and women compete in one class, but 23-year-olds race against 60-year-olds. In our 2020 edition of the Vendée Globe race, the Paralympian Damian Seguin, who was born without a left hand, delivered an outstanding race, coming seventh overall in a non-foiling boat. Our sport requires a full performance from every facet of human ability, and above all, we lead with our brains. When a huge physical response is required, we must adapt and respond with a technique that works for us as individuals in the circumstances we find ourselves. It may take me longer to tack my boat or to change a sail, but in a race that lasts three months, there are multiple other opportunities to make that time back through sailing smart or recovering well from adversity. As the weeks tick away on our circumnavigation of the globe, every one of us loses muscle mass and strength. I lost 9 kilos on my race: by the time I got to the end, my muscle bulk had completely disappeared, and every task took longer and challenged me more. One may even argue that those of us who are smaller, or physically weaker, could hold an advantage in the long run, as we do not need to adapt our style once our body begins to waste away. Because we are never able to rely on brute strength to solve a problem, we are accustomed to sitting back and thinking a plan through before we dive in, to ensure it will succeed. Maybe this, too, delivers a higher proportion of successful outcomes.

At 2am on 8 December, in the pitch dark, with no moon and a building breeze, the tack line on my Code Zero broke. I had been watching the wind slowly build from my beanbag down below. This is often how I spend my nights: sheltering from the cold and the wet, reclining on the floor, propped up against the beanbag behind my head and staring at a screen full of numbers. If the numbers are within limits, I will sleep, after first setting my alarm for 30 or 45 minutes. Then I'll wake and check the computer screen again. If the numbers are marginal, I continue to doze, eyes closed. Drifting in this almost-sleeping state, my mind relaxed yet alert to a change in the angle of heel or an increased rush of water past the hull, I listen out for any indicators that the breeze is on the rise.

When the wind reached 27 knots, I upheld the deal I had made with myself to never be lazy when I needed to change sails and hauled my body out of the beanbag (no mean feat against gravity, the slippery beanbag sliding and reforming every time I tried to push myself out of it). Drysuited and booted, I trudged on deck with a head torch and safety harness. Once there, I was struck by the close, impenetrable night. The combination of no moon and heavy cloud cover creates a kind of darkness that is like having a thick blanket draped over your head. There is no definition to the blackness surrounding the boat; it is almost impossible to make out any but the closest of waves; the horizon simply does not exist, and without the power of the torch neither does the top of the mast. This loss of perspective makes everything close and oppressive. The sound of breaking waves, beyond the limitations of my vision, was menacing. Flicking on my head torch reduced my world further. These head lamps are over 1,000 lumens in strength, which is ten times the power of the average torch. The focused beam allows me to pick out details on the front of the boat and at the top of the rig from the cockpit. When it is on, it bathes me in a pool of bright white light, making work at night possible. However, it also accentuates the sensation of blackness, nothingness outside the sphere of my light. I have no ability to predict the motion of the boat, as I cannot see any oncoming waves, so I stagger around the deck, often knocked off balance. There could be a sea monster just 10 metres away from the boat and I would be completely unaware. The disorientation these black nights deliver can be so bad that at those times when I am physically depleted, I have not trusted myself to react to the unseen and sudden movements of the boat. I resort to crawling around the deck on my hands and knees to ensure I do not fall over the side. This night I was on my feet, the boat was sailing well, and it felt good to be on deck, in control of the power. I needed to put a reef in the mainsail, drop it down to the boom, and tie off a slab at the bottom of the sail to reduce its size and power. With the right reduction in sail, the boat would continue at the same speed, or might even be faster, and the risk of damage, or the autopilot losing control, would be greatly reduced. Dropping in a reef was not so much about physical strength as it was about good technique. I needed to read the boat, ease the halyard that held the mainsail up the mast in time while the boat was surfing, then pull on the lines that held the sail down and make them secure. I was standing by the mast, locked into the motion of the boat, and as the last few metres of main halyard fell, there was a loud bang. At first, I didn't realise what had caused the noise. It seemed to have come from the back of the boat. I scanned the deck and saw that the outrigger (a carbon pole fitted at right angles to the boat's hull at the back and designed to project the sheets of my gennaker as far outboard as possible, mimicking a wider boat) had shifted from its usual spot. I immediately assumed that one of the linkages holding it in place had broken. As I scanned for obvious signs of damage, I could feel *Superbigou* becoming a little wilder, heeling over more, slightly less controlled. It was obvious something was wrong, and I could see the tiller starting to move more erratically as the autopilot struggled to cope with this new power. My mind instantly imagined the boat wiping out, me at the mast hanging on, away from any of the control lines that would make a difference. Vulnerable in my ignorance of the situation, I took a breath. One job at a time, I told myself, my methodical sailor-brain asserting itself firmly. Reaching for my autopilot remote control, which I always wore on an elastic band around my left arm, I sent the command to steer 10 degrees lower, an action that would instantly reduce power in the sails, decreasing the apparent wind and calming everything down. I needed to finish the job in hand: I had a half-reefed mainsail that, if left unkempt, could flap itself to ruin. Whatever had happened with my headsail, I could not risk losing my main. Be calm, get the job done, then move on.

Once the mainsail was under control, the boat sailing slowly and as flat as possible downwind, it was time to investigate. Even if a line had just slipped or jolted, I needed to reassure myself that it was safe to power up and carry on. In the middle of the night, it is easy to miss details; you never have the luxury of the full picture. Sometimes the most obvious things simply do not get seen. All it takes is the beam of a torch 50 centimetres to the left, and you may miss a rip in the sail or a broken piece of equipment. Sound becomes so important to us in these situations. The first indication of a problem is often a noise, and we need to search diligently until we can report its source.

I checked the cockpit and outriggers first, then headed up to the bow to look at the sail itself. My big gennaker was flying up in the air, around 2 metres above its normal position, with the tack line (which holds the bottom front corner of the triangle of sail) broken. I was surprised the incident had not created more drama, but the sail was still being held in place by the furling line, which stretched under the metal frame of my pulpit and around the furling drum. This line, normally operated from the cockpit, is designed to furl the sail and roll it slowly around its cable. It was not designed to be load-bearing, so would definitely not cope with the several tonnes of load this sail could exert on the tack line. The furling line had stopped the sail from flapping wildly once the tack line had broken, avoiding a huge amount of damage, but this situation couldn't last. The force of the barely secured sail was already bending the metal framework of the pulpit upwards.

My mind raced as I went through several scenarios for how this could go. Somehow, I needed to get this sail under control, stop any further damage, and then swap the sail to my spare tack line so we could get racing again. The immediate option appeared to be taking the gennaker down, but the risk in doing so would be huge. Normally, we roll these sails up into a tight sausage before lowering them to the deck; with very little windage they are manageable, and more importantly, small. But with the tack line broken, I was not able to furl this sail, as the front edge would need to be stretched tight between the tack and the head in order to perform the manoeuvre. I imagined the technique of dropping without furling, visualising the steps in my head. It was hard at the best of times, and it relied on speed and perfect timing. I'd need to synch the dropping of the sail with the rolling of the boat, so that as the sail swung over the footprint of the deck I'd have to loosen the halyard quickly to ensure the sail did not go in the water. It was barely conceivable: one small person in the middle of the night, battling with the full surface area of the sail in 27 knots of wind, trying to drag 150 square metres of canvas out of the sky? I could not see or feel the roll of the boat, my head torch would restrict my ability to see the whole picture if things went wrong, and even if I were to land the sail, it would likely be caught by the wind and drag its way into the water where, considering the speed of the boat, it would be ripped out of my hands for good, pulling me with it if I refused to let go. I could see a few outcomes – some lucky, others not so lucky – and all of them carried risk.

I needed another solution, but I needed to work fast. Right now, I was at an advantage. The furling line was, while the pulpit remained in place, holding the sail in position, albeit high in the air. This gave me a short window of stability, but it would not last.

At some point the furling line would break or the pulpit would rip off, and the escalation of damage would have exponential consequences for me and the boat. For the moment, the tack was still under control but out of my reach. If I were able to bring the tack of the sail down low enough for me to reach it safely, I could put my spare tack line on to the sail and haul it down that way. I needed to act quickly.

In the back of the boat, I sorted out the necessary blocks and winches, carefully tying ropes off, re-leading lines, trying very hard not to rush. I couldn't afford to make any mistakes, because if I got a rope jammed or put an extra load on anything it would only lead to more difficult problems. My heart was thumping hard; it wasn't difficult work, just stressful. Very slowly and with extreme care, I started to wind on both sides of my furling line, looking forwards with my torch to check for the moment the sail was low enough to grab. It was hard not to race up to the foredeck the minute it looked remotely in reach. The more I pulled down on the furling lines, the more the sail powered up and the more load I put through these lines that were not designed to take it. Too much and it would break, not enough and I would waste time going to the front of the boat and back again to finish the job. I also knew that working at full stretch would be a danger to myself. I needed to be planted solidly on the deck, ideally on my knees, as I worked with both hands to sort this problem out. If I were to set the tack at the extent of my reach, I would have no defence against an unseen wave rolling the boat and taking me over the side with it.

I held my nerve and wound the tack down, going forward only when it was close enough to reach. I took a safety line with me and tethered it from the bowsprit to the base of my flying sail. I was then in a position to work at a relaxed pace when I changed my tack lines over, the sail flying above my head all the while, and *Superbigou* chasing down waves that launched a deluge of water over me and the deck. I had bought myself time, and I needed to breathe out and finish this job carefully and well.

RACE BLOG, 8 DECEMBER 2020

The night was still black and I sat for a moment thinking about how lucky I had been. Lucky the line had broken while I was on deck, lucky I had not had to battle with taking a full-size flogging sail out of the sky, lucky that Superbigou *is such a strong boat to cope with these mishaps. I have now put a system in place where there are always two tack lines on my furling sails. Those lines are put under one hell of a load, and those sails will be my workhorses for at least the next six weeks while I am racing through the Southern Ocean. With a second 'safety' tack line in place, I will be able to sleep safe in the knowledge that the sail will be contained until I am next on deck. In this way,* Superbigou *and I are evolving, we are adapting, we are learning.*

Rushing in to wrestle that sail out of the sky would have been the wrong answer, and I wonder if, had I been bigger or more physically strong, I might have been more inclined to try. It is not always easy to step back from a crisis situation and think. It requires a calm state, a confidence to withdraw momentarily, and the ability to put aside your feelings of fear or stress to focus clearly on finding a solution. This is something I have learned to do through my sailing career. I know well that icy grip of fear, and how it has the ability to paralyse you and turn your brain in circles. But when you are alone on a boat in the middle of the ocean, there is simply no one else to take charge. The fear cannot take control. It keeps you sharp, but you must learn to suppress it. There is a methodology I follow in every crisis situation. First, you must reduce escalation. In some situations, this means your first action can seem counterintuitive, and from an external vantage point may even seem that you are not addressing the problem at all. In the scenario above, I was in the middle of the ocean, miles from land or other vessels, all the problems were on board with no risk from external factors, and I was physically in no danger. The situation simply had to be contained. To have left the half-reefed mainsail unattended while I searched for the source of the noise would have meant giving up control of another element. A quick risk assessment told me that the consequences of ripping a mainsail outweighed those of ripping a gennaker. I had other sails I could use at the front of the boat (albeit of different sizes and shapes), but I only had one mainsail, which was in use every second of every day.

Text message to Joff, 8 December 2020

I've finally got the new tack system in place after hours of messing around. I had no idea it would be possible to rig it wrong or get it snagged in so many ways. I think I have walked at least 3 miles backwards and forwards up the deck.

Another memorable case of calm under pressure happened in the horrific conditions of the Vendée Globe of 1996–97 when, south-west of Cape Leeuwin, Australia, at 51 degrees latitude south, British sailor Tony Bullimore's keel fell clean off, weakened from the bashing it had received in the Southern Ocean. Without a keel for stability, Bullimore's boat capsized completely, rolling over 180 degrees. One minute he was drinking a cup of tea and smoking a hand-rolled cigarette, the next he was standing on the cabin ceiling, cigarette in hand and still alight. He took a few puffs while he coolly weighed up his options. Could he somehow cut a hole in the hull and push his EPIRB up to the surface, from where it could transmit? In the event, however, he never got the chance to find out, because a moment later the swinging boom smashed the cabin window and the interior was flooded. Bullimore's first thought had been to find his survival suit and put it on, because in water that cold you'd die of hyperthermia within a matter of hours. Throughout his ordeal, which seemed almost hopeless, he employed an engineer's logic, which I think every one of us Vendée Globe sailors possesses when a pressing problem requires a solution. In a makeshift hammock, he crouched in the freezing upturned hull for four days in the dark, nibbling chocolate, until finally he heard the knocks of a diver from an Australian frigate that had come to his rescue.

When asked the question 'Did you feel fear?', I think it's probable that most solo sailors, like Bullimore, who have found themselves adrift in the hairiest conditions imaginable, answer 'No'. In my blog of 8 December, I discuss my own relationship to fear:

RACE BLOG, 8 DECEMBER 2020

I don't consider myself to be a particularly brave person, I don't think this is a characteristic you are born with. I think my sport has taught me how to control my fear and think clearly in a crisis. I do this not because I enjoy the stress or want to be a hero, but because I love my sport. I am driven to compete at the highest level I can possibly achieve, and with the euphoria of screaming through the world's most beautiful oceans on a beautiful race boat comes the acceptance that at times I will be challenged and I will be scared.

14

STITCHING TO SAVE NINE

During my race I had been asked a lot about Time – whether it had gone quickly, or if I noticed the passage of the hours and days. I think people wanted to know whether I was marking off the days at sea, or the days till I got back home. But the reality is that time took on a completely different meaning out there on the ocean, a meaning especially pronounced at the point in the race when I was heading east and the dawn came earlier each day.

At home, our concept of time is governed by key markers in the day: starting work or school, lunchtime, home time, TV programmes, meeting friends in the evening, bedtime. Any 24-hour period is constructed so that most activity happens during daylight hours, and we sleep through the night and wake up with the dawn. During the race, although I chose to do most of my jobs during the day, there were no communal markers to denote for me the passage of time. I ate when I was hungry, slept whenever I had the opportunity or when I could no longer function at the level I needed. I worked when there was work to be done. And the real joy was that there were no other demands on my time: I was just there to sail. I kept a note of the days and weeks as they slipped past, merely as a reference to the outside world. In reality, what I was interested in was the passage of geography and weather. To have the time and the space in my life to be totally absorbed in something I love, free to give it everything that I had, was such a unique pleasure, and something hard to achieve while still attached to the land and the drumbeat of life around us.

> ### RACE BLOG, 13 DECEMBER 2020
>
> *I am aware of how many hours I sleep, I know how long the night-time is, I know how long it takes to change a sail. My food is in day bags, my clothes in week bags, and I am being disciplined enough to stick with this regime. But other than these practical markers in my day, I hardly notice the passage of time. I exist in a bubble, where the date and the month do not matter. I have one job to do, day or night. I never notice the hours going past in a day, just the jobs being ticked off, the speed of the boat, the rise and fall of the barometer, the change in direction and speed of the wind. It is a world with no frills but full of purpose. Every action I take, whether trimming a sail or taking a nap, has an impact. I am only out here for one reason, and I spend every hour of every day fulfilling that objective. In this way, time passes quickly because I am happy and fulfilled.*

Local time is, of course, based around the passage of the sun, with noon being the time at which the sun is highest in the sky. Longitude is calculated from the difference in hours and minutes between the sun reaching its zenith in any given location in relation to noon UTC. I kept my time on board the boat to UTC (GMT) – not so I could measure longitude, but because all weather forecasts are issued in UTC, so it made sense to run my ship's time in the same zone. My small shore team are based in the UK, my sponsor Medallia was in the States, so to avoid any confusion in our communications we kept all timings to UTC. That way, with my dawn breaking earlier and earlier every degree I sailed east, the hour of the day held less and less relevance to me, other than at those times I followed the weather reports.

> ### RACE BLOG, 13 DECEMBER 2020
>
> *When I went out on deck to gybe the spinnaker this morning, a foggy, damp dawn was just breaking. I glanced at my watch, which is still set to UTC, as I went on deck: it said 0100. I've*

been working up there for a couple of hours and am now back at my computer, trying to warm my fingers around a hot drink (which is actually a disappointing experience with a thermal mug). The time now reads 0310, and the day is fully upon me.

Wrapped in a contented, purposeful calm, I moved about the boat, putting it to rights as we made our slow progress in the last of the sun. I knew there would be times in the forthcoming weeks where the passage of time would not be such a gentle affair. With the wind howling through the rig, the boat endlessly battered by the sea, I knew that I'd be sitting, watching the hours going past, willing the storm to abate, and feeling every excruciating second.

By the second week of December, we had passed the first cape of the course, the Cape of Good Hope, South Africa, and made our way into the Indian Ocean. The initial depression that propelled us into the Southern Ocean had given a taster of the challenges ahead, but rather than lining up for the next depression to land, I found myself stuck in a ridge of high pressure. The boats ahead had stretched their lead even further and were now heading north to avoid head winds, while Didac and I became stuck in the wind vacuum between systems, leading to some very strange weather. For over a week, we were meandering along in light winds and sunshine, uncharacteristic for that part of the ocean at that time of year. A full week of light winds when I should have expected strong tail winds inevitably had an impact on the overall time in which I might have expected to finish the race. I gave a nod to the fact that my race finish time looked as if it could be a week longer than I had hoped for at the start, but as I wasn't counting down the days to the finish, it had no real effect on my morale. Simply an acknowledgement that the weather had changed the goalposts – something to be understood and accepted as normal by any offshore sailor.

RACE BLOG, 10 DECEMBER 2020

If you had asked me to close my eyes before the start of the race and imagine what I would be doing during my first week in the

Indian Ocean, today would not have been anywhere close to my visualisation. Once again, we are bereft of the big breeze to push us east; the skies have been clear and I even had my shorts back on in the middle of the day today. It's been hot.

Now I love the sun. I love to be warm, and I love the huge amount of positive energy sunlight brings into our lives, but this last two days it has felt like my race has been on pause. I have struggled along at a walking pace, stuck in my own little weather vacuum, while the boats ahead and the boats behind all make up their miles in their own weather systems. I feel like I am in a bubble, almost suspended from racing. I am still doing everything I can to move Superbigou *forwards and to pick the right route, but when there is no more than 10 knots of wind on offer, I seem to be proceeding around the world at a crawl.*

I knew that I wasn't alone: the whole fleet was having a hard time with weather systems not quite as we had imagined. It would have been so easy to get frustrated, with hopes of a quick time to the finish being dashed and new records hanging in the balance, but there was so much more of the Southern Ocean to sail, and I was determined not to get hung up on any of that.

Instead, I did what I always do in these quieter times: I tried to use my time wisely. It can feel odd to take your sails down for a repair while you're engaged in a race – and in this case I lost several hours of progress by having to sail a suboptimal course while I was doing the patching – but it was the right thing to do. We can still find much truth in old proverbs, handed down through the generations, their meaning never seeming to wear thin. I knew that a stitch in time would undoubtedly save nine, so I went ahead and dropped the mainsail, putting patches on a couple of areas I'd noticed were being rubbed by the lazy jacks. I also took out each of my downwind sails, inspected them for damage, adjusted the leech lines (control lines that run down the back of the sail to stop it from flapping as the sail gets older and starts to stretch), and repacked the sails with care. I accepted the fact that being focused on getting the job done rather than on sailing would have an impact on my speed. There was always enough to do in quieter times, and I tried to make it my objective for *Superbigou* to be on best form when the breeze finally arrived, so that we could make the most of every extra knot of wind with no concerns.

RACE BLOG, 10 DECEMBER 2020

Now our pack has split up, just Didac and I are left together. The distance between us goes up and down, and I am needing to adjust my focus between pacing with him and the big picture ahead. Both yesterday and today, I lost miles while I was working. But I need to keep reconfirming with myself that this is an investment in the future: it is necessary, and a small loss now is a small price to pay.

Unlike the Vendée Globe, the Ocean Race is a fully crewed, round-the-world yacht race where boats of a similar size to our IMOCAs are raced by teams of 11 or 12. This has the advantage of allowing utter focus on the part of each sailor, who can give their full-time attention to driving the boat hard and fast. The crew includes a full-time navigator, and those with the expert knowledge to troubleshoot electronics and IT. The race is sailed in legs, with stopovers to refit the boats and refresh the crew. The Vendée Globe race is a whole other level. Not only is it single-handed, but it is also non-stop. This compounds all the long-term wear and tear on a boat, heightening the risk of critical damage, and stretching the human being to new limits. Even sailing a boat like this quickly is enough to take the energy and attention of a full crew, but I had to cover all the other duties, too, as well as keeping the boat safe – I had to do it alone. I'd write my job lists on the walls around the cabin, so I would never forget what needed to be done, and I would cross them off, marking them with dates so I had a reference for the future. I also exchanged job lists with Joff, who was my 'conscience' on shore. I had to split my time in a million ways. Managing the boat's performance, ensuring I had the right sails up for speed and power; downloading the weather and planning my routes to stay out of trouble; and trying to get ahead of the competition. I had to build short- and long-term strategies, while keeping the boat performing. I had to keep up with my media commitments, telling my story, and communicate regularly with my sponsors to ensure they were getting all they could from the race. On top of that, I needed to look after myself, feed myself, get enough sleep, treat injuries or illness, and make water to drink and to wash in.

If I totted up the number of tasks that I knew I had to perform at some point in any 24-hour period, I would always have too much to do, and choosing to focus on one job at the expense of another would almost always have a consequence. To prioritise and deliver what is important in any given moment, keeping an eye on the big picture, while ensuring we were going in the right direction, demanded a method of triage to help me understand the right thing to do.

Each day I triaged my activities by asking myself three questions:

1. Am I safe?
2. Am I going in the right direction?
3. Am I going as fast as I can?

The answers to each of these questions would dictate what I did and when.

AM I SAFE?

This question could relate to me, the boat, or my strategy to cover the next few days. Am I on the red line for sleep deprivation? Can I rely on myself to make good dynamic risk assessments? Am I feeling strong enough to wrestle a sail to the deck if I need to? Then the boat: is it working as it should? Is something broken or close to breaking – which could put myself or the fate of my race in danger? Am I safe to push hard or do I need to throttle back and make repairs? And, finally, the weather: is there a system coming that could damage the boat? Am I protecting my position in the fleet?

If any of my daily tasks left undone could risk either my personal safety or the finishing of my race, these were the jobs I would address first, and at the cost of all others. The choice could be painful at times: it could mean sailing in a different direction, or allowing a competitor to get away while I focused on making necessary repairs. The meaning of 'safety' covered geography, meteorology, my personal well-being, as well as the condition of *Superbigou*. But these were mission-critical jobs, and I had to do them. When staying physically safe becomes the priority, performance is put aside for the moment, because finishing the race is always the first objective.

Once these critical items on my job list have been ticked off, I can move on to the next question. However, the process is far from static. As my boat crashed its way through the Southern Ocean, a job that fell into the 'Am I Safe' category could appear at any time, and in that moment would demand all my attention.

AM I GOING IN THE RIGHT DIRECTION?

This question is courtesy of the first sailing coach I worked with when I started to train for solo sailing in one of the big French training centres. He pointed out that it was better to be going slowly in the right direction than quickly in the wrong one. He hammered the lesson home by making us sail around a course of buoys, where we made our way to one, then turned around it to sail to the next. The normal way to set up a yacht race has the course given out before the start, each leg of the race at a different angle to the wind, requiring crews to change sails at each mark to ensure best performance. However, the exercise our coach gave us had us given the first leg ahead of the start, but we only found out what our next buoy would be minutes before our arrival at the previous one. Those in the squad that reached for the biggest, fastest sail, without giving time for calculation, found themselves flying off under maximum power only to realise they were heading in the wrong direction and would have to take their sail down. The ones that did well worked out where they needed to go first, then put up the right sail.

In ocean racing, the 'right' direction will change depending on what you are trying to achieve. It may be finding the best wind on an ocean, avoiding a landmass, or going somewhere calm to make repairs. The goal is always to finish the race – but when the race is around the world, the fastest route is not always the most direct. The 'right' direction in any given moment must be determined by our own calculation of risk and opportunities, together with an assessment of the state of the boat and our own well-being. There is a constant stream of work involved in downloading weather forecasts and reports, which generally update two to four times a day (satellite imagery is available in real time). In the best of all worlds, we'd have time to scour the internet for reports from ships and weather stations, compare measured wind to forecasts, run multiple different scenarios on our routing software – after all, in a fully crewed race, a navigator is assigned permanently to that role. It is hard not to get sucked into spending hours at the computer searching through the what ifs, running routes over and over again. At some point we need to be brave and confident, to pick a route and move on. It is easy to stay with the pack – following other boats takes away the stress of having to make a decision – and it can be a valid strategy should there be other priorities to deal with.

AM I GOING AS FAST AS I CAN?

If the first two questions have been addressed, it is time to put the pedal to the metal. And this is always the part I love. It takes an incredible amount of self-motivation and passion to get ahead, because it always involves the extra effort of going out into the elements, changing sails, trimming, moving weight around the boat. You are not accountable to others; no one really knows just what is happening on board. Going fast uses up energy, and in the middle of the night, when you are cold and tired, it can be painful. But the rewards are direct, and the buzz of knowing I am pushing to the limits and the thrill of overtaking a competitor make it all worthwhile. It is what I live for out there. The answer to this final question – 'Am I going as fast as I can?' – can never be 'yes', however, because there is ALWAYS going to be a way in which a boat can be tweaked or tuned to make a difference. And the sailor managing life alone doesn't have the luxury of total focus on sailing. We have to be content with fast averages, while we look for opportunities to work at the rest of the job list once the boat is going safely, quickly, and in the right direction.

Since finishing the Vendée Globe race in 2021, I have used this triage system to great effect in business and other areas of my life. Working with multiple sponsors, scaling up our team at Pip Hare Ocean Racing, working to create and deliver the best performance programme possible to the deadline of the 2024 Vendée Globe race, all the while maintaining the dual roles of company CEO and team skipper, I am once again faced with what can at times seem like an insurmountable volume of work. I triage my day-to-day job list using the same three questions. Only this time 'Am I safe?' refers to our cashflow, the work environment of my employees, our contractual obligations, as well as the qualification process to ensure my place in the next race. 'Am I going in the right direction?' translates to my overall objectives and values for the business. 'Am I going as fast as I can?' drives me away from complacency, encourages me to stretch out of the comfort zone and keep pushing our business forward to new ground. Staying true to these three questions is always of greater importance than getting ahead quickly.

15

KEEPING THE EGO IN CHECK

By the third week in December, I had sailed one-third of the straight-line distance around the globe – 8,000 miles – and we were approaching the longitude of the Kerguelen Islands, French-owned small, rocky outcrops in the south of the Indian Ocean. The race leaders were some 3,200 miles ahead of my position, already traversing the waters below Australia, but I was more than happy with my ranking within the fleet, having climbed to 18th place during the five weeks we had been racing, and over 400 miles ahead of the group I had originally benchmarked as my competitors. With the second oldest boat in the fleet, any position above 32nd in the fleet of 33 would have been outperforming my boat.

I had been sailing in company with Didac for nearly all of the five weeks of sailing. A great pacer, he was on his second Vendée Globe race, in a boat he knew inside out. I knew he would make good decisions on navigation and would not be shy about pushing. In this way, he helped me grow my confidence as we separated from the other 2007 generation, non-foiling boats, leaving them behind us. Even so, once you cross the start line there are limited times when you may see your competitors again. We quite often race in close proximity, just out of sight, over the horizon. Sometimes, if close enough, we can monitor each other's progress using AIS (Automatic Identification System), which uses very high-frequency radio to send and receive position, course, and speed data between boats, with a range of up to 10 miles at times.

Text message conversation with Didac, 13 December 2020

Pip: *Hola! Buenos Días – accompanied by picture of 'One planet, One ocean' showing up on my AIS screen*
Didac: *Hola, Hola! I try to see you in the morning but not. Let's go to Cap Leeuwin!*
Pip: *That's a good plan! I've seen enough of this part of the ocean. I am ready for somewhere new!*
Didac: *I can see you now with no screen!*
Pip: *Yes I see you too! It's so strange!*
Didac: *Uau ... It's always incredible the meetings in the middle of nothing*

It was an incredible confidence boost when faced with breaking new ground every day to have someone to chase or to nip at my heels. Didac, it seemed, was also enjoying our proximity. He told me that during his previous Vendée Globe race in 2016, he'd had to return to Les Sables d'Olonne due to technical difficulties and restart six days after the fleet. After that, he had sailed most of the race alone.

After a couple of unseasonably light patches, I was delighted when *Superbigou* and I finally hooked into some breeze. The top of a low-pressure system was rolling underneath us, and I was determined not to let this latest opportunity escape. While I had the energy and confidence, I would push as hard as I could to stay in contact with it, determined to learn from my previous experience and not to back off too early and let the strong winds pass over the top of me. I had been looking after *Superbigou* carefully in the light wind days, and was confident that we were both strong and in good shape to push hard. The sail plan was simple: starting with the jib and main, as the breeze shifted behind me, I would transfer the jib to the outrigger and eventually hoist my Code Zero, the bigger sail at the front of the boat, which would boost my speeds and rake in the miles. From the look of the forecast, the passage of the majority of wind would happen between midday and midnight, and I would be on my gennaker within 12 hours.

As the pressure dropped and the wind started to strengthen behind me, I was excited at the prospect of a good run, but also desperate to execute the best performance I could in the face of this opportunity. I didn't set out like a maniac, just with the desire to push the boat on the set-up that I had. The wind quickly accelerated to more than forecast, gusting up to 44 knots, but *Superbigou* took it in its stride. As the breeze built, we continued to fly, bow up, autopilot steering a hard but steady course. I tucked in another reef and wondered about changing down the headsail, but there seemed little need. Everything was under control. Every now and again I would command the autopilot to bear away 20 degrees and sail downwind, flat and slow, so I could wander around the deck reassuring myself the stack was tied on, the tack lines weren't chafing, the sheets weren't rubbing. It was fine, and there was no need to back off.

RACE BLOG, 15 DECEMBER 2020

I had been averaging 16 knots for the first part of the afternoon, regularly surfing at 20. When the breeze had eventually gone far enough round for me to put the jib on to my outrigger, I put the bow down, went forward and set the pole with a new sheet for the jib, then came back and transferred the sail outboard. When all was set, I dialled the pilot back up 40 degrees to course and it was like someone had pressed the turbo button. Superbigou literally leapt forward on a gust of wind; the speed accelerated through 20 knots, up to 24, and then sat there for over a minute. I was standing in the cockpit, gripping on to the edge of the cuddy, and the expression on my face must have been one of total shock and amazement. A tonne of water came over the bow. It didn't take its normal route down the side deck and into the cockpit: it covered every surface of the coach roof, a huge moving body of water that slammed into me, pushing me against the back of the cockpit. I adjusted my position to stand behind the coffee grinder, grabbing hold of it with both hands, staring at the screens in front of me, head down to the oncoming waves, watching in amazement as Superbigou continued to sit at speeds in excess of 20 knots.

Superbigou seemed to have a new definition of speed. I had never felt it move like this before. This 20-year-old boat seemed to be absorbing the energy from around us and transferring it into a bone-shaking, white-knuckle speed. Sometimes we would take off, bursting out of the top of a wave, with the bow piercing into thin air, but equally it could be like I was racing a giant snow plough, the hull pushing water out of the way, up and over the deck and out to the sides, far from skimming over it. I will happily admit that after my first shock at how fast we were going, my second thought was 'you'd better put that jib back where it was ... this is too fast'. But already my brain was calculating how many miles I would make if I could keep this speed up even for 12 hours. In the tracker updates, I could see I was consistently posting speeds in excess of Didac's and had slowly started to pull away. My competitive self was greedy for those miles and would not let them go without a fight. I wrestled with my caution, making a mental checklist of every element of risk, identifying each reason I had for slowing down, mentally ticking off all the possible areas of the boat that could be put under strain by this new level of speed. As logically as possible, I reassured myself that this was not outside my capabilities or those of the boat.

Though I had been sailing in the IMOCA class for two years, my experience of sailing at these sorts of speeds was limited. In my first year with *Superbigou*, I was on a shoestring budget: the boat badly needed a refit, and I knew that to push hard in big breeze would be a risk to the whole project, so it was out of the question. Between the end of my refit, when I received my new sails, and the start of the Vendée Globe, I'd been lucky enough to get those two weeks of big breeze training days in the English Channel outside my home port of Poole, and for that I will be eternally grateful. But out here in the Southern Ocean, a thousand miles from land, and with the huge waves, it was a completely different experience and I was a total rookie.

As we continued to charge along, tonnes of water crashed over the deck. I couldn't stay on deck. No one could. But I couldn't settle down below. There was no way I was going to take off my foul weather gear. My mind was going over and over all the things that might break, hounding me with the question: how much is too much? I wanted to be ready to spring on deck at a moment's notice should disaster happen. I sat in the conservatory (the small person-sized space created by a plastic awning that hung over the exit to the cabin) for a while, listening intently to every noise the boat was making. Then I realised I was so cold that I was shaking – I hadn't eaten or drunk anything for hours – so I went below and made a meal, all the time watching the numbers, the boat speed, the wind speed, the rudder angle, and how hard the pilot was working.

That feeling that I was pushing the very limits lasted for a little over six hours. During that time, I sailed *Superbigou* harder than I had ever pushed it in the two short years of our acquaintance. I was on high alert the whole time, exhilarated by the speed, terrified by the implications of getting it wrong, but unable to stop. After all, this was exactly what I came out here to discover. I might not get a chance to push *Superbigou* that hard again, or maybe the chance would arise in the next few days. But I needed the courage to challenge myself and get a glimpse of what the next level of 'normal' might look like.

RACE BLOG, 15 DECEMBER 2020

I am writing this just after dawn on what I think is a typically white, cold, dank morning in this part of the Indian Ocean. I am cold, my clothes are all damp, my hair is matted, and when I woke up this morning I had the imprint of the foam matting on my face where I had eventually fallen asleep on the floor. Last night Superbigou *and I achieved our highest ever top speed – 27 knots – and we put in a 4-hour run with an average pace of over 19 knots. Wow! That was incredible ... It's not often that I speak proudly of my own achievements, I am a strong believer that pride goes before a fall and so I have an aversion to any sort of statement that could be considered boastful. I am still slightly in shock, a bit groggy and feeling like I'm waking up from a massive impromptu party that happened at my place last night.*

The next day, there was a lot of action with a bucket, sponge and bilge pump. *Superbigou* had a few persistent leaks that regularly needed my attention, so I knew that I'd be crawling through the black carbon tunnels doing my rounds of bailing out. The bonus to this was that it got me all around the boat, so that I could inspect other things as well. I was delighted to find that, other than a lot of tidying up to do, we were in good shape after our boat-shuddering performance. All the while I was working on the boat, I had my eye on course and boat speed, aware that Didac was just to the north of me. But for the time being, there wasn't a lot to do other than sail fast and enjoy the ride. The sea was flat, the wind had finally dropped to only 22 knots, so I had the big zero up and we were making the most of the conditions. I promised myself that after the next big blow – which wouldn't be far off – I would wash my hair and break out a fresh set of thermals. Definitely something to look forward to. However, that would be longer than I envisaged. The big blow turned out to be bigger than I'd bargained for, and a whole lot wetter.

By 18 December, Didac and I were nearing the longitude of Western Australia and incredibly we had caught up with the pack of foilers that had broken free from us two weeks earlier. We were sailing hard and matching or beating the speeds of the boats ahead, and I was loving the competition. Every minute of every day presented a new opportunity to learn, to develop, to redefine what 'good' looked like for me. I was grinning from ear to ear, laughing a lot of the time, and completely absorbed in racing my boat. It wasn't easy or comfortable, but it was exactly where I wanted to be. I would happily deal with the consequences of pushing my old boat hard, and that was a good thing because there were many. *Superbigou* and I were at war with water, and for a while it seemed that the water was winning. All IMOCAs are wet boats, and mine was no exception, but without a closed cockpit the hardships were that much greater. I had to work extra hard to ensure that my life on board didn't descend into a soggy pile of ruined kit. In these big conditions, if I wanted to do anything at all with the trim of the boat, I would bring water back down below with me, as I was as dripping wet as if I'd just got out of the sea. My living space was small, and as I slept on beanbags on the floor and sat and worked at floor level, it was really important to try and keep the area dry. Before going on deck, I'd religiously pick everything up off the floor and put it in one of the storage areas. I relied on so much electronic kit, which could be ruined if I leaned over and dripped water on it from my sodden foulies. If I was going to stay below for any length of time, I would take my top layer off, carefully hang it out of the way, then mop up the floor, pull out my beanbags, and push my foul weather gear trousers to my ankles before I sat on my beanbag in my dry mid-layer. If I needed to go on deck in a hurry, I would have to calm any urgency, taking time to put the beanbag away and pull on my foulies properly, no matter what hell appeared to be unfolding outside. Soaking myself would be adding risk of hypothermia to the mix, and my supplies of dry clothes were short. If I thought I would be on and off the deck a lot, I stayed kitted up and sat on the bare floor, because if my chair or beanbags got wet, they'd stay that way for the rest of the race. When we were really going for it, I slept on the floor in my wet kit. You can endure a lot of physical discomfort when you reach exhaustion.

RACE BLOG, 19 DECEMBER 2020

I spend many minutes every day with a sponge and bucket, soaking up every last bit of water on the floor of my living accommodation, just trying to keep everything as dry as possible. Though we have now got to the stage where 'dry' has become a relative term for 'less wet than another thing'.

Every sail change seemed to be either in the middle of the night or at dusk. If I started without a head torch, I'd only lose time fumbling round in the dark, so it was better to pause to go and get one. One night I had to go out to the end of the bowsprit three times due to various snags on the sail change. It was a crazy sensation out there in the pitch dark, with my head torch lighting up only the details around me. The water beneath the sprit was matt black; I could see the boat behind me, but looking forwards there was no definition between sea and sky. I was balanced outside the guard wires of the boat, with my legs wrapped around the bowsprit, braced on the bobstay, the cable that held the end of the sprit to the boat. Working with both hands to free a snag, I had to trust myself to stay seated in place. I was in a harness, tethered on, but with the boat constantly surfing down waves, even at reduced speeds it would be hard to fight the pressure of the water should I fall off the sprit. I had no way of knowing what we were sailing into; the water washed over me, and I tried to ignore it; my heart rate was high, the cold was biting into my hands. It was as if we were sailing in a black hole. My balance is terrible at the best of times, but on a night like this I had no sense of the direction the boat was travelling or the approach of any waves. I staggered around on the foredeck like a drunk, struggling to get from one spot to the next, resorting to crawling on my hands and knees between jobs. There are no prizes for style out here, and no one to see me anyway.

Every time I pushed *Superbigou* hard in the Southern Ocean, I was besieged by leaks springing up all over the boat. We had been so careful to prepare and test in the time available before the race, but nothing we could have done, short of sailing through the Southern Ocean on a practice run, could have replicated the onslaught of water that found its way into the boat. It seemed just when I had cleaned up and plugged one leak, another would develop. Sometimes I just wanted to ignore the water, to settle into my beanbag and have a break, but there was no one else to mop it up. My experience knew that a small leak could develop into a bigger one: water left to wash around the boat could reach the craziest of places, damaging electronics, ruining kit. So no matter how tired or beaten I felt at the constant workload, I had to pick up the sponge, turn on the bilge pump, and crawl into whatever dark, small cavity needed my attention.

On 19 December, I decided to change my definition of 'normal'. I'd been pushing *Superbigou* hard for a couple of days and gaining confidence that the boat and I had more in the tank. I was impressed by our speeds relative to the three foilers ahead, and they seemed tantalisingly close. I never imagined I would be chasing these boats as part of my race, but now I had caught back up, Cali, Stéphane Le Diraison, and now Alan Roura seemed like fair game. I could see no reason why I should not put targets on their backs. The problem was that in the big breeze conditions, when their foils made the most difference, it would not be possible to catch up through speed alone. I was sailing *Superbigou* foot to the floor, and just about managing to hang on to the coat-tails of these faster boats. If I was aspiring to get ahead, I could not merely follow them – I'd need to think for myself and sail a different route. Recalling my brief studies of Southern Ocean meteorology, I knew that the longer I could stay with a weather system, the more miles I would gain in the long run. We had back-to-back systems on our run towards Australia, which meant I had the opportunity to try something different. So far, our peloton had been sailing along similar lines of latitude, and the safety that came of being with them had been of some comfort, but if I wanted to move forwards, I would need to push into a breeze that was a little stronger, but would hold out for longer. That meant sailing south for a few hours, while the rest of the pack continued on the route east. When the time came to make my move, I had already run and rerun my routing what seemed like a hundred times. It was clear there would be an initial drop in relative position as I headed south, but once I had positioned myself to the south of my competitors and turned to sail a course east again, I should be faster and stay with the wind for longer. It would be a win in the end.

There were many reasons not to make this move. I was already in an incredible position, lying 18th in the fleet. I was keeping pace with or ahead of the positions recorded by the leading three boats of the 2000 Vendée Globe (of which Britain's Ellen MacArthur was placed second, a race achievement unrivalled by other British sailors until 2016, when it was equalled by Alex Thomson). My boat had been launched in 2000, so I was using these stats as my benchmark for excellence. A huge part of me challenged this need to take a risk, but I had come here to discover what I was capable of, and I could not turn my back on this opportunity to learn. I had set my own goals, but halfway through the race I was already adjusting my expectations and moving the bar higher. I had been coy about sharing my goals at the start, and lucky in the fact that no one expected anything from me. In general, I was viewed as an adventurer, not a serious sailor. I had chosen only to share my performance target with an inner circle of friends. I understood all the reasons I might not achieve that goal; I could sail an immaculate race, but then have some gear failure that could take it all away in an instant. Once you share a race position as a definition of success, that position will also allow others to define failure. So I figured it was best if I kept my performance target a secret.

Text message conversation with Lou Adams, 17 December 2020

Lou: *Paul [Larson] rang me today, him and H are very excited, he is reading Ellen's [MacArthur] book and plotting where you are against her and you are well ahead. He wants me to put it out on social media but I said we had decided not to*
Pip: *Paul knows how I feel about it. It just adds a whole heap of pressure I don't need*

Pip: *And it sort of makes success look like a binary option*

Between midnight and four in the morning on 19 December, I split from my pack. With every hour that I sailed a different course to the group I had been with for more or less six weeks of the race, I felt a little sicker. In my head I knew it was right, but my inner voices of doubt were fighting the decision. To sail away from a pack you have been inching up on feels wrong in every way while you are doing it. Just before 0400, I lost my nerve and gybed back to head east, and was then dogged by the idea I had bottled out too soon, tormenting myself that I had not gone far enough to make a difference. It seemed that I had just allowed my competitors to sail away unnecessarily. At 0530, I gybed again to the south, watching the wind slowly build and sitting in a miserable, nauseous stress-ridden state until I could bear it no longer. I gybed to head east, in the same direction as the others. The extra two gybes cost me time and energy. I was an exhausted, depleted wreck by the end of my seven-hour split, but I had to know if I could make a difference.

Within 24 hours of making my move, I had moved up to 17th place, recorded as the second fastest boat in the whole fleet over a four-hour period. I moved from a state of low morale and exhaustion to feeling elated, so proud at having thought the problem through, then executed my move. Daring to be different in this way bolstered my ambition. I was determined to keep redefining my limits. I was out here to be the best version of myself – no excuses, no backing out – and I loved it. I believe one of the greatest strengths of humans is their ability to continually develop, and so redefine their personal definitions of what 'good' looks like. Out on the ocean I got to experience that in abundance, with no interruptions, free to break through levels of performance, to make mistakes, learn, and recover. Far from being terrifying, this stretch of the Southern Ocean seemed to be delivering what I hankered after most: endless opportunity.

Over the next week we would cross the halfway mark in the race, pass our second cape, Cape Leeuwin on the south-western tip of Australia, and enter the Pacific Ocean. All the while, I was pushing hard, increasing my lead on the boats behind and gaining on Cali, who was less than 25 miles ahead and next on my list of targets.

Extract from interview in *Tip & Shaft* with The Ocean Race Europe-winning skipper, Yoann Richomme, 24 December 2020

'I want to salute the very good race of Pip Hare who, with a 1999 boat (Superbigou, built by Bernard Stamm), a late and modest budget, stands up to skippers benefiting from newer and updated boats with foils. Her routes are beautiful and smooth, we can see that she knows how to use the weather and navigate, I find what she is doing is quite fantastic on a high level'.

On 26 December, I noted a low-pressure system was developing some miles behind me to the west, due to move south in a couple of days, but what really worried me was a large and very active front associated with this system that stretched up to the north, towards Tasmania. It was travelling east rapidly, catching up with my position. I had been tracking these systems for a number of days, and this particularly aggressive front was forecast to have winds of 35 knots at its peak (which would mean a gradient breeze of 45, with gusts of 50 or above, like that first front I had crossed in the Biscay). At first, it looked as if there was no way to avoid it, and I considered taking a different route to minimise its impact, but then the forecasts changed. The passage of the front had slowed down, and a route was opening up that might keep me ahead of the worst of the wind.

Every day I pulled in updated forecasts, checked the routing, ran variations, and changed the parameters, as I tried to understand all possible scenarios. I wondered: what if I don't sail fast enough? What if the wind is less? What if the wind direction is 15 degrees different? All routings suggested that *Superbigou* could stay ahead of the big breeze, but I'd need to sail fast, make no mistakes, and take every opportunity to push my boat hard. If the front were to move more quickly, or if I sailed slower, the safety cushion would be eroded.

Race Blog, 26 December 2020

It's a pretty intense feeling and I am hyper-aware of how the boat feels and watching the numbers on my instruments several times a minute. Today I sat on deck for over an hour, engulfed by the water running down the deck and just watching, listening and feeling Superbigou *as the pilot carved its way through the waves. Watching the route the pilot takes through the ocean helps me to understand how loaded up the boat really is. When we leap off the back of a wave and surf at 24 knots to the next one, we don't always jump over it but sometimes plough into the back of it. The boat lurches forwards, everything loads up. It's when watching how the boat recovers from this sudden loss of speed that I can really get a feel for whether I am pushing too hard.*

On all previous boats I'd sailed, whether racing or cruising, the instant way to understand if the boat was overpowered was to take the helm and feel the balance. Even in 2019, while I was getting to know *Superbigou* properly, I still needed to have the helm in my hand to understand completely the power, balance and load I was putting the boat under. Now in the Southern Ocean, it was better not to steer, and I found that I didn't really need to. On deck I could watch the wave patterns and understand exactly what it was that made us lurch, heel over or load up; I would watch the rudder angles as the pilot steered the helm from side to side, also listening to the rhythm and cadence of the autopilot ram motor to gauge how hard it was working to keep the boat on track. I would note the wind strength and angle, and was starting to build a database of previous conditions that would form the basis of my decision-making. When the boat was set up just right, I found it mesmerising, watching the data stream to my displays, feeling the motion of the waves and listening to the autopilot respond. The energy from the wind and the ocean seamlessly transferred itself to the boat, and the motion was powerful but fluid. It was a rough ride, and I got thrown around by every wave, but the boat didn't feel out of control. When there was too much sail or too much heel, when the course or balance wasn't quite right, the feeling was more edgy: rough and unpredictable. Most of the time there was something I could do about it – change or trim sails, or adjust the course – all the time looking for that perfect balance between maximum speed to take me east and managing the risk of breaking something by pushing too hard.

In the same way I balanced the power in the boat, there would be plenty of times during the race when I had to balance the prompts of my ego – that competitive little devil on my shoulder – with the need to stay safe and be prudent.

RACE BLOG, 28 DECEMBER 2020

Sometimes, launching off waves, managing to equal my boat speed to the wind speed, I am holding on tight and my stomach is in a knot – is this too much? Am I taking too many risks? – but it's addictive. I won't lie – I get a huge kick out of seeing Superbigou *somewhere near the top of the leader board on a 24-hour run. It is so very unexpected, and I know I should not really be there. But now I am curious to see what else we could do.*

But there always has to be an off switch, I know that. I was a very long way from home, and we were only halfway, with so many more miles to sail, problems to solve, storms to encounter.

RACE BLOG, 28 DECEMBER 2020

I have to trust myself to know where that red line is. I can normally feel it. Like now, for example – literally, just as I wrote these words the boat heeled just a little bit too much. I looked up, and sure enough the wind speed has snuck up. Just two knots, but I have registered a number that I haven't seen for a while. It's noted. I am now on amber alert.

I constantly monitored average wind angle, wind speed and boat speed on the computer. I've never been great with numbers – I am more of a words kind of person – so I used graphs to show averages and give me an overall picture of what was actually happening. The higher up the fleet I clawed, the hungrier I was to see if I could go further. Just another hitch to the south, hold my nerve for a couple more hours with a big sail. I wanted to keep pushing my personal boundaries; this was my chance and I would take it. But at the same time, the better I did, the more the risk seemed to weigh heavy on my shoulders. I was in a great position, why be greedy? Why not bank it and stay with this new pack? I had much to lose, but I needed to remind myself that I was not sitting at a roulette table in Vegas, placing wild bets with an unknown outcome. If this was even close to gambling, I was card counting at the blackjack table – and I was still cautious and diligent in my approach. Every four hours, I would slow the boat to a crawl, do a quick walk of the deck for a two-minute health check, then back on the breeze again. Whenever I did concede and change down, I made sure to use the time wisely. If I had to change to a smaller sail, I would steer up a few degrees to bank some height. Not only would it open up more possibilities for using the zero later, but it would give me a chance to sleep, do a few jobs, and, at the very least, allow my brain a little chance to relax.

I constantly wondered if I was pushing too hard. It was a question that bugged me day and night. I knew that it wasn't about beating other people, it was about finding out who I was, how I could perform with what I had, and always based on my fundamental belief that it is always possible to do better. But I knew I had to keep my ego in check. I didn't want to be the knucklehead with my foot on the gas who sailed her boat till it broke.

16

CELEBRATING WITH TREATS

Transcript from video message, 25 December 2020

'[Shouting] – Merry Christmas – [wild laughter] – It's Christmas Day and look what I got! Look at my present. It is, like, the most beautiful sailing day. I can't believe it, it's been like this all morning and I have been beating myself up all night because I gybed too early ... This is the best present EVER. To everyone everywhere all over the world, I hope you can have a Christmas Day like this, and if it's not sunny, I'm sending you some sunshine from the Southern Ocean.'

On Christmas morning, 2020, I had the extraordinary experience of opening my presents live on BBC's Breakfast TV show via a satellite connection. I'd already opened most of my haul of tiny presents, as the UK was a half-day behind, but I'd kept a last gift to open on air – carefully chosen to have the least risk of causing offence on national TV. I chose well. It turned out to be a packet of chocolate-covered coffee beans from an independent chocolatier in Swanage, a coastal town 10 miles from my home. The beans were a real treat, a taste of luxury and decadence among the freeze-dried monotony of food on board. I ate six beans, one after the other, sucking the chocolate off the outsides first, then crunching into the bean inside, noting how well its bitterness contrasted with the smooth chocolate. Having had no sweet treats for seven weeks, eating those beans really felt like a celebration. I certainly experienced the after-effects – six in one go had me bouncing off the walls of my tiny cabin, and the caffeine hit stopped me from sleeping for the next 24 hours.

The presents had been smuggled on to the boat in the final stages of race preparation at Les Sables d'Olonne. After a week of racing, I came across the ziplock bag, no bigger than the size of a laptop, full of small, wrapped and labelled gifts, with instructions on what they were for and when they should be opened. I hadn't considered how much I might need little offerings like these, chosen with love and care, each one conveying special thoughts from home. But they became essential to maintaining morale at various stages of the race.

In addition to the presents, the bag held a small container of Christmas decorations, party poppers for New Year's Eve, and a memory stick with videos recorded by my family for key moments in the race. Just knowing how everyone must have planned far enough in advance to get them to me, managing to deliver the items to a locked-down France, was enough to make me happy.

Over the course of the Vendée Globe, I came to be known as 'the happy skipper'. The French media called me 'La Rayonette', meaning 'ray of sunshine' – a title with which my friends still take great delight in teasing me. There was a good reason for my smiles. Even taking into account the levels of fear, discomfort and stress, I knew I was exactly where I wanted to be, and the feeling was only heightened with the knowledge of what life ashore was like, as the world struggled through a second, then third wave of the Covid-19 pandemic. Although I never looked at the news, I knew things in the UK were bad. Lou Adams (now the team's full-time operations director) was working for the campaign three days a week during the race, the rest of the time running an NHS emergency department in one of the south coast's busiest hospitals. From her, I heard of the horror. Wave after wave of ambulances turning up at a hospital that, quite simply, had no more room, as well as the impact of the crisis on the mental health of her team. I'd felt guilty that she was working on our campaign, but she told me later that it had provided a much-needed balance, a distraction from the horrendous reality of the situation at the hospital that winter. There were certainly times when I felt it was disrespectful to flaunt my freedom so brazenly, but Lou always told me it was a tonic and encouraged me to share my happy moments with her three daughters, whose questions and comments made me laugh and who punctuated my own weeks with 'fun fact Fridays'.

Over the course of my race, I discovered how much joy can be found in small material things. Living day to day in a sparse environment put together based only on need, never want, changed my definition of 'treat'. I learned to take pleasure from and celebrate things that would seem very run of the mill in normal life. I found myself using everyday items to change my mood, give myself comfort, or simply to enhance a feeling through the ritual of celebration.

Food and drink, of course, was a major part of every day. Some skippers had taken cans of beer – Jean Le Cam famously had a bottle of red wine most days – but I've never enjoyed drinking alcohol while sailing, even in small amounts. Others took treats of cured meats or tinned pâtés, but as I don't eat meat, that was out. The majority enjoyed cakes, sweets and chocolate as a pick-me-up – all of which would send me into a sugar low when tired and exhausted, so they were banned from the boat. I had enough fresh fruit to last the first month of the race. Knowing my limited supply was precious, my daily apple became something I very much looked forward to, so that I would be bitterly disappointed if the apple turned out to be excessively bruised or floury. Towards the end of the race, I started to become incredibly bored with my menu. Many of the freeze-dried meals – though given different names like Mexican Vegetables, Mediterranean Rice, Italian-style Couscous – turned out to be identical blends of rice or couscous and vegetables. My taste buds would cry out for any different flavours to stimulate my palate. Whenever I opened a 24-hour food bag and found a meal that was different – Fish and Potato or Nettle Curry were my favourites – I would do a little dance and plan my day around eating the meal. One day a week, a can of sardines was included in the bag, and I was surprised at how much I looked forward to eating that oily fish straight from the can. It was all I could do, through the middle stages of the race, not to go rifling through the as-yet unopened food bags and pull out all the good stuff to eat. I restrained myself by imagining how hard it might be in week 10 if I was faced with no possibility of variety. By the time I got back to the North Atlantic, I finally gave myself permission to ransack the food supplies, ripping open the bags, doubling up on my daily dried fruit rations and seeking out anything that wasn't couscous.

On their return to Les Sables d'Olonne, skippers are presented with the meal they most desire, a traditional part of their victory celebrations. Near the end of my race, within two days of the finish line, the Vendée Globe race organisers contacted Joff to ask what I would like as my meal. I suspect I was the only vegetarian in the race, and I know most of my fellow competitors had opted for steak and chips or pizza in their craving for anything chewy and full of flavour. Joff had little idea what I might like to eat, and only knew that I was a vegetarian. And so it was, after walking down the dock, I was ushered into a small room where a table was laid for one. I was presented with a tray on which was a plate of couscous and vegetables, looking almost exactly like the meals that I had been trying desperately to avoid for the last three weeks of the race. Thankfully, Lou, who knew me better, had also thought to order me a platter of fresh fruit, and she sat with me in that tiny room, laughing at the untouched couscous, and watching as I inhaled every piece of vibrant, zesty fruit.

Tea, rather than food, has always been my preferred treat when sailing. I cannot think of a situation that has not been made better by a cup of tea. I've always found that it tastes better outdoors. Whenever I was working hard on deck, I'd carry a thermal mug with me, and take sips between moments of exertion. In the south, when it was really cold, I would use the promise of a cup of tea to spur me into action on deck. While working in the dark, on all fours, with my hands raw and stinging through the pain of the cold, I would create an inner dialogue: 'Just get through this sail change and you can go below and warm up with a cup of tea.' It always made sense to focus on the good times I knew would be coming my way. And then, when every last item had been completed, the boat checked, strapped down and sailing fast again, I would go below to collect my reward. I had two mugs for my tea, each with different levels of thermal insulation, one for the deck and one for below. The on-deck mug could keep tea hot for up to an hour, even when deluged by icy waves, its outside cool to the touch. Unlike the down-below mug, which, having less thermal insulation, didn't keep my tea warm for as long but acted as a comforting hot-water bottle. I would make a cup, place it inside my jacket, which I'd zip up and enjoy half an hour of body warming before drinking the tea. Absolute heaven.

Other small acts managed to enhance my physical comfort, too, making a huge difference to my morale and mood. My obsession with anything that was dry or warm only heightened as the race went on. Changing clothes or breaking out some clean underwear became almost ritualistic in nature, and I started to use those times to celebrate something or as a way of rewarding myself. The relief of removing a ten-day-old pair of long johns, so ingrained with dirt and sweat that they scraped against my skin when I moved, was incredible. As I gently cut open the vacuum-sealed plastic bag, the smell of detergent escaping out of it was heady. The aroma seemed wholly out of place on a boat in the middle of the Southern Ocean. It brought an exoticism to the space – the promise of something impossible to obtain out there on the ocean. As I pulled on the thermals, the fabric of the merino wool felt warm, soft and malleable. So luxurious, in fact, that it was as if my skin was celebrating with every inch the wool moved up my legs. I could feel every nerve ending on my legs relaxing. I would then hurry to get my waterproofs on over the top, terrified of making the long johns unnecessarily wet.

Text message to Lou Adams

I LOVE MY LEGS today. It just makes me happy to look at them, I have on a brand-new pair of stripey merino wool thermals.

It seems insane to devote a whole paragraph to thermal underclothes in the real world, but the comfort I felt was so deep, intense and long-lasting that it deserves describing. When the boat was stable, with no chance of deluge, and I judged it safe to have periods of solid time down below to recharge my batteries, I would remove my foul weather gear altogether. It was then that the treat of all treats would be brought out of its dry bag: my huge down jacket. I would put it on, find a dry hat, then wrap myself in my blanket and let the feeling of warmth and security make its way through my body and mind. As an extra sweetener, one of my friends had given me a pair of cashmere gloves as a Christmas present. Initially, on opening the packet halfway through the race, I thought 'That's a strange present to give someone who's battling water all the time', but those gloves became one of my most prized luxury items. I would put them on before I had a 'dry sleep', and each time the softness of the wool was such a surprise. Sometimes I would just lie my face on top of my hands to feel the silky wool on my cheek. These physical feelings were so gentle and different from everything else I experienced on the boat, where I was surrounded by cold, sharp, scratchy, hard, wet, unkind sensations. The gentle touch of a cashmere glove on my face was a tiny moment of tenderness.

Text message extract

I dried my boots on the engine today and put them on when they were still hot! Now THAT was a highlight.

Celebrating landmarks on a journey – rites of passage marking the progress of the route – is something expected, a tradition among sailors. Despite their practical natures – often quite engineer-like – sailors often tend towards superstition. It is most likely a factor of having to face unknown and unpredictable perils at sea. Tradition holds that they should never sail on a Friday, whistle on board unless they're looking for wind, or have bananas on the boat – and they must always make an offering to Neptune on crossing the equator. A traditional crossing-the-line ceremony involves casting libations into the sea. When Ellen MacArthur, 26 miles behind Michel Desjoyeaux, crossed the equator during the Vendée Globe race of 2000, she 'threw her second-to-last packet of ginger nuts as an offering to Neptune', thanked the sea god for letting her pass safely, and finished her prayer off with 'Thank you for putting Mich in a windless hole. I know that's not nice, but thank you.' (*Taking on the World*). Isabelle Autissier, on the other hand, in a more flamboyant, French sort of way, threw flowers and champagne into the waves on her 1996 race. I did nothing at all, except throw myself into my work and plan on opening a bag of dry thermals once I got a breather.

RACE BLOG, 29 DECEMBER 2020

The landmark days are coming thick and fast at the moment, and today I crossed the antimeridian for the second time only in my sailing career. I was primed to mark the occasion, glancing occasionally at the GPS reading 179, but once again was engrossed in some other work and completely failed to watch that moment flash by. It is great to be in the Pacific and at the moment the weather is being kind with a moderate breeze and the third day in a row of bright, warm sunshine. This is giving me some breathing space to work on the boat and get us both back in shape for the next big shake-up. I even managed to change into my halfway thermals today, my water tank is full, and if the sun is shining tomorrow, I am definitely going to treat myself to a shower in the cockpit.

What we deem to be a luxury changes throughout our lives. It is a reflection of our environment and our relative balance of want versus need. Being at sea for long periods has taught me to appreciate small things, to engage with how they make me feel, and to allow myself time to indulge in those good feelings. I note them, and memorise the sensations to amplify the good times. There is nothing wrong with wanting material objects. My boat and its equipment are expensive, technical, complicated items, and I love all of them unequivocally. Every time I walk down the dock and look at my IMOCA, sitting bow up, just above the water, I get a shiver of excitement. That boat makes me happy beyond belief. For me, the trick is being able to engage in how an item makes you feel – whether it's a diamond ring or a clean pair of socks. In itself, the item cannot make you happy, it is all about the way you relate to it. It always surprises me how quickly I revert to my harder-to-please self when I'm on shore. I certainly don't get excited every morning by the thought of putting on a fresh pair of socks, but I still tend to lean towards *experiences* rather than *things* when I choose to celebrate.

Transcript from video update

'Drinking tea, chilling out, enjoying being here without feeling I'm under attack from the waves ... I have learned that we have these really intense periods of hard sailing, which take it out of you, and you think "I'm not doing a lot, so why am I tired? Why is it taking it out of me?" But I guess it's just the intensity of it, you know – my mind is working all the time and the boat is just surging and rushing and banging, and so I suppose it is just tiring you in a way that you don't immediately recognise. These slow days, of course, are important for maintenance and repairs to get the boat back together again so we can be ready for the next big breeze, but also I am learning that I need to give myself a little bit of time on these days, too. And, actually, just coming out here, drinking a cup of tea, chilling, looking at the waves and doing nothing in particular – it's OK, I give myself permission, and I don't do that often. But it's a nice day.'

As I described in Chapter 8, Feeding the Spirit, music accompanied me through most days of the race. I used it as a tool to keep me going, to enhance my mood, to help me create memories for the future, and to celebrate the good times. On the days I was working hard on deck, had pushed through some difficult weather or completed all of my daily chores, I would give myself permission to flop on to my beanbag with a cup of tea or a drink, and do nothing but listen and sing along to some great tunes. Interestingly, after coming back from the race, I was interviewed by a PhD student who was writing a thesis about sound and memory. It was he who told me that hearing is widely believed to be the last sense we lose as we approach death. And how sounds can evoke memories and feelings in patients suffering from Alzheimer's, and other forms of dementia. He interviewed me about the sounds I remember from when I was at sea, how I interact with my soundscape, and what memories a sound evokes when I am on land. Sound is critically important to solo sailors, of course. A bang, a squeak, a repeated clicking or scratching can permeate even through sleep to alert us of a problem. Some sailors won't listen to music, claiming it disturbs their interaction with the boat, but I would not be without it. In the latest generation of foiling IMOCAs, the noise levels inside the boats are horrendously loud, and many of us are turning to noise cancelling headphones to get some respite from the cacophony. In this new environment, music has an even greater role in maintaining my mental health.

Initially, I felt self-conscious about my small celebrations. It always felt wrong to be self-congratulatorily early in the race, knowing that anything could happen. But celebration is also about sharing, and as the race went on I came to understand just how much sharing these moments meant to the locked-down real world. So, I threw myself parties with music and decorations to celebrate crossing the equator, passing each of the capes, crossing the antimeridian (the 180-degree line of longitude), Christmas, New Year and my birthday, recording each moment in a video to send back to shore. I let myself be proud and happy, because that is what people wanted to see. In doing so, I let our race followers be proud for me. Sometimes I would not feel like making a fuss if I was tired, feeling flat, or just not in the mood to show or share emotion. But, without fail, as soon as I had put on some good music and thought about what I might say on my update, my mood would change. Just speaking good news out loud made me engage with it.

I know that in my everyday life I do not spend enough time celebrating. It's one of the downsides of driving hard to a far-off goal. I don't always mark the milestones – feeling time pressured, my mind has normally moved on to the next thing as soon as one task on the list is completed. When I finish a race, I am already thinking about how I would do it better next time, or running through the boat job list and prioritising upgrades or repairs before we are next on the water. That is not to say I am never satisfied or happy – as mentioned in previous chapters, I thrive from taking joy in everyday moments, drinking it in, appreciating my situation, and this is what enables me to carry on through the hard times. But I need to remember to stop and take the time to acknowledge achievements. A driven mindset served me well through the 30 years I was working towards the Vendée Globe race alone, but now that we have a team I have had to learn, as team leader, that celebration is important, not only for positive feedback but also for regeneration. Many people get their energy through the positive reinforcement of sharing achievements. Marking success or milestones with celebration is an important part of any team dynamics.

Video message, New Year's Eve, 2020

'Happy New Year, everyone. I have been on my own now for 53 days, so I am getting pretty good at parties for one. Erm, but I am not really on my own, because I've got so many people following me and supporting me. It's incredible. So, wherever you are, whatever you are doing, goodbye 2020, hello 2021.'

[I point and fire a party popper at the camera.]

17

RUDDERLESS

By day 59 of the race, I was flying high, though managing on less and less sleep. Since passing New Zealand, I felt like I had fully hit my stride. Through careful navigation and pushing the boat hard, I had managed to jump another two places in the rankings. Giddy at my 15th position, I was relishing the bigger breeze and waves, now leading a new pack – comprised of Cali and Alan Roura – along the top of the ice limit in the South Pacific. For the past three days, we had been battling our way through a depression, reduced to tiny sail plans as we negotiated the huge seas. It was by no means comfortable: the temperature inside my cabin was 6 degrees, and a squall had brought sleet and snow with it. When we shared stories via WhatsApp, it was clear that each of us was starting to feel the strain. We were losing weight, as well as sleep, and were constantly having to deal with various levels of malfunction on our boats. Alan, *Superbigou*'s previous skipper, had a continuous hydraulic leak from his keel ram, which made it impossible for him to power up fully at times, and I had lost my wind data a week earlier when both units at the top of my mast failed. Climbing the mast hadn't been an option in the severe conditions, and my deck level emergency wind wand was dropping out constantly so could not be relied upon. Not only did the lack of wind data make sail selection difficult, but it also eliminated the option of having the autopilot steer to a wind angle. Having to guess wind strength and direction had been manageable but exhausting, requiring a large degree of human intervention to keep the boat going well.

On 6 January, the three of us had sailed south of Point Nemo, the most remote spot on the planet, closer to the international space station than to any continental landmass. Feeling our isolation acutely, the relentless grey of the Southern Ocean was finding its way into our heads and souls. Despite that, I was heartened: my course time was now several days ahead of the winning race times of 2000, and I had gained a good understanding of the rhythm of weather in the south and learned how to capitalise on every system that came over. The thought of the boat breaking at this point in the race was never far from my mind, but my anxiety was starting to ease. The home run was tantalisingly close. With only 1,500 miles to Cape Horn, I had started to imagine what life might be like when I turned the corner and headed back up to the Atlantic equator. Judging from the forecast and my current speeds, I believed I could make it in less than a week. How wrong I was.

At dawn on 7 January, the wind dropped slightly and I ventured out on deck. I turned *Superbigou* downwind, and we slowed to a rolling, pedestrian gait that allowed me to walk the 50 feet to the bow on a deck clear of water. I inspected the boat, bow to stern, checking the ropes, blocks and rigging, looking for problems, maintenance needs and breakages that might trip me up. All good. But then, just as I got to the last 5 feet of the deck, I noticed that my port rudder stock seemed a little low compared to the other.

I had two rudders steering the boat, a common design feature of wide boats like IMOCAs. When the boat heeled over, one rudder was fully immersed while the other was out of the water. They were mounted underneath the hull of the boat, 1 metre forward from the transom (rear end), and if I hung over the end, I could see the backs of the rudder blades. The stocks, to which my steering gear and autopilots were attached, came through the bottom of the boat into a compartment under the back deck. The top of the stocks exited through the deck – where I was then standing. I decided that the rudder must have slipped down slightly, and that the clamps holding it in place might require a turn to tighten them. To do this, I'd need to attach a rope to the top of the stock, pull the whole rudder up, then crawl into the back. The job itself would not be too difficult – it was getting into the rear underdeck compartment that was the hard part. I texted Joff to tell him the plan, and he agreed to it.

I assembled all my tools in a bucket, then posted myself through the small hatch in the back of the cockpit that led into the steering compartment. As usual, there was quite a bit of water sloshing around inside: this part of the boat leaked constantly (at its worst, I would have to climb inside four times a day to empty it). Moving my body into a high plank position, I launched myself headfirst through the second bulkhead and landed next to the rudder stock in the very back of the boat. In the dark and the freezing cold, the thin carbon hull providing no insulation against the icy sea, I sat in the tiny wet space with my tools. On inspection, it didn't seem that the clamps were loose. My heart sank. Something wasn't right, but I couldn't work out what. I took out my phone – always in my pocket during boat inspections – and snapped pictures and a video of the stock via WhatsApp to Joff. Later, as I emerged blinking into the daylight, I saw the double tick of my message turn blue. He had received it. Minutes passed. Tendrils of anxiety curled around me, my arms starting to tingle, as I waited to hear back from him. Usually, he'd send a response immediately, but this time I knew he was trying to figure something out. I sensed it would not be good.

The reply came back, with a screen grab from the video I had sent him. Part of the rudder stock was ringed by a messy green circle. 'Is this a crack?'

I felt oddly calm. I knew he was right. I hadn't seen the crack myself, but the inevitability that something would trip me up had been hanging over me for days. I had been pushing *Superbigou* so hard, and had been waiting for something to break. It was a strange sort of relief now that it had. I had been carrying a tension around with me, the dread of some catastrophic failure. The further I had climbed up the ranks, passing other boats, the worse the fear had become. I knew I was pushing *Superbigou* hard, risking damage, and the knowledge had weighed on my conscience. There's a sick part of your brain that always wants to tell you that something's too good to be true, that the glory days won't last. And now my fears were confirmed. It had happened.

And here I was, thousands of miles from shore, between storms, and I had broken a rudder.

It was partly due to the boat's previous owner, Alan Roura (in this moment, my closest competitor), that we had a spare rudder on board at all. The Swiss sailor had competed with my boat (then named *La Fabrique*) in the 2016 Vendée Globe, and he had broken a rudder in almost exactly the same geographical location during his race. I remember chatting with him following the Transat Jacques Vabre race in 2019, when we compared our experience of *Superbigou*'s quirks, and he described how he'd replaced the rudder during his Vendée. I'd listened to him carefully, wondering at how he had managed to achieve this incredibly complicated feat alone on the ocean, all the while thinking: 'I couldn't do that. I'm not strong enough...' Afterwards, the fact of his rudder change continued to niggle me. I was carrying his replacement rudder, and another that dated back to the year the boat was built, which was, naturally, a point of weakness. In our build-up to the race, we were always struggling with budget and cashflow. I'd known a spare rudder was important, but for a long time it had been a long way down the list of priorities. It had finally worked its way to the top of the list when we signed Smartsheet as one of our sponsors, and I'd had a new rudder built one month before the race start. We hadn't had time to fit and test it, though, as that would have required lifting the boat out of the water. On balance, it had made no sense to disrupt the geometry and impermeability of the steering system and rudder bearings when we knew everything was working well. It was a compromise, and though we did eventually rehearse a rudder change in the race village just days before the start, we had gambled on the old rudder making it.

RACE BLOG, 8 JANUARY 2021

It always amazed me that Alan was actually able to change a rudder in the Southern Ocean. I couldn't imagine how hard it must have been. But every time I thought of him changing it, there was doubt in my mind as to whether I would be able to do it.

To change the rudder alone at sea was a challenge that required a properly thought-out solution. Joff, having already sent five skippers successfully around the world in older boats than mine, had developed a technique. For this, he ensured all equipment was on board, and had packed my rudder, inside its custom-made garter, ready to be swapped. At Les Sables, we had practised the method of lowering the box of anchor chain over the back of the boat, using it as an anchor to overcome the rudder's buoyancy. We'd then pulled the broken rudder down and out, leaving a tracing line through the empty bearings, before reversing the procedure to carefully guide the new rudder into place. I remembered that cold morning when I'd tried to follow instructions, all the while feeling overwhelmed and uncomfortable. I was now going to have to do it for real, 1,500 miles from Cape Horn, in a howling wind and raging seas.

It was hard to choke back the tears when I made my video update that day. I tried to put on a brave face, reassuring everyone that I was fine and safe, and that it was just a setback. But I broke down when I talked of how I would have to pause racing. It wasn't the broken rudder that was devastating me – I wasn't scared for my life or worried that I couldn't solve the problem – it was the thought of losing my 15th place. Forced to stop sailing fast, I'd had to take my sails down, and was now sitting there, waiting for the others to catch me up.

There was some comfort to be taken from the situation as a whole. I reminded myself that I'd noticed the problem while I was on a port tack, so the cracked rudder hadn't been the one under load. I could keep control of the boat with the starboard rudder, and hopefully there would be no further damage to either the stock or the steering gear. If I hadn't spotted the rudder problem, in the next three hours I would have gybed back on to starboard and sailed hard in 30 knots of wind. The rudder stock would have inevitably failed at some point afterwards, with the boat loaded up under full sail. Looking at it from this perspective, I'd had a lucky escape. Wiping out in such circumstances could have caused a lot more damage.

RACE BLOG, 7 JANUARY 2021

I am now sailing very slowly east, with just my small jib up, making way but under minimal load. My main objective now is to find suitable conditions to make the switch. This is challenging in this location, as the sea state needs to be relatively calm. Yesterday it looked like there might be a window later on today.

I knew I had to change the rudder. I knew how to change the rudder. The biggest decision I had to make was when and where to do it. We had practised the procedure in flat, calm water, and I understood immediately the huge risks of doing it at sea. The rudder needed to hang directly under the boat to align with the holes. If the boat was moving forwards, the rudder would trail behind at an angle such that it wouldn't line up. If the waves were big, the boat might come down on the top of the stock while I was trying to guide the rudder, and the impact could break the stock or rudder bearings, or even puncture the bottom of the hull. I needed to find flat water, but I was in the Southern Ocean, so that would be no mean feat. I would need to scrutinise the weather forecasts and sail towards an area where a calm was predicted, before attempting to make the change. The course of the race would have to take a back seat. No matter that I'd been aiming for Cape Horn – the only priority now was to replace my rudder, and if that meant sailing in the wrong direction, so be it.

The rules of the Vendée Globe race state that a skipper may not receive performance-enhancing outside assistance. In this situation, it meant that Joff was allowed to help me with the physical process of changing the rudder, but he could not give me any coaching advice, or opinions on where or when I should do it. That was down to me.

Two options appeared to be available. Option 1 was to sail 400 miles north, out of the path of the Southern Ocean depressions, to an area where a high pressure would establish itself in about four days' time. At that point, hopefully, there would be minimal wind and the sea state would drop quickly and substantially. The high pressure was forecast to last a few days, which would give me plenty of time to make the change. Option 2 was less obvious. If I continued on my current course for another 24 hours, there could well be a small lull between gales, caused by a finger of high pressure pushing up between depressions. The GRIB file (a type of weather forecast file) showed the wind would drop to 10 knots for six to eight hours. Perhaps, just perhaps, the sea state might drop enough during that short period as well.

On the face of it, option 2 seemed the riskier, but option 1 would mean sailing an extra 400 miles to get up to the high pressure, and another 400 back down once the rudder had been changed. Not only would I lose my pack, but all the boats behind me would catch up. I had opened a gap of 1,500 miles between me and the back of the fleet, and in my estimation, I stood to lose five places should I take that first option. As always, I asked myself where the greatest risk lay. I could not and would not give up my position in the race without a fight. For me, the greatest risk in that moment was losing my hard-won result. The high pressure to the north would stay for a few days, so as there was no risk of losing that option 1 opportunity, why not go for option 2? I would stay where I was, making slow progress towards Cape Horn, while I waited for my weather window to arrive. If it did, I would go for it. If it didn't, I would admit defeat and head north. Yes, I would have sacrificed 24 hours in the process, but at least I'd have tried everything to keep my race ranking.

When the time came, on the morning of 8 January, I felt sick with apprehension. Still flip-flopping about whether to try the change or not, I knew that once I started there would be no going back. If I damaged the new rudder, it could mean the end of my race. The wind had been slowly dropping, but conditions were far from ideal, with the sea state failing to calm. Now I was playing a game of chicken, knowing that I needed to wait as long as possible to allow the waves to decrease, but if I waited too long, the next gale would be upon us. I had talked through the procedure, over and over, with Joff, who had sent me instructions and diagrams. I had slept as well as I could, making the most of our slow speeds the night before, and had assembled everything I needed in the cockpit, ready to go. Now I just needed to pick my moment. I just had to slow the boat down enough to get the rudder in, but even with all sail down, *Superbigou* was making 5 knots, just from the pressure of the wind on the mast and hull and the momentum of the waves. Eventually, the wind dropped a little more, and I threw my sea anchor (like a water parachute) out of the back of the boat. It slowed us down to 2 or 3 knots. I took a deep breath, sent Joff a text, and went for it.

The whole procedure took about an hour and a half, with many hours of preparation and packing up before and after. My heart was in my mouth for the whole time. I moved around the cockpit, winding winches, pulling ropes, sliding over to the back of the boat to grab, yank, and manhandle rudder ropes and anchor chain. Once I was committed to doing it, there was nothing going to get in my way. There were some tough moments, and I had to plead with my boat and the ocean a couple of times, but when that new rudder stock finally came shooting up through the deck level bearing, the out-loud whooping that came from me could easily have been heard for miles around ... if anyone had been there to hear it.

RACE BLOG, 8 JANUARY 2021

Every part of my body aches. I have bloody knuckles on every finger, bruises all down my legs, and muscles I didn't know I had that hurt, but YES!!!!! The new rudder is in and Superbigou *is back in the game ... humming along at 15 knots, and I can't quite believe that I did that.*

Now can I please have a pass out of the Southern Ocean? I think I am done here now.

PARK IT WHILE YOU SORT IT

My natural tendency, when sideswiped by a difficult event or faced with enormous disappointment, is to shrink from the world. When we are hurt physically, we respond with a cry of pain, sometimes tears, and we naturally attempt to protect ourselves from further injury by pulling back from the thing that hurt us. Emotional or mental pain can trigger exactly the same response.

Through my first years of solo sailing, I really struggled to recover when things went wrong. I couldn't seem to get out from under the problem. It would weigh me down, holding my focus in a negative way. My confidence wobbled easily. I was quick to doubt my ability and to create a narrative that told me I would not recover. I'd dwell on my problems, allowing them to distort everything. But one of the incredible things about being alone at sea is that you are forced to be the solution to your own problems. When there is simply no one there to make things better, you must step up and work it out yourself. Over time, I developed my practical ability to problem solve, building up a knowledge bank as I continued to learn from experience. Sometimes, my life would depend on it.

However, although my practical knowledge kept growing, I still struggled with the emotional aftermath when I suffered disappointment or fear. Even after I had solved a problem, I found it hard to let go of the vision of what might have been or how I had failed myself by getting into the situation in the first place.

For me, the turning point came during the second week of my 2013 Mini Transat race. I was mid-ocean, after ten days of racing a 6.5-metre boat alone across the Atlantic. I had been pushing hard through some difficult weather, and in the space of five hours had managed to tear two of my three spinnakers. Not willing to be forced into submission, I had hoisted my third and final off-wind sail in the lashing rain and gale-force winds. Two hours later, I was down below when the autopilot misjudged a wave. Just for a second, the machine turned the wrong way. My little boat ended up out of control, loading the sails up so that I heeled over at 90 degrees, the halyard holding up my spinnaker breaking in two. By the time I'd got the boat back on its feet, the spinnaker was dragging through the water behind the boat. I slowly brought the sail into the boat, tugging against the weight of the water, only to reveal it had a huge hole in it. I'd broken down and sobbed. I was soaked; the sail was soaked – and it was in pieces. With no other big off-wind sails, I could no longer race. And not only that: I would have to climb the mast to fix the halyard, and the spinnakers were so wet it would be impossible to get any repair materials to stick to them. I imagined my competitors sailing away from me in the big breeze, while I had to waddle slowly with small sails. I sat outside in a big pile of soggy spinnaker, letting the waves wash over me, and wept for at least half an hour. My internal dialogue went something like this: 'Why is this happening to me? Why am I so stupid? Why did the autopilot have to jump? Why did the halyard have to break? Why me?' But after these laments had circled my head a while, I had a curious experience. I listened to myself and felt a bit silly. The boat was going slowly, yes. I was tired, yes. But fundamentally, I was fine – and yet I was doing absolutely nothing to make my situation any better.

This was a huge learning moment for me. I looked down on myself: a sobbing sailor in a small boat, a thousand miles from help. It was then I realised that in order to move on, I needed to change my internal dialogue, to acknowledge the situation and not waste energy railing against a situation that had already happened and I could not change.

With the bad experiences, the disasters, come the opportunities to learn. By the time the Vendée came round, with my rudder adventure, I knew that the best way for me to approach any problem was to first acknowledge that it had happened, and then to accept my new situation as the point from which I had to continue.

Yes, it sucks. Bad luck, other people's actions, being in the wrong place at the wrong time – all seem deeply unfair when it's not your fault. But you can't go back in time, you can't change what has happened – the only thing to do is move forward. When I am in the middle of the ocean, I need to ensure all my energy is focused on that forward motion, no matter how aggrieved I feel. Processing emotions is distracting; it saps our energy.

I know we need to process emotion – grief and disappointment – and understand why things went wrong so we'll know what to do next time. But that sort of mental cogitation has its time and place, so I have learned to park it until I have time to deal with it. I refuse to let it get in the way of picking myself up and moving onwards.

All this is much easier on the water. There is an immediacy of the situation when I'm sailing on the ocean, and the awareness that I alone have to be the solution.

I was overtaken by both Cali and Alan when I changed my rudder. I'd dropped back into 17th place, but was determined, with over 7,000 miles of racetrack to go, that I would still have a chance to come back at them. Changing the rudder had taken a lot out of me, physically and emotionally. I knew I did not have the same energy I'd felt before the break, and was playing catch-up in every way. The leader of the race was now 2,500 miles ahead of me, the frontrunners making their way back up the Atlantic in various states of disrepair. The race had already broken all records, taking the competition to new levels. It was exceptionally close – just 500 miles separating the top nine after two months – and many of the foiling boats had been in sight of each other through the Southern Ocean.

While I was battling to the Horn, Isabelle Joschke, who had been hanging just outside the top ten, announced her retirement from the race. A crushing disappointment, but with her keel swinging freely beneath the boat and no possibility of fixing or canting it, she had no choice but to sail to the Brazilian coast for a repair. I didn't want to imagine what she must have been feeling – we were all just a step away from that. Soon after, I was passed by Jérémie Beyou, one of the sailors who had been tipped to win but had been forced to turn back three days into his race after having broken his backstay. He had restarted nine days later, and as it had been inevitable that he would catch me in his state-of-the-art big foiling boat, I didn't feel such a wrench at losing another place to him.

It snowed a lot in the second week in January. The boat was wet, and I was longing for Cape Horn, where I would finally say goodbye to the Southern Ocean and be on the homeward stretch, but the day before I rounded the famous promontory, I was to reach the lowest point of despair in the race so far. The day had ground me down from the very start. The breeze was difficult, the sky full of squalls and lulls. Without my wind data, I was struggling to maintain boat speed and sail a consistent course, which in itself was enough to frustrate. The rudder bearing on the side that I had changed, so triumphantly, had developed a leak that was steadily worsening. By 12 January I was in the back of the boat every hour, bailing out over 40 litres of water washing from side to side. It wasn't hard for Joff and me to guess the diagnosis – one of the seals in the bearing must have dropped out when I changed the rudder – but without access to the bottom of the boat, it would be impossible to seal. And because the water was moving from side to side with the motion of the boat, I could not leave a bilge pump (like a giant water hoover) running alone; one minute it would be under water, the next in the dry.

All day I was in and out with a bucket, trying to work out whether the leak was stable or getting worse. Each time I had to first bail out the compartment, then crawl in with a torch to inspect every surface to ensure I knew from where the water was coming. The work was demoralising, and climbing in and out of the back of the boat exhausting. I couldn't imagine doing it at this rate for another 35 days, but the leak was not going to get better by itself. On one occasion, a squall came up behind just when I was on one of my tortuous expeditions into the underdeck back compartment. Normally, I would be wearing the pilot remote control on my arm, and if I sensed any changes in the boat's movement, I could command the autopilot to adjust course to keep the boat stable while I carried out my work under the back deck. As *Superbigou* heeled over and took off like a bat out of hell, I was thrown face forward against the back of the boat. I could immediately feel that the wind was shifting as we started to roll to windward, and I knew I needed to alter course to keep the boat safe. I reached for the remote, only to discover it wasn't attached to my arm (I must have left it in the cabin). I would need to climb out of the back of the boat to get on deck to the nearest pilot control as quickly as possible – not easy when you have to crawl through a hole in a bulkhead, bisected by one of the tiller bars, so small that the larger members of my team could never manage it. The situation was insane. Here I was, trapped in a tiny compartment at the back of a 60-foot boat careering, almost out of control, through the Southern Ocean. One stupid mistake had put me in danger, and I was scared. Contorting my body in a mad scramble to get through, I fought to get out, but it was too late: *Superbigou* crash-gybed. I was thrown once again across the boat, landing on the downhill side of the hull, followed by the entire 40 litres of water that had accumulated from the leak.

A gybe is always a potentially dangerous manoeuvre. The mainsail and the heavy boom to which it's attached must be brought from one side of the boat to the other. The manoeuvre is normally carefully controlled, taking me around 40 minutes to execute from end to end, where I put the keel into the centre of the boat so that the bulb is directly underneath the mast, then bring the boom to the centre too, closing the angle of the mainsail to the wind blowing from behind the boat. In this way I minimise the load, and the mainsail doesn't have so far to swing across. A crash gybe is the out-of-control version of this manoeuvre, normally due to a failure of the autopilot. In this scenario, the boom swings wildly across the boat, landing against the mast rigging with the full force of the wind from behind. A crash gybe can dismast a boat, rip a mainsail in two, and break carbon battens. In short, it can end a Vendée Globe race.

I picked myself up, head spinning. The boat was pinned on its side, mainsail against the backstay, the keel now on the downhill side, ensuring that *Superbigou* stayed down with the mast at 70 degrees to the water, unable to bob back up. I was stuck on the low side of the steering compartment, the hatch to the cockpit over 2 metres above me. Up to my knees in water, standing on the side of the boat, I could not reach that hatch. In moments like these, I always find new strength, and although I was exhausted and have never been able to lift my own body weight, I knew I just *had* to get out of that hatch. I was not going to end my days stuck in the back of this boat. I could hear the Code Zero sail flapping and flogging at the front, and it was only a matter of time before it ripped in two. Somehow, I managed to propel myself upwards, using one of the steering rods to push away from, and leapt for the rim of the hatch, which, luckily, had swung open. Grabbing the rim, I hauled myself up, pushing my feet off the bulkhead behind me for traction. It was agony getting through – the sharp edge of the hatch cut into my now fatless frame – but I made it.

On deck, it was carnage. The Code Zero was wrapped around the forestay several times, but at least the mainsail was unbroken. I started the slow, methodical process of getting *Superbigou* back on its feet so we could race again. Luckily, nothing was damaged, and I was able to get the zero down relatively easily, though as it wasn't furled I wouldn't be able to use it again until the next windless day when I could put it back up and furl it properly. It had taken me two hours to sort the mess out, and by the time I'd finished, the back compartment was once again full of water. It felt as if some malevolent deity was playing a perverse game with me.

RACE BLOG, 12 JANUARY 2021

It's like someone is repeatedly knocking you over. Every time you stand up, another blow comes. Will this be the one that keeps her down? I have been knocked down hard today.

After consultation with Joff, and a lot of bailing out, I managed to create a taller and more robust temporary boot to go around the rudder and stop the water from getting into the back of the boat. When conditions would allow, I planned to laminate a more permanent solution in place. For now, I hoped that would be an end of it, because I had Cape Horn to think about.

At 57 degrees latitude, Cape Horn is the reason most sensible sailors use the Panama Canal to circumnavigate the globe. The dreaded rocky promontory, however, is an experience that any sailor braving the wilds of the Southern Ocean wouldn't want to miss. The lows of the Southern Ocean funnel through the Drake Passage, between the Horn and Antarctica, causing some vicious sea states and currents, not to mention the hurricane-force winds that hurtle off the Andean glaciers. Over the centuries, tens of thousands of ships foundered off Cape Horn as they made their way from Europe to the west coast of America. Cape Horners – those intrepid sailors who successfully sailed around it and lived to tell the tale – were allowed to wear a special badge of honour: a gold earring in their left ear, the ear closest to the cape as they rounded it.

For many Vendée Globe sailors, like me, the cape comes as a wonderful relief after the weeks of slamming across the Southern Ocean. Miranda Merron, who ended up finishing 22nd in our race after a 101-day voyage, described her rounding of a Cape Horn suddenly bathed in sunlight so beautifully:

'I could smell damp earth and it was just divine. It was the first land I had seen in 69 days and there are no smells at sea, beyond whales and fishing boats' diesel and the smell of ships ... and so, when you have that incredible smell of damp earth, it is just bewitching, and you breathe in great lumpfuls of it.'

Many never see the Horn as they pass, either from being too far offshore or having low cloud destroy visibility. My route would take me close into the shore and, in the twilight of a grey evening, making out the iconic shape was just the tonic I needed. It had been a long day for me – and for my friends at home, many of whom had been hoping to stay up and watch me round the Horn in real time, but who eventually sent me rude WhatsApp messages either telling me to get a move on or that they had already toasted me and were going to bed.

The wind died away as I got closer to the shore and the black outline of the headland against the grey cloud became firmer. I was emotional at the sight of it, feeling very proud. When my VHF radio sprang into life, I almost jumped out of my skin. I had not heard a human voice over the radio for 63 days. It was the lighthouse keeper, and I greeted him in poor Spanish before speaking to his wife in English. It was a wonderful moment. I thought of all the sailors who had rounded the cape and marked the occasion, both those of old and my own heroes. I had followed their stories hungrily, hardly daring to hope that one day I might race around the world and join their number. Although I'd have to sail a few hundred miles north before I would technically leave the Southern Ocean, I felt a sense of relief that the perils of the south were done. At that moment it felt like, maybe, everything was going to work out. Just the return leg up the Atlantic. Surely, the hard bit was done. But what a foolish sailor I was.

RACE BLOG, 12 JANUARY 2021

I think the Capes are named the wrong way round, because this one definitely brought me hope.

18

FACING FEAR

As ocean-racing skippers, we are in a constant battle to stay in control of our environment. It's never a surprise to see the most celebrated skippers on their hands and knees sponging up the tiniest cupful of water the minute they see it on the floor of the cabin. We know these small details matter. Unmanaged, they can spark off a chain of events that can lead to a loss of control, especially once the boats have become ravaged from weeks at sea. We flex and adapt to suit conditions, always working to maintain control at a level that allows us to perform. But sometimes it is taken from us, and with that loss of control comes fear. The two are inextricably linked.

I love being at the helm of any boat, the tiller in my hands, in touch with all that is happening. Looking out from the helm position, I will see incoming gusts of wind as streaks of dark water, I'll watch waves break, and notice the tiniest variation of sail shape. My personal database of ocean experience, built up over 30 years at the helm, allows me to pre-empt and react to the natural environment, so I can maximise speed and course. But though I love the tiller in my hand, you have to embrace the truth that on an IMOCA your autopilot is absolutely vital to safety and success. Sailing solo in the Vendée Globe race, with daily job lists to cover all roles on the boat, there was no time left to steer *Superbigou*. And the truth is that the machine could steer a lot better than me in all but a handful of occasions. It didn't get wet, tired, cold or distracted, and though it couldn't see the waves, it could judge exactly how to ride them, its multiple sensors picking up the acceleration and heel of the boat. It's an incredible machine, but is reliant on a constant stream of data to perform well. Take away one element of that data, and the result is like blindfolding a human helm. During the course of the race, I had burned through all my wind data sensors, finally losing the last one at the beginning of January in a dramatic crash gybe.

RACE BLOG, 2 JANUARY 2021

Mid-morning, I was rudely awakened from a snooze by the pilot crash gybing the boat, which is never a good way to wake up. Once I'd clambered on deck and got us back on our feet again, checking for damage, I engaged the pilot again only for it to dive off towards another gybe. A quick check revealed that the wind data was absolute rubbish, so I set us up to steer to the compass and wandered to the mast to look at my wand. I'm still not really sure what has happened. From deck level with the binoculars, it looks like a cup is missing off the speed sensor, but neither the cups nor the wand are rotating at all, they are both stuck solid. Very strange and definitely not the conditions to go aloft and check it out.

This was bad news, as my second wind wand fell off during the first big front we encountered just three days after the start. Without wind data coming from the top of the mast, my performance would suffer. Sure, I could sail safely without it, if I was conservative with my sail set-up and by using my powers of observation and the barometer to get a sense for wind strength and direction. But to perform without this data is hard. It is the nuanced changes that make a difference, particularly the analysis of my polars (how well I'm sailing against my theoretical best performance in any given wind conditions). Without this point of reference, I was forced to guesstimate whether I was sailing fast or not, which was definitely detrimental to performance.

By day 71 of the race, I was making my way back up the Atlantic. The front of the fleet had crossed the equator and were on their way to the finish in a tightly fought contest. I'd lost contact with my Southern Ocean peloton, having had to stop north of the Falkland Islands to execute a six-hour time penalty given by the race jury after my outside life raft had been washed off the back of the boat in the south. The penalty felt rough, but I used the time to laminate a tube over my leaking rudderstock, which would put an end to my four-hourly trips to bail out the back of the boat. In a way, the break was just what I needed. I was still reeling from being overtaken by Cali and Alan when I changed the rudder. I'd been desperately trying to harness the power to chase them, but without wind data, and with the leak in the aft section (which, if left unattended, filled the back of the boat with as much as 100 litres of water), *Superbigou*'s performance was compromised.

On 18 January, when faced with a depression there was no way around, I had to sail through the centre of the storm with no wind data, manually adjusting the pilot constantly to find the best course to steer over the steep, aggressive waves.

RACE BLOG, 18 JANUARY 2021

Passing through the eye of the depression on Friday night was an intense experience. It was pitch dark, total cloud cover blocking even the light from the stars. As I got closer to the centre the wind built and built, until finally I was on deck, pulling the mainsail completely down in wind that I could feel pushing my body. It is incredible just how much your world shrinks in those circumstances. You can see nothing outside the footprint of the boat; when I looked up, my head torch merely illuminated the water droplets filling the air and reflected light back in my face. The waves were confused, and having no vision outside the boat, it was impossible to know when and which way you were going to be knocked next. I spent most of the time crawling around on hands and knees; my balance is so bad I struggle to stand up on a moving deck on a good day. I felt like I was feeling my way through the darkness. I had a map in my mind of my route through the depression and not being able to see it physically I had to use clues to guess where I was. The barometer, in a steady fall then stable. The wind direction, which I was mostly deducing from my course and the trim of my sails. If the sails started flapping, I knew the wind had backed.

Text message conversation with Joff, 18 January 2021

Pip: *At least I didn't know if it was over 50 knots*
Joff: *Definitely something to be said for not knowing if it's 50 knots*

Passing through the storm had inflicted yet more damage on the boat. I'd lost two blocks (the pulleys around which ropes turn) and had broken one of my reaching poles. During the height of the storm, my leg became trapped inside the daggerboard casing on the foredeck, resulting in a huge bruise to my calf (and a fresh pair of dry socks ruined). After the storm had passed, the sea state was horrendous, and again the pilot struggled to find a good course.

RACE BLOG, 18 JANUARY 2021

The waves were big, coming from three different directions, and with a really short wave length. Every time Superbigou *started to move, I would feel us launched up on to a wave and then dropped off the back of it, into thin air, falling a few metres with the most gut-wrenching crash. The rig shook, the boat sounded like it was splitting in half, I was thrown across the cabin or cockpit, wherever I was. Exhausted having been up all night getting through the low, I put* Superbigou *on a conservative course at reduced sail and was trying to sleep on the floor when we came down hard off a wave. Another gut-wrenching crash, then all manner of kit rained down on me from the windward side of the boat. I was pinned on to the leeward side, the boat heeling over crazily, and I knew exactly what had happened. In the constant pounding, we had broken one of the keel lines. It took about an hour to replace the line. I had to get into the compartment with the keel canted to the wrong side, and while I worked I was liberally hosed with seawater.*

I recollected my foolish joy at rounding Cape Horn, when I'd had the fleeting thought that it would be 'downhill from now'. *Superbigou* was starting to show her age, and I was increasingly being worn down by the never-ending stream of problems. By 20 January, I was still lying in 17th place. The storm conditions were well behind me, and I had sailed into the semi-permanent cold front that extends from the Brazilian coast, marking the transition from the tempestuous weather systems of the South Atlantic to the warm, wet trade winds. The wind got lighter and shiftier as I continued north, and it became clear that leaving the autopilot to steer to compass course wasn't going to work. With no reliable wind data, I had to stand on deck looking at the sails to work out which way the wind had shifted, steering the pilot up and then down on the remote control. I was locked into that role – unable to sleep, eat or navigate – because the moment I left the pilot, the wind would shift or we would hit a wave. And then the ache in my head would return. For a while, things seemed a little more stable, so I tried to bank an hour of sleep, but the minute I lay down, the wind dropped and the boat felt too flat. I got up, dropped the keel, lay back down, and the wind shifted forwards; from my beanbag, I steered the boat down a couple of degrees with the remote, then the breeze picked up and we heeled over too much. There was no way on earth my brain could turn off enough to sleep, so I embraced the fact that *Superbigou* needed me.

For the first time in many weeks, I hand-steered *Superbigou*, and it was magnificent. I took a cup of tea, some great sounds (Daft Punk and Muse), and sat on deck steering my way through the shifts and the waves for five hours, until night fell and my neck and back were tired, and a big ugly cloud rolled over the top of us and stole all the wind. Despite being very tired and frustrated, I did relish the opportunity to helm. I have always been a very active helm when solo racing. In all my previous boats I have spent hours and days locked into position, feeling every part of the boat. It gives me a truly deep connection with weather and conditions.

> RACE BLOG, 21 JANUARY 2021
>
> *Taking the tiller in my hands yesterday alleviated the ache in my head; I was taking control, using my own brain to react to the many changes on the water, steering a way through the disturbed conditions, and that made a difference. I have not yet been totally superseded by a machine.*

I knew I couldn't hand-steer for the rest of the race. Once the conditions became more stable, the pilot would once again take control, but for now I savoured the opportunity to feel my boat fully.

My progress over the previous day had been slow. There was no way around the light patch of wind that extended across the Atlantic. Slowly, *Superbigou* ground to a halt. Cali and Alan were suffering the same fate to the east of me. What really hurt, however, was watching the boats to the south cruising up to us in a good breeze. On the midnight update, I painfully noted that Stéphane Le Diraison, who had been 550 miles behind me two weeks previously, had reduced my lead to just 50 miles and was now travelling 15 knots faster than me. It hurt so much; I was silently screaming. And every tracker update gave me another jab. All those miles I battled to gain, in Southern Ocean conditions, were now melting away in the Atlantic heat.

I knew enough about myself to do everything I could to fend off that horrible feeling of despondency, the sense of powerlessness. The only way to counteract it was to find positive things to do that would help me perform once the breeze filled in. I made a list of all the jobs I could do in the light winds that would benefit me in the final four weeks of the race. There were multiple routine items that I gleefully ticked off my list, but one job had been hanging over me for a while – the one huge thing that would really improve my performance to the finish. A job where those twin monsters of 'loss of control' and 'fear' would meet to fight it out.

From initial analysis, as I gazed at the top of the mast through binoculars, it looked like the wind wand could be repaired. The only way to find out for sure was to climb the 28 metres to the top of the mast. No solo skipper enjoys climbing the mast. It is something we do as a last resort when no other solution presents itself. Even moored in the marina, it scares the pants off me. I had already done a halfway mast climb in the early stages of the race, and going to the top now filled me with dread. In lesser boats, or with larger crews, many sailors climb the mast as part of their routine drill – a general inspection during relatively stable weather to check the various fittings, especially if the boat has been under stress in a storm. But an IMOCA's mast is over 100 feet tall (30 metres), so climbing it while at sea alone is an action carried out only in extremis. I can summon the courage to do it when there really is no other choice. There is nothing about the process that feels safe; you are giving up a fundamental level of control by placing yourself above the deck, hanging from a single rope, unable to change the course, manage sails or influence any aspect of how the boat sails. You must place your life in the hands of machines and equipment and trust they are up to the job. The experience when you're out at sea is very different to when you're moored in a harbour: the motion of the boat on the waves, however slight, causes a wild swinging and jerking at the top of the mast, like some vast pendulum.

Unlike some cruising boats, we don't have steps fixed into the mast to help our progress. We have to self-belay our way up with ropes, using the same equipment as tree surgeons, hanging for hours in a climbing harness that cuts off the circulation to our lower limbs. On *Superbigou*, I use a hand ascender and foot loop to inch my way up. I live in fear of being separated from the mast. If I were to lose contact and the boat heeled over, I would be swung away from the rig, out into thin air, held there until the boat came upright, when I would come hurtling to meet the hard carbon mast with bone-breaking impact. I use a strop around the mast to keep me close when climbing, but despite this, I am driven with desperation to hang on with legs and arms. I sometimes end up clinging to the mast like a koala, which makes it impossible to continue climbing. At the point when I am actually engaged in fixing whatever is broken, I must force my hands to let go, relying on the strops and my knees and thighs to keep me in position while my hands work. The experience is always frightening, and the very thought of it can cause my body to go into an adrenaline cycle of shaking and hyperventilation. Every part of my being tells me to keep my feet on the deck.

On 21 January, with a solid forecast of light airs, I eventually galvanised myself enough to climb the mast.

RACE BLOG, 22 JANUARY 2021

When I have something big like this to do that I am scared of, I tend to sit around for a bit. I think about it. I try to imagine myself doing it. To an outsider it must look like I have just given up, sitting staring into space. Then at some point in this little ritual I think I get embarrassed at my own procrastination, and without warning (sometimes even surprising myself), I will get up, get my stuff together and just go and do it. Once I have started, I will finish. It's always the starting that is the difficult bit.

Extracts from text messages to shore

Pip: *Are you there?*
Joff: *Yes, of course.*
Pip: *I'm going to have a go at the wind wand*
Pip: *It's all in place I just need to kit up*
Pip: *If I get scared I'll come down*

Joff: *Ok, I'll let RM [race management] know*

My climbing rope was attached to the spinnaker halyard lock on the windward side. My main worry was that I would get thrown around the front of the mast by a wave. My safety strop would keep me close, but I knew it would be tough getting back to the windward side again. Now, as I managed to pull myself up, I kept on the uphill side of the mast in those sections where there was rigging to hold on to, but when it was just the mast, I had to attempt to hold on to the mainsail. A couple of times I was thrown around the front of the mast and had to scrabble and swing my way back, mid-air. During one set of aggressive little waves, I had nothing to hold on to, so I did my best koala impression, wrapping arms and legs around the mast. When the waves subsided, I tried to continue the climb, and that is when I realised that I was stuck.

My right leg had slotted between the mainsail and the mast during a brief lull in the wind. Now the wind strength had increased, the sail edge had stiffened and would not give way. I couldn't get my leg out, which was now trapped between the luff (the leading edge of the sail) and the mainsail track. My knee was too big to bring back through the gap. I struggled for a few minutes, but the sail was too heavy and tight to shift: I was powerless against the grip of this 200m² sail. Realising that I was firmly stuck, I ventured to let go entirely. Gritting my teeth, I took hold of my knee with both hands and tugged. It barely shifted, and the feeling was as if blood vessels, bone and cartilage were being relentlessly crushed, my knee grinding violently against the mast track. I continued to pull, knowing it was short-term pain and trusting my body would not allow me to create serious damage. It worked – though I wasn't sure my leg ever would again.

RACE BLOG, 22 JANUARY 2021

Success. And some impressive bruising ... Afterwards, I adjusted my technique to push back and out with my toes on the track ... koala is not to be recommended. The rest of the climb was pretty quick after this. I was scared enough to just want it over with. Working at the top of the mast was far easier than the climb or the descent. I finally made it down to the deck, very bruised, a bit sunburned, dehydrated, and very sure I never want to go up there again.

The good news was that having successfully managed to replace the missing part, I once again had wind data. Ahead was a stretch of 1,000 miles reaching, and *Superbigou* always struggled against the more modern boats in those conditions. But it was in good shape, and still fighting, trying to push the limits of what was possible to achieve in a 21-year-old boat.

RACE BLOG, 22 JANUARY 2021

I might not be able to compete against the newer boats on speed over the next section, but I can compete on effort, tenacity and bloody-minded never giving up. We are still Game On!

FACING FEAR

One of the frequent questions I'm asked by people curious about why on earth anyone should put themselves in such a precarious position as to sail around the world alone is: 'Don't you get scared?'

The truth is that my job does scare me. Not all the time, of course, but there are moments in every solo ocean race when I expect to feel the dry mouth, elevated heart rate, pounding in my ears – the fight-or-flight grip of real fear as my 60-foot boat races through the dark, smashing over waves, careering across the ocean with me inside, feeling more like a passenger than a master.

Early in my solo sailing career, I hid my fear. I thought people would think I was weak or incompetent if they knew I was scared. So, I put on a front and pretended to be an old hand who knew it all. As my career has developed, I have realised that just the right amount of fear is an incredibly powerful tool that demonstrates I understand the risks I am taking and am therefore in a good position to manage them. Risk-taking goes hand in hand with never settling for what I know, but forging into the unknown in order to keep improving and learning. Fear, you could say, is a step on the path to growth.

Being scared at some level has become a normal feeling for me. I have learned to understand my fear and have developed techniques to stop it from swallowing me whole when I am alone, exhausted, and unsure of how things will pan out. It can be isolating. If I were with other people, I could share the load. Knowing someone else is by your side in difficult times significantly reduces the stress of what you're experiencing. Even having someone on the end of the phone to talk to can make a difference.

When I started out solo sailing, I could not afford satellite phone airtime, other than in case of emergency, so I had to learn to overcome my fear entirely on my own. These techniques still serve me well both on and off the water; they have helped me to take and manage risks, deal with the unexpected, and manage my way through previously unencountered challenges both in the sailing and business worlds.

The first thing I do is admit to myself that I'm scared. I often say this out loud: 'OK, I'm scared.' Just saying it makes the fear less powerful; it gives me some sort of control; it feels like a step towards defeating the monsters.

Next, I talk myself through why I am scared. Slightly unconventionally, that involves listing all the bad outcomes that could occur as a result of the thing that is scaring me. This feels unconventional, because most common wisdom encourages us into positive visualisation. Instead, I look the negative outcomes square in the face. I don't pretend they won't happen; I pull them out of the shadows and take a good look at what could really go wrong and admit that what I am doing is risky. In this case, on that particular day of the mast climb, there were many reasons to be scared about doing it alone. What if I fell, or got separated from the mast and swung out of control away from the boat as it heeled? What if the autopilot stopped working and the boat tacked and I got trapped? What if the weather changed while I was at the top and the boat started to be overpowered? One by one, I name all the things that could go wrong.

Once I identify the negative outcomes, I talk myself through all the mitigations I have put in place and all the logical reasons that they will not become a reality. I find this incredibly helpful because as well as tempering my fear, it is like doing a dynamic risk assessment – an audit of training, experience, skill and expertise that gives me the green light to move forward.

In the case of climbing the mast, I would have noted the following:

- I had the correct equipment and it was well maintained, so there was no reason it would suddenly fail.
- The rope I used to climb had held sails of 400 square metres in the air, so my 68kg weight was not going to cause it to break.
- I had trained and practised my technique, so I could trust myself.
- I use two tethers to keep me attached to the mast, so I would always have one around the mast to keep me from swinging out.
- The weather conditions were perfect, with very little wind, no sign in the forecast it would change, and the horizon was clear.
- If I saw clouds as I climbed, I could come down.
- The autopilot had been driving my boat around the world for nine weeks without a problem. It was irrational to think that it would suddenly stop working now.

I always say to myself that if after running through my audit I am still not able to convince myself that the worst will not happen, then maybe I need to listen to my fear. Perhaps this will be that time when I need to be cautious and change my behaviour to protect myself and my boat. Sometimes, fear has a place.

The final piece of the jigsaw is thinking about what will happen if I don't take action. Quite often, this is what spurs me on the most. In the case of my mast climb, I knew that if I didn't change my wind instruments, my performance would remain hampered: I would lose any chance of catching the boat in front, and would lose places to those behind. I had an opportunity to change this. I had worked so hard to get my place on the start line and had battled all the way around the world. I could not live with myself if I took the easy option at that moment. I had to keep fighting, I had to try. And so, after two hours of reasoning with myself, I finally climbed the mast, and I am proud that I did.

There were many moments during my Vendée Globe race where I surprised myself, feeling immense pride at how strong and creative I could be. I often look back to that race and wonder if I could replicate my rudder change or that mast climb, or whether there was some spark ignited in me by those conditions that may never be lit again. Right now, typing these words, I don't feel my strength so tangibly. There is something about being on the ocean alone that brings out my most powerful self. When there is no other option, we must all step up.

19

PRIORITISING HEALTH

When we started to prepare for the Vendée, it was with the absolute knowledge that things would go wrong ... with the boat. But at no point in my visualisation of the race did I imagine that I could be the weak link. Before the race, I was required to have medical examinations, including blood tests, stress tests, echocardiographs and echocardiograms. Every skipper had to be certified fit to race by the event doctor, as well as having bespoke medical training appropriate to the circumstances in which we would be living at sea. The race doctor issued a list of contents we had to pack in our medical box, which was subsequently checked off and approved. Lou helped me to prepare myself in case of accident on board, but I don't think I properly contributed to this process. With Joff, I already had a database in my head full of past failures and existing concerns, so I was fully engaged in the preparation of the boat. Maybe I had a blind spot or was in some sort of denial, but I couldn't visualise that I might break down physically. I had experienced small injuries before – broken ribs, a crushed finger, cuts, burns, and skin complaints from sitting in the wet for days on end – but nothing more than that. So, when my health started to unravel in week 11 of the race, I felt unprepared for it.

I remember watching the drama unfold after Yann Eliès was injured in the 2008 Vendée Globe race. He had been changing headsails the morning of 18 December, bracing himself on the pulpit of his IMOCA, *Generali*, when the boat surfed into a wave, buried its bow, and came to a sudden halt, the impact of which caused Eliès' thigh bone to break. He managed to crawl back along the deck to make a phone call to the race organisers.

Stranded in the Indian Ocean, 900 nautical miles south of Fremantle, Western Australia, Yann had to wait two days until he could be rescued, while his boat continued on autopilot. In too much pain to move, he was confined to his bunk on a diet of morphine. Marc Guillemot, on *Safran*, was tasked to stand by, as was Sam Davies, then on her first Vendée Globe race. Neither could do more than offer moral support, as they weren't in a position to rescue an immobile Yann. Two days later, thankfully, he was safely evacuated by a Royal Australian Navy frigate.

I knew it could happen. When it came to medical problems, I understood there would be little to no solution for broken bones, save painkillers and immobilisation. I had to accept the possibility of a break, in the same way I accepted that the mast could fall down. I was confident that I could treat any small injury, and I didn't even consider that I might become unwell in some other way. Lou and I had spent two days in my back garden (under COVID rules), going through the contents of my huge yellow medical box. Should I suffer some injury at sea, I knew I'd need to be the nurse, surgeon, anaesthetist and patient, all on a moving wet platform. We worked through every medical procedure, adapting techniques to allow for rough seas, including the need to strap my arm to my thigh to prevent it from folding in two while inserting a needle for canulation.

Other than losing so much weight, I had no health problems in the first ten weeks of my race. By Lou's own admission, she had been having an easy ride. But when the problems came, they were so left field. I'd always embraced that 'next level' concept of a challenge, but I am not sure a biblical-type plague was what I had in mind.

On 17 January, I sailed through the centre of a huge depression off the Uruguayan coast. It was a challenging time, and the boat was damaged by the constant pounding from oncoming waves. As we went through the centre of the low, it was pitch dark, so I hadn't noticed the fields of blue jellyfish sweeping over the deck at the height of the storm. It's almost laughable now – imagine fighting for survival against the elements, and then just when you think it couldn't get any worse, a plague of poisonous creatures is thrown into the mix. When dawn broke, as I was working through the aftermath of the gale, I came across dozens of tiny Portuguese men o' war jellyfish stuck in rope bags or attached to the rigging. One by one, I carefully picked them up with my pliers and dumped them over the side. After that, I thought no more about it.

A day after these strange little invaders littered my deck, I felt a burning sensation on the back of my neck. I reached round, to discover blistering skin under my fingertips. I thought it odd – the soreness had arrived so suddenly – but concluded that it must have been a reaction to the rubber neck seal of my dry top and the fact that I had not washed my hair for weeks. I took a photo of the back of my neck and sent it to Lou, then put some cream on the sore patch of skin, washed my hair, and again thought nothing more of it.

Text message conversation with Lou, 18 January 2021

Pip: *It's the kind of thing that could get infected though. Especially seeing as I really am a festering dung pile at the moment. The smell from my foulies is quite extraordinary*
Lou: *Yup ... pour some fresh water over it and don't keep touching it. Take a photo in next couple of days and will tell you if worth popping*

A day later, after a wonderfully productive session of on-board DIY in the sun, I lay down on my stack of sails to take in the beauty of the evening. When I stood up again, I noticed my back was hurting. Assuming sunburn, I reached around my back to have a feel and was met with a big, bulging blister. Mystified, I contacted Lou again. I took a photo of the blister, stretching my phone round with some difficulty, and sent it to her. As we texted back and forth, my back became increasingly red, the blister growing, the skin around it more and more aggravated.

Extracts from text message conversation with Lou, 19 January 2021

Lou: *Ok that's weird... anything that could have rubbed that?*
Lou: *You've not been stung by anything?*
Pip: *Nope there's nothing out here*

Lou: *Ok ... Are you feeling generally well?*
Pip: *Yep a little bit lightheaded*
Lou: *Are you showered?*
Pip: *Yep this morning*
Lou: *And in clean clothes?*
Lou: *Have you got a jellyfish down your t shirt?*
Pip: *Oh fuck, I think I know*

Though Lou's last question was delivered with a comic twist, in a former career she had worked as a medic in Australia, where reactions from 'bluebottle' stings are common. One of the jellyfish had clearly washed over my head in a wave during the storm, and I realised that there must have been others tucked into the folds of the sail bags I had lain on earlier in the day.

RACE BLOG, 20 JANUARY 2021

So now I have what is effectively a chemical burn, which I am trying to treat with my hands behind my back, and I need to keep reasonably dry and clean to avoid it getting infected. Just to add a little bit of extra complication to the rest of my race. I am laughing about it, despite the pain, as I think only I could have managed to come up with such a problem on top of sailing solo around the world ... Laughing is the right response, the only other option would be to curl up in a foetal position while hoping the wind eventually blows me back to LSD.

By 23 January, I had climbed the mast and was badly bruised from getting my leg trapped, the blisters on my back and neck had spread to my arms, and as I travelled north towards the equator the stifling heat appeared to be aggravating my skin further. I was in constant pain and had started to feel incredibly unwell. Lou prescribed me a regime of antihistamines, anti-inflammatories and painkillers. We agreed I should stay out of the sun where possible, and I had to wait for the medication to start working.

The one day in the entire race when I doubted my ability to continue was 24 January. By now, the rashes and blisters had spread to my legs, arms and wrists. I could no longer lie on my back to sleep. Any touch of fabric on my skin hurt. Feeling weak, I worried that I wouldn't be able to handle the boat should something unexpected happen. Lou, concerned at the escalation of symptoms, turned to her own network of specialist doctors to discuss how we should progress. The strength of my painkillers was increased, and she added a steroid medication to the mix. We agreed a check-in schedule, and she messaged me the times and quantities for each medication. I had to message back, affirming what I had taken and when. Remote diagnosis and treatment of a patient is a huge exercise in trust. Lou had to trust that I was giving her the whole picture; I had to be honest about how I was feeling. And for a person who is used to internalising pain, this was not easy. On this darkest of days, I asked Lou if she thought I should be in hospital, and I had already decided that if she said yes, I would head straight for Recife, 250 miles away on the Brazilian coast. She answered firmly, 'No. Just give yourself time to heal. It will get better.'

My condition got worse before it got better. Over the next week, my back went into spasm as a result of sleeping on my front on an uneven surface and the constant slamming of the hull; my face and eyes swelled up; my vision became blurry. At one time I had trouble breathing, but my steroids had run out and the antihistamines were getting low. I was still in shock at how badly my body had let me down, terrified that I would prove to be the weak link that stopped me from finishing the race. During those weeks of being unwell, powerless to fight back, I was overtaken by the remaining two foiling boats.

Lou, at least, had confidence. Yes, my situation was extreme, but I could and would get better. I was in no imminent danger, unlike some of those that came through her hospital doors. One morning, however, during my third week of sickness, I wobbled that confidence.

From an interview with Lou Adams, team medic and coordinator:

'*My alarm that day went off at 0530. I got up, checked my phone, looked to see when Pip was last online: 0120. I was surprised, but continued with my routine ... scrubs on, black coffee, and the long drive to the hospital. I got to work at 0650, checked my phone again. Nothing – no sign that Pip had been online. We had arranged a BBC live interview for that morning, so I sent a text, quick and simple: "How's your back, burns, face, pain score?" I watched the two ticks appear, indicating that her phone was connected to the satellite, but they didn't turn blue. The what ifs came screaming into my head: what if she's knocked out? What if she's been knocked overboard? What if, what if ...*

'*I had to calm my thoughts. At the hospital we were in the thick of the global pandemic; I was in for a full day. My inner dialogue took over: "Compartmentalise your thoughts, Lou. Focus on today." It didn't work: this didn't feel right. I had half an hour before my first operations meeting; I checked the tracker and the boat seemed to be on the right course. A quick call to Joff for reassurance. I was not reassured. He explained that the boat could sail for days on its own if Pip was unconscious, overboard or injured. He called Pip on her satellite phone. Nothing. I called her mobile: nothing. This was not good. The BBC interview was missed, I had no answers, and had to start my day.*

'*Just after 0900, I received a text: she had overslept. As I looked at my WhatsApp, feeling the power of those two blue ticks, I was relieved and furious with her. It was an emotion I would never fully be able to express, which had taken me to a dark place, thinking the worst. I realised then that we had been holding our breath for this entire race.'*

On reading Lou's account and seeing the incident from her perspective, I was conflicted – not for the first time – about the emotional fallout my team, friends and family experience because of my chosen career. I was sick for over three weeks during that final run up the Atlantic. It sideswiped me in a way I could not have imagined. Over the course of the race, I had grown to see myself as the master of my own solutions – strong, powerful, resilient. One tiny jellyfish revealed my vulnerability.

RACE BLOG, 25 JANUARY 2021

I've been reflecting on just how much I have put my poor body through in the last 77 days, and I am, as ever, impressed at what we human beings can do.

I have set up, hoisted, and dropped off-wind sails – sometimes ten changes a day – dragging them into position, fumbling with small catches and levers in freezing conditions, taking ice-cold water over my head as I hang off the bow to pull in a tack line, hauling against the halyard with all my bodyweight, being yanked off my feet by the spinnaker refusing to be tamed. I have staggered or crawled up and down the deck to the mast to put reefs in and out, crawled my way out along the boom to unhook reefing lines, stood bent forwards over the coffee grinder, arms pumping, for what amounts to hours, eased sheets out only to pull them in minutes later, top-wound furling lines on sails that seem to go on forever and ever. I have dragged heavy, wet sails from one end of the boat to the other, lifting them out of the hatch at the front and over every obstacle that may catch them on the deck. I have crawled in and out of tiny, dark, damp spaces in temperatures over 35 degrees, slick with sweat, while trying to do up bolts or thread a line in a corner I can only reach with one hand. I have slept on the floor for sometimes only minutes at a time, eaten from pouches and bags – some meals only a mouthful managed before I am needed on deck again. I have been shivering with cold, exhausted with heat, and yet still when the boat calls, my body will jump into action ...

The incredible ability of a human to endure short-term physical discomfort never ceases to amaze me. We are both physically and mentally capable of so much more than we believe.

20

KEEPING THE DRUMBEAT GOING

The weeks from my mast climb on 21 January to my birthday on 7 February were the darkest of my race. It felt like everything was slowly crumbling around me. It was hard to stay positive with my body suffering and the escalating boat problems, not to mention the raw mental pain from falling all the way back to 19th place. In my lowered state, the news that Britain was likely to be in a third COVID lockdown at the finish of my race, and that those friends and family whom I had missed so much at the start would not be there to welcome me home, threw me into extreme emotional turmoil. At some point, though, I realised I would be consumed by my own thoughts if I didn't develop a strategy to get me through each day. I still had my usual tools of job list triage, risk management and anxiety control to fall back on, but these dark days required something else. I had neither the energy nor the capacity to continue at full bore. In order to survive, I needed to reduce the pressure. Something had to give.

On the evening of Wednesday 27 January, Charlie Dalin on *Apivia* crossed the finish line at Les Sables d'Olonne. The finish was relayed to me by my family onshore – and what a finish it was! Through that final day of racing there were five skippers still in the running, with the narrow margin you might expect in a shorter, coastal race. Amazingly, there were only a couple of hours between the top three. It was so close that Dalin emerged out of his covered cockpit only after he crossed the line. Ordinarily, the winner would have enough time in hand to come out on deck and wave to the spectators in their boats on the approach to Les Sables, but not so Dalin, who knew he might not end up being the

211

winner once calculations for lost time had been awarded for the hours spent in the search and rescue of Kevin Escoffier.

At first it looked as though Boris Herrmann would win the day. Running in third place on the water, once he'd been awarded his lost hours he was within his six-hour margin to win against Dalin. But then disaster struck. Not long after Dalin crossed the line, Herrmann's boat collided with a fishing boat while Boris was asleep below decks, having not woken up to his AIS alarm. Happily, he was OK, but there was damage to his starboard foil and rigging, which meant he had to limp towards Les Sables at a much reduced 7 knots. He didn't make it in time.

Yannick Bestaven, racing into Les Sables on *Maître Coq IV* at 18–20 knots, was ultimately declared the winner, as he had a ten-hour time advantage due to time spent in Kevin's search.

THE TOP FIVE

1. Yannick Bestaven in *Maître Coq IV*: 80 days and 3 hours
2. Charlie Dalin in *Apivia*: 80 days and 6 hours
3. Louis Burton in *Bureau Vallée 2*: 80 days and 10 hours
4. Jean Le Cam in *Yes We Cam!*: 80 days and 13 hours
5. Boris Herrmann in *Malizia-Seaexplorer*: 80 days and 14 hours

RACE BLOG, 28 JANUARY 2021

I hardly think anything I have to report today is of note following the intense drama of last night. But just so you know ... I am back in the north!

I got to experience Charlie crossing the line almost live, through the relayed messages of friends who were watching live at home. It was ridiculously exciting just then, hearing about him coming into the line at speed, then the wait to see how the rest unfolded. And who could have predicted a finish like this?

Watching the drama unfold that night was a great reminder that in the 3,250 miles of racing I still had to go, anything could happen. In our own little pocket of performance, the dice had been rolled, and the six boats now in my pack had picked their respective longitudes to take on the doldrums. We were now powering north to try and break through. I was the furthest west in the group, which gave me a slightly worse angle coming into the north-east trades, but I was hoping that the trade-off would be a more solid breeze to drive me through the area.

RACE BLOG, 31 JANUARY 2021

I am hot, sweaty, being shaken and slammed around, and feeling that this part of the course is relentless. I've been three days now in the NE trades, and have at least another three to go, and it is taking a lot of my emotional energy to stay sane and focused. Superbigou *is heeled over hard and regularly bouncing off waves, so moving around is difficult and the ride down below is far from smooth. The sun shines directly into the cockpit and there is no shade on deck. Down below is airless and climbs to temperatures in the high 30s during the day. Doing anything below soaks me in sweat; on deck I am baked by the sun and drenched by the waves. There is nowhere to hide from these conditions.*

Though we had largely kept my medical problems away from the public eye, friends following from the shore had already noted how much weight I had lost and could see that technical problems were getting more frequent and severe as the weeks progressed. During the final month of the race, various friends messaged me, encouraging me to take my foot off the gas: 'You have proved yourself. Just come home safely.' Their messages made me sad. I wasn't ready to give up. I still had over 3,000 miles to sail, and wouldn't settle for my current position in the race. At the same time, I recognised that I was stuck in my own circumstances. I believed I would get better, and that the opportunity to push again would come, but for the time being, I needed to find ways to get through each day until that moment came.

Emotional resilience is the fuel that allowed me to battle through the dark clouds that were forming at this stage in the race. There were times when my world shrank until I was just a small person, not coping, in a dark, cold, wet boat. A cage would slowly build around me, trapping my negative emotions and keeping them close. I learned quickly to recognise when my world had reduced to this state, and I understood that at those times I needed tools to pull me out of the darkness and give me the emotional energy to get back up again. I didn't even need to get up and fight, I just needed to get out from under my problems and recognise that things could and would get better. I've already described my mental technique of 'zooming out' in Chapter 5 (Tackling Uncertainty). With it, I could remind myself that not only was I moving through the ocean, but I was moving through time as well. This difficult period was just that – a moment in time – and things would change.

Extract from my workshop on Resilience

Zooming out and recalling what the good times felt like was the emotional rocket fuel I needed to keep moving forwards.

However, this was such an extreme period in the race that my usual positive visualisations – how far I'd come, how lucky I was to have this extraordinary opportunity – weren't sufficient to fight the circumstances. Tools like these are helpful to change a mindset, but now that I was dealing with multiple levels of stress and pain, I had to respond with physical actions to stop things from getting worse – to accelerate my recovery in every sense of the word. In weeks 12, 13 and 14, I had to accept the fact I could no longer operate at full capacity. It was then that I turned to my practical knowledge of systems management to help me manage myself.

The following analogy helps to explain the idea: *Superbigou* ran all its electrical systems on three 12V lithium ion batteries. The electrical systems on board were critical to both survival and performance, feeding power to autopilot, watermaker, navigation systems, satellite communication, data sensors, instrument displays and much more. I had three ways of charging the batteries: through solar, hydrogenerators, and using the alternator on the engine. Each day I monitored the battery banks, never allowing them to drop too low before I engaged one of the charging methods to top them back up again. When I'd lost one of my hydrogenerators earlier in the race, I had recognised the risks. I couldn't continue to burn through the boat's battery power at the same rate, so I turned off my electrical demands one by one, analysing each machine in order of priority to unload the system and give me time to make repairs.

In the same way, now that I was struggling as a human being, I needed to recognise that 'unloading' myself would help my recovery. I shut bits of myself down when I was going through my worst weeks. I had to let go of my competitive desires, and just keep the drumbeat going. It's normal for me to manage layers of performance while I am racing. We are not machines, after all. With natural cycles of energy and creativeness, our capacity to deliver varies even within a 24-hour period. I thought of my ability to perform as a sliding scale, which I could adjust according to circumstance. At the very top, I was racing hard, seeing to the media's requirements and the boat's technical needs efficiently. At the very bottom, I was simply being safe, marking time until the situation improved.

In this way, I turned off the bits of me that were not essential while I tried to recover from my allergies. When my back was in spasm and my skin at its rawest, I had to accept the fact I couldn't spend time on deck during the day, so I reduced my trimming to a check once every few hours. I chose a sail plan that was slightly underpowered for conditions, in order to reduce the possibility of sail changes or reefing. Crawling through the boat with blisters on my arms and back was agony, so I reduced my internal boat checks to once every five days, relying instead on my hearing to warn of imminent problems. At night, I would try to improve performance, spending time on deck in the cool night air, but when my face became swollen and my back was bad, even this was too much to handle. Items remained untouched on my job list, as I never made it past the 'Am I safe?' stage of triage. Each day, my only requirement was to keep going and move in the right direction. Despite the stifling heat of the equator and a total lack of appetite, I committed to eating at least one and a half times my food rations, forcing it down mouthful by mouthful, and drinking at least 4 litres of water a day, which I marked off on my whiteboard. The routine and rhythm helped me work through the hours and minutes. I had small benchmarks to hit every few hours, but I no longer expected my capacity to be open-ended.

I backed down on my communications with the shore, going for days without sending an update. When I did, I was careful to film myself from far away or in the dark so that no one could see my swollen face and blistered neck. I stopped writing detailed blogs, and only covered off the live media demands. My team on the shore were able to take up the slack, turning my voice notes into update posts, sharing media we had already created, keeping race followers informed with a stripped-down level of information. I didn't want to share how hard I was finding things, and faced with the option of either lying or just not talking about how it was, I chose the latter. Most people thought I was too busy to give detail. Only those who were really close to me knew how much I was suffering during those weeks.

In the really bad moments, I thought of the weather. I would think back to the blackest of scary storms, where I huddled below, full of anxiety and fear, watching the wind instrument data climb and climb, as I listened to the boat crash and crack around me. In such moments, I always reassure myself that the front will pass over, and on the other side the weather will be better. In this way, I comforted myself during these dark days of the Vendée, telling myself that my feeling of helplessness was just a moment in time. Only that. Eventually, things *would* get better, because – like the weather – everything always does change. All I had to do was to keep that drumbeat going.

When things did start to change, it was in the most unpredictable way. By 3 February, eleven boats had crossed the finish line. I was chasing a pack of four foiling boats up the Atlantic, nearing the Azores, with 2,400 miles left to run. Didac had made up ground during my illness. On the tracker, he had overtaken, knocking me into 20th place (though we would have to sail a circuitous route

216

around the Azores' high-pressure system, so the trained eye could still put him behind me). The good news was that the air had grown cooler, my skin getting better every day, and I was able to bandage the worst blisters to keep them protected. My energy was starting to return, but I was still struggling emotionally, so when I started getting messages from my shore team asking me to look at a video they had sent me, I put them on ice as non-essential traffic. Eventually, my phone buzzed into life with a call from our comms lead, Isla. Caught off-guard, I picked up. She asked me how I was. Unable to answer, I sat in silence, the tears rolling down my cheeks. I couldn't lie, yet I didn't want to admit how beaten I was feeling. Eventually, I told her I didn't want to talk. She said she understood, but she *really* needed me to watch the video.

Curiosity pulled me out of myself, and I clicked on it. At first, I didn't recognise the man with white beard and glasses, who was staring at me, standing in front of a cabinet, which I later realised was full of movie memorabilia. He fiddled with his computer, then started to speak. 'Happy birthday, Pip. I hear you are sailing around the globe.' My jaw fell open. I started to laugh, then stopped, then laughed again. It was the unmistakable voice of Hollywood actor Russell Crowe:

Message from Russell Crowe, 3 February

'Now just this morning, I was kayaking up Coffs Creek. I had a paddle, which made it significantly easier, so it's a similar journey, I imagine [laughs]. I'm just sitting here thinking about the incredible challenge in front of you and how overwhelming that must feel some days. But just keep going. What an amazing feeling you are going to have when you can say you've claimed the globe. Happy birthday, Pip. Sail well.'

The whole thing had come about through the actions of Steve Harris, the breakfast show DJ of our local radio station in Poole. Steve had been following my campaign since 2019, giving regular updates to listeners. Knowing I'd be at sea on my birthday, 7 February, he had decided to get together a collection of birthday messages from people that I admired to share on air. As well as soliciting messages from famous British sailors, such as Sir Ben Ainslie and Dame Ellen MacArthur, he had a message from comedian and sailor Griff Rhys Jones, and from ultra-marathon champion Jasmin Paris. My team on shore had told Steve that I'd always loved the film *Master and Commander* and that I had a picture of Russell Crowe as Captain Jack Aubrey on the wall of *Superbigou*. Steve tweeted the actor and was somewhat surprised when he got a reply – but not as surprised as I was.

Extracts from text messages to Lou, 3 February 2021

Pip: *It was a lovely surprise. Well actually, it was way more than that. I am a bit confused and stunned. But it made a difference*

Pip: *The truth is I am really worried about the next week. It's going to be really tough and I think I'm going to end up in one of the worst storms yet and I don't feel at my best to deal with it and that is a big concern*

Pip: *I'm trying to get back on it. About to wash my hair. Eaten two meals today. I just need to keep moving forward*

Russell's message was supposed to be kept a secret until my birthday, but it had become impossible to keep a lid on things. The media frenzy that followed was surreal, to say the least. I had a full day of live interviews with mainstream national news, describing my reactions at receiving the message. Others who had contributed birthday messages were somewhat overshadowed by Russell's gesture, but it meant a huge amount to me that every person, famous or not, had bothered to take time out to think kindly of me and record words of solidarity and encouragement.

The change had arrived. I was ready to fight again.

21

Running Up That Hill

Race Blog, 9 February 2021

If the finish was 'just over there', I'd be taking this all in my stride.

Many extreme athletes experience a gruelling form of mental torture on top of their physical pain as they get closer to the finish. Time becomes elastic suddenly, so that instead of feeling closer to their goal, the finish line seems further away. They have a sense, too, that the prize – tantalisingly close – will be whipped away when it is almost within their grasp. In olden days, sailors might have fancied Neptune was playing a cat-and-mouse game with them – and it is true that I sometimes get a superstitious sense that we elite skippers have got above ourselves in thinking we can conquer the seas, no matter how high-tech our yachts. I have often suffered a persistent, niggling voice in my ear telling me that pride comes before a fall.

Over the course of the Vendée, I'd lost 9 kilos in weight. Not eating enough early in the race had caused irreversible weight loss, and by now my clothes swamped me. I'd built up extra muscle pre-race, but it had wasted away, and I was to discover that basic tasks took increasing amounts of time to achieve. In preparation for the race, I'd regularly run long distances off-road, which demanded similar physical discipline and mental fortitude to solo sailing, but I wasn't at all sure I could rely entirely on my endurance fitness to see me through. Of the mental techniques that helped me, there was one I use when running up hills that adapted itself very well to this gruelling last stage of the race when the distance to my goal was difficult to predict. The trick is to run *over* the hill, not *up* it. If you focus on a point beyond the hill summit as the finish, it helps with managing energy and expectations.

The race was never going to finish with a gentle saunter to the line. With just over 2,000 miles to go, I could feel my fight coming back. There were four foiling boats ahead of me that I had been leading in the Southern Ocean, and I was 168 miles behind my nearest rival, Alan Roura. At this point, my competitive spirit lifted its head and roared. I was still close to the winning time of the 2000 race, which had been my benchmark for excellence, and I was not going to quit now, even if there was nasty weather ahead. As always, I asked myself, where is the risk? Surely, the biggest risk was to throw away this last opportunity to make an impact.

Certainly, the weather in the North Atlantic carried a degree of risk. It looked evil as we made our way around the Azores high. Ahead, there was a succession of low-pressure systems barrelling their way from Nova Scotia towards northern France, with a web of complex fronts spiralling off each one, making for huge, rough sea states and changeable conditions. My fragile and sleep-deprived state didn't make matters any better, and after three months at sea the wind and waves would find any weakness that had been developing in the boat. My steering was making some odd noises, and I had to keep reminding myself that it didn't matter how close to the line we were: I was only a step away from a race-ending mistake.

RACE BLOG, 6 FEBRUARY 2021

I guess I am nervous because the stakes seem high, but I need to trust that I can get through this well. I never doubted myself before and it seems a bit odd that I feel this way now.

If I honestly believed I could still reel those four guys in, there was only one way to find out. I brought *Superbigou* on to a course that put me in the strongest breeze, and on 6 February was once again the fastest boat of the 11 that were still left racing in the Vendée Globe.

Extracts from text message conversation with Joff, 6 February 2021

Joff: *Afterburners lit* 🚀
Pip: ☺
Pip: *The forecast is so flipping shite*
Pip: *Was it too much to ask for a straight line run home?*
Joff: *Evidently so*
Pip: *Balls!*
Joff: *How is the body holding up?*
Pip: *Ok. Better for having something to do – less time to think about it. But I do look like I've been dragged around a field a few times on the back of a tractor.*
Pip: *How is France?*
Joff: *France without restaurants. What's the point?*

On 7 February, although I experienced my birthday fuss, with the huge wave of virtual birthday love being directed at *Superbigou* from around the world, the weather, which shows none of us favours, did not care that I had just turned 47, and the wind was already up to gale force with 5-metre seas. I had just over 1,000 miles to the finish and had gained 60 miles on the pack of boats ahead. The night was inky black, with dark, sodden clouds blacking out any light from the small slither of moon. I was back to my Southern Ocean ways, waiting down below, fully kitted up, as I watched the instruments intently, like a cat about to pounce. It was 4am when the time came to furl, then drop my Code Zero. Stepping on deck, I was hosed by a wave. I cursed myself inwardly for not changing my head torch: it wasn't well charged, and the light was weak. I told myself to trust my process, and started the furl anyway, although I couldn't see the bow of the boat from the cockpit, but I failed to see the masthead halyard, which had come loose at the mast, swinging around at the front of the boat. So many crises are caused by one small detail, gone unnoticed, which escalates in a matter of minutes. The rope wound itself around the Code Zero as I made the furl, eventually getting to the limit of its length so that it constricted the sail at the top, leaving a bulge of sail open to the wind. From the cockpit it felt like the furl was normal, so I released the tack line and went forward to drop the sail to the deck. This instantly caused a wineglass-shaped mess, the sail partly furled, partly bulging and flapping. Worse still, I could not drop it, because the masthead halyard wound around it was holding it up there.

RACE BLOG, 8 FEBRUARY 2021

There is always a tiny second of panic that comes over me in these situations. It's really quick and hardly registers, but it's a jump inside, with the question, 'What happens if you can't sort this out?' The answer is always the same, so the moment is only short. 'I have to sort it out, one way or another.'

There followed two hours of trying various ways to get the sail to the deck. Each new approach would involve staggering backwards and forwards up the bouncing deck between cockpit and foredeck, winding ropes on, letting them off, then going forward to see if it had made any difference. Eventually, I managed to unfurl half of the sail, enough to unwind some of the restrictive halyard and create enough slack to drop the sail to the deck. Trying to pull all 165 square metres into the deck with one arm, while easing the halyard with the other, was immense physical work. I knew that if the sail went in the water, I would either lose it, the force of water ripping it, or it could take me over the side with it. By the time I was finished I was exhausted and bruised, as well as angry and disappointed with myself. I had put everything at risk by not charging my head torch. Such a stupid, unnecessary mistake, and now I had a half-furled sail stuffed down the forehatch and a furler in bits in the cabin. Anything but shipshape for the mother of storms ahead of us.

By 9 February – day 93 of the race – I had 563 miles left to sail. Fourteen boats were home, and our pack of four was heading into the Bay of Biscay, where a huge low-pressure system was on a converging course with us. We'd need to sail fast to get in ahead of it. Behind me, Didac Costa, blocked by the wind and waves that preceded the depression, was forced to take avoiding action to stay out of the worst of it. By now I had almost caught up with Stéphane and Alan, reducing their lead to 74 miles, but conditions on board were terrible. Even my 'running over that hill' mental trick was barely effective as a morale booster. With every new weather file, my route to the finish seemed to get longer or more complicated. The prospect of a finish had been shown to me, then cruelly taken away. Through most of the race, the finish had been too far away to visualise, so I was mentally able to accept the open-ended nature of the race and pace myself accordingly. But now that the end was in sight it felt like a final sprint, but one where someone kept moving the finish line. Since I'd started looking at my potential finish dates five days before, my ETA had slipped by three days.

RACE BLOG, 9 FEBRUARY 2021

It is relentless out here. Squall after squall. Multiple wind shifts. Waves coming from every direction ... The conditions are so volatile, with wind speeds spanning a range of 25 knots in the space of an hour, that I need to change gear a lot. With these constant changes it is impossible to keep to the speeds my routing options suggest. Every time I swap headsails I lose a bit of ground, then when the breeze dies and I am underpowered I lose ground while I wait to see if it is a temporary lull or here to stay ...

Also worth noting that if the finish was not 'just over there' then I probably would not be in this system at all or would have got out of it pretty pronto. But the answer is to look beyond the finish.

I have not just sailed 97% of the way around the world to be broken now.

During those last two days of my race, I could feel my world starting to unravel around me. It was clear by now that I would not be able to catch Cali and Koji, but Stéphane and Alan were still fair game. My competitive spirit was alive and kicking, so I decided to choose a different route to the finish. While they sailed north into the Biscay, mirroring each other's zigzag course, seeking out less wind, I chose a more aggressive option. I would take a southerly route into the bay, staying in stronger winds, and skirt around the top of Cape Finisterre. My navigation software was able to run routes for my competitors, and I could see that if I pushed hard there was a chance I could beat them over the line. After all, I had got past them before like this. The plan was reliant on my being able to push hard with my downwind sails. The big one was still in the forepeak, half unfurled, but the little one would do the job. I set off on my new course, excited at what might happen and full of hope for a dramatic finish.

The drama, when it came, was very different. At lunchtime on 10 February there was a huge bang. The boat lurched and slowed. I ran up on deck to see my sail halfway down, dragging down the side of the boat like a huge fishing net. The strop holding the halyard lock in place at the top of the mast had finally worn through after 94 days of swinging and rubbing against the top of the mast. The top of the sail was still being held up by the thin halyard, which fortunately had been wrapped around a winch. I walked to the foredeck, grabbed the edge of the sail and foolishly tried to pull it on deck. An impossible task, as the fabric was under tonnes of load, held down by the weight of water dragged along with it as the boat continued its path through the waves. Next, a sound caught my attention – a straining and pinging – and I looked up to see the bowsprit was being bent down at an alarming angle, the weight of water in the sail about to snap it in half. I ran back to the cockpit and let the tack line run free. As the rope rushed out, the sail washed further back down the boat. But now the furling line was under huge tension. For a moment I watched in horror as it started to rip the pulpit (the metal frame on the front of my boat) off its mounts, first squashing the metal, then pinging the frame from the deck. The dragging sail was about to cheesewire all the fittings from the side of my boat – it was quite literally ripping the deck apart. I cut the furling line. The sail washed back some more. Now it was pulling on the halyard alone, but it was dragging the boat down on one side and was in danger of wrapping around the keel.

There was no way I could get that sail out of the water with my own muscle, so I spent the next five minutes considering my options. The most obvious involved cutting the halyard holding the sail up. I would take off, leaving the sail in the water, unless I could think of a clever way to recover it mechanically. This first option did not appeal. Not only did I not want to lose the sail or leave it as junk in the sea, but I was painfully aware that it could still end up tangled around the boat's rudders and keel. The next option came to me more slowly. It would involve somehow emptying some of the water out of the sail, enough to move it. If I could capsize *Superbigou* over the other way, leaning it right over with the mast close to the water, the Code Zero would be on the high side. Maybe, that way, enough of the sail would be lifted out of the water for me to handle it. Worth a try.

I headed to the back of the boat and pinned the mainsail into the centre and prepared my backstays. I gingerly manoeuvred the boat through a gybe, so the wind was hard on the opposite side of the sail. The boat heeled over hard, leaning at around 70 degrees. I could hear everything I had left out down below clattering to one side. At this crazy angle, I could barely climb out of the cockpit, but managed to cling to the guardrails on the high side and made my way forward. Lying down, I peered over the side of the boat. My sail was hanging under the hull, and it was now empty of water. I had no time to lose. With one foot on the mast and the other on deck, braced so I could not fall down the steep slope to the water, I pulled the sodden sail on deck in half-metre sections. I had no choice but to keep going, a bit at a time, and after an hour of back-breaking work the sail was finally on deck.

Although I had lost four hours of sailing time, and had both of my off-wind sails stuffed into my forepeak and no fractional halyard left, I was still not willing to give up. In reality, I had lost my chance of overtaking my two competitors when I dropped my sail in the water, but I soldiered on, setting the boat back on course using my jib, then getting to work repairing the furling line, re-running the tack line, so that everything was in place to hoist my sail again on the remaining halyard. Even if I couldn't catch the two boats, I still wanted to know what *my* best time looked like.

Superbigou was tired. I had pushed the boat so hard and it was old. Within 24 hours of the finish line, there was another terrible bang. This time, one of the ropes that moved the keel head from side to side had broken. Now, as I approached the coast, the keel was swinging down to leeward, heeling the boat aggressively. The wind had swung around, now ahead of me, and in the rough water there were increasing amounts of traffic in my way. I had no choice but to crawl to the wet box in the front of the boat, far away from my displays and the boat controls. The keel was swinging around underneath the hull, and *Superbigou* was heeling over at an alarming angle. I needed to find a replacement rope and rig it up.

When I got inside the keel box, I realised all the blocks (pulleys) that the keel rope threaded through on one side were broken. When I had capsized the boat in order to recover my Code Zero, the head of the keel must have fallen down against the blocks and crushed them. I would have to put new ones in place as well as rigging a fresh rope. Thigh deep in water, I got inside the keel box. If I was on a collision course with a fishing boat, I would have no idea from inside the box. All I could hear was crashing and banging and the sound of the water sloshing around my legs. The head of the keel, taller than me, was supporting a three-tonne pendulum at its other end. Each time it swung on to my side, I had to duck out of the way to avoid getting crushed. I worked by the light of my head torch with cold fingers, sick with anxiety. At one stage I got tangled in the rope, and as the keel swung to one side the rope tightened, squeezing on either side of my chest, and lifted me off my feet. I yelled out, then was dropped back down with a splash. After that, I sat against the side of the boat sobbing for a while, my stomach cramping painfully. Finally, so exhausted I could hardly move, I crawled out of the keel box and back to the cockpit. The wind was up to 35 knots; I needed to watch for sea traffic, but by now I could not stand up straight as my stomach pains were worsening. I was so afraid *Superbigou* wasn't going to make it. On the shore, Joff was having the same concerns.

Text message conversation with Joff at 2315 on 11 February 2021, an hour and a half before the finish

Joff: *We have been trying not to come out to you for the last 40 miles. Don't want you having to rescue us.*
Pip: *It really is shit conditions out here*
Pip: *Right now I am more stressed than any other time. Even the rudder swapping*
Joff: *Me too*
Joff: *Feel sick*
Pip: *I have had agonising stomach cramps for about four hours*
Joff: *That will be the stress then.*

22

THIS IS NOT THE FINISH

The end, when it came, was nothing like the big Hollywood blockbuster finish one might imagine. When I crossed the line at 0057:30 on 12 February 2021, I felt nothing but a strange and dislocated numbness. I had carefully prevented myself from visualising a triumphant entry into the French harbour – cheering crowds, flares lighting up the sky, tearful smiles of my loved ones – and I was glad about that. Not only would it have been more disappointing for me if I'd failed to finish the race, but I do wonder if an experience of any magnitude ever quite matches the fantasy.

In the more distant past, of course, I had imagined how it might be. In my early twenties, I had watched the coverage of previous races, allowing myself to drift into reverie, picturing what it would be like to come down that famous channel in Les Sables d'Olonne. I had seen pictures and videos of yachts returning home to crowds of thousands lining the breakwaters, the skippers tired but victorious, arms held aloft, a red flare in each hand. I had watched them fall into the arms of their loved ones and been gripped by the famous footage of Ellen MacArthur crying, reluctant to leave her boat, kissing it as she stepped off. Back then, when I dared to imagine myself crossing the line, it was a montage of those scenes: a swelling pride in my chest, a welcome home from the proud people who loved me the most.

The reality was much less romantic. Shaking with stress and doubled over with pain, I limped towards the line. *Superbigou* was sailing slower than usual because I could no longer cant my keel to counteract the heeling moment of a bigger mainsail. With every crash of the bow smacking into the waves, I experienced a painful stab in my stomach. The night was pitch black with no moon, the sea an aggressive chop, the lights of the French shore visible ahead of me as I squinted through the darkness with spray in my eyes, trying to make out the navigational marks that would indicate the finish line. In the distance, I could see the glaring reds and greens of the navigation lights – so many of them – and suddenly they were rushing towards me, disorientating, confusing. As *Superbigou* approached the line, floodlights lit up my boat, then the roaring of engines as several RIBs swooped around the back of my boat and pulled in alongside. The noise seemed unnatural to me after months at sea. Confused, I felt all eyes on me, aware that these strangers were expecting something from me – an emotion I felt powerless to deliver. I had expected to be hit full and hard by a wave of elation. After all, the great race was over and I had achieved my dream of 30 years. But, in truth, I couldn't feel anything at all.

I had been so immersed in every moment of the last three months, feeling such a sense of belonging and purpose. I had known what to do in every moment, and never questioned how I should feel or what I should do. But here I faltered. What do they expect of me? What should I do next? Until now it had been just me and *Superbigou*, *Superbigou* and me. But all at once there were other responsibilities, a whole new set of pressures bearing down on my worn-out body and mind. I knew I had to be seen, so I climbed out of the cockpit and walked along the deck.

Looking back now at the footage of my arrival, I realise how tiny I looked. My once well-fitting drysuit swamped my frame. I looked like a child in an adult's clothing, a diminutive presence on the deck. *Superbigou* was floodlit, and with the bright lights shining in my face there was nowhere to hide. I couldn't even see the finish line – pinned here on deck, unable to hear the radio and without my charts, I had no way of knowing when I would cross it. *What do I do now?* Almost on autopilot, reaching towards those mental images of other races, I punched the air. Boats sounded their horns. I punched again, jumped up and down. And then something unaccountable and wonderful happened. The physical act of celebrating for the cameras lit the vital spark in me. My brain released its grip on my stress, my stomach pain vanished, and only then did the thought creep across my mind: 'You have finished the Vendée Globe.'

I had finished in 19th place: the first British sailor over the line. I became only the eighth woman in history to finish this race and the tenth British sailor. My race time of 95 days, 11 hours, 37 minutes and 30 seconds would have put me in third place in the year 2000, the race for which my boat was originally built. I finished within 24 hours of four foiling boats, with a gap of just 200 minutes between me and the 18th placed boat. On paper, my boat should have been second to last in the fleet. Instead, I would finish 16 days ahead of that position. *I'd made this happen.* Once I let myself absorb that thought, I let it become real in my mind. Now I no longer worried about how I should behave or what people expected of me. I didn't make any comparisons – why should it matter that this race finish was so different from every other I had watched over the history of the Vendée Globe? There were no crowds lining the breakwater, and my loved ones and supporters were prevented by lockdown rules from travelling to France. But this was my finish. My moment. And I let myself feel proud and happy.

I have always been a person with big vision. I believe in progression, pushing hard, working hard. I refuse to place restrictions on the possibilities of what I might achieve. I kept my vision hidden from so many for so long, never feeling brave enough to share it in case I was met with scepticism or derision. Over the course of my life, I have learned that vision is the engine that drives me uphill hard. Vision gives me purpose to try what others say is impossible. It allows me to pick myself up every time I get knocked down. It gives me purpose and clarity to make it through the hard times. By contrast, and perhaps against received wisdom, visualisation has not always been such a helpful tool, and I've learned to use it carefully. When I am imagining something that I have already experienced, visualisation can be a positive thing. When I make a manoeuvre on board, I visualise how it will go; I mentally rehearse how I will move, and the sequence of every rope pulled, button pressed or winch wound. I imagine how the action will feel when done well: the motion of the boat, the timing, the sounds. This form of visualisation is based upon known experiences, well-trodden paths. But when I have no personal reference from which to draw, my imaginings must inevitably be based on the experience of others. And I have found that the act of visualising my role models' activities, perceived from a distance, has not always served me well. At times, it has led to disappointment or a wrong footing on my journey. Early on in my career I was trapped in the starting blocks by the glossy perception of other sailors' paths to the top. I could see only the fully funded campaigns, the beautiful boats, big teams, and stress-free skippers polished to perfection. I believed that the route to success had to look like theirs, and I am sure it held me back. At some point, though, I realised that my journey and my race were always going to be different, because I was different. My journey from 17-year-old schoolgirl to 47-year-old Vendée Globe finisher has been original – all mine – and I'm proud that I have laid every paving block myself.

My welcoming party numbered eleven people in all. Happily, my team had arrived early to quarantine in Les Sables, having been granted travel permits, and with a small number of friends who had managed to travel to France before the borders closed, I was blessed with the sight of familiar and friendly faces. After crossing the line, my team piled on board from their RIB. For a short while they stood at the back of the boat, and we all looked at each other, not entirely sure what to do next. Paul broke the stand-off, swooping down into the cockpit and hugging me, followed by Joff and Lou. For a while it was pandemonium as everyone crowded into the space that had been mine exclusively for three months. There was plenty to do, but people were in the way. Sails still had to come down, and we needed to put extra diesel in the fuel tank to get me up the channel, but it was dark, my team hadn't been on the boat for a while, and I was not used to giving instructions. All of it is a blur to me now, but I know we muddled through. I remember a fresh apple thrust into my hand, which I devoured, and as we were motoring into port I went down below to video-call my parents, knowing there would be no time once I got to the dock.

As we entered the start of the breakwater, accompanied by a fleet of small boats, I was once again filmed, and that footage was livestreamed around the world. Joff took the helm so I could go and stand on the deck in sight of the cameras. A few people leaning out of apartment windows shouted and cheered; a rubbish truck emptying bins by the canal-side honked its horn, its bin-men waving. But otherwise there was no one to wave to as we progressed up the waterway. Standing there like a lemon, I suddenly felt awkward again, until Paul came to the rescue once more, appearing at my side with a glove, bucket of water and flares. He gave me the glove, pulled the trigger, and the intense bright-red light burned and grew. Repeating the action I had seen my heroes make so many times before, I held the flare aloft. Another spark, another flare. Now I had one in each hand, and suddenly it didn't matter that there was no one there to see. My team were smiling, some were crying, the support boats were alongside, and my pride and joy bubbled up inside me, growing more and more intense until I felt like I could burst.

Halfway down the canal, another boat came alongside and French sailing legend Jean Le Cam, who had finished fourth in the race, jumped on board. He hugged me hard, breaking off to tell me in French how well I had done, that I was the spirit of the race, then hugged me again. I was a little shellshocked, unsure of what to say. But then my team grabbed me back and walked me to the front of the boat. I don't remember coming alongside at the dock, but I do recall my theme music blasting out: Aretha Franklin's *Respect*. There was a small gathering of people – cameras, microphones – and although it was raining and two o'clock in the morning, they were singing along and clapping. I was given a huge magnum of champagne, which I sprayed around, and when I took a swig the bubbles instantly went up my nose and made me cough. But I couldn't stop smiling. *La Rayonette* was alive and well.

During the three months it took me to sail around the world, I felt the most free, the most strong, the most confident and capable I'd ever been in my life. I had pushed my old boat relentlessly, increasing my knowledge of ocean racing along the way, as I experienced new conditions in parts of the world I had never seen before. Alone, and already ahead of the back of the fleet, I could have taken my foot off the gas in the Southern Ocean. Accountable only to myself, no one else would have known how much or how little effort I was putting in. For three months I had been living in a beautiful flow state with minimal outside interference, at the edges of my capabilities – in my 'stretch zone'

– with total permission to be focused, 24/7, on racing my boat. What a privilege that had been. Every painful step I had taken to the start line had been worth it, and I was proud to acknowledge that I hadn't wasted a single opportunity during the race. Stepping off the boat on to the dock, I was asked a final question by a member of the press: 'So Pip, what's next?' Of course I knew.

After any great enterprise, a great black hole can open up to engulf the unwary. I'm sure that every one of the skippers who took part in the Vendée had to be careful not to step into it. It is the black hole of anticlimax, of let-down, of feeling 'what was it all for?' It's the voice that whispers to you that nothing you ever do will be as exciting, colourful, fulfilling or inspiring again. That dark place into which you can get sucked is one of dislocation, of purposelessness. We are bound to feel out of step with friends and family who cannot hope to understand the enormity of what we've just been through. And it is not just the mind that suffers: the body has its own reaction, too. It is only fair to expect minor collapse after such a lengthy period of unmitigated stress. We aren't superhuman.

To prevent myself falling into the black hole once I got off that boat, I knew I would need a clear direction and purpose. When every second of the previous two years had been taken up with moving my project forwards – not to mention the nine years I'd worked tirelessly to climb the ranks of solo sailing – I knew very well that I could be a casualty of the black hole if I didn't at once embrace a new plan. Luckily, it is in my nature to always have a vision of where life can take me next, and even before the beginning of the Vendée Globe race I was thinking about 2021. Once again, I asked myself three simple questions: Am I capable of more? Do I want to continue? Have I got the energy to go on? *Yes, yes, yes.*

At the start of the Vendée Globe race, I was a complete rookie. I'd never sailed in the Southern Ocean, let alone around the world. I had been happy to turn up and race on any terms to prove my worth, to find out if I had what it takes to really excel in the sport. I found a way to benchmark my performance, but it had always been capped by the age of the boat, the lack of funding early in the programme, and the limitations of my own experience. With no idea of what to expect, I had been learning as I went. Now twice the sailor I had been at the beginning, I had grown from my mistakes, and had already identified areas where I wanted to upskill. I had cut my teeth with my old boat and demonstrated my competitiveness, and now I wanted to know if I could be better. Give me another chance to race around again – this time with a full cycle of preparation, a team to support me, a newer, faster boat – and I could really prove my worth. I had made so many compromises in my preparation for the race that I had hardly invested in my own development. Instead, I had ploughed all my energy into fundraising, then piled every penny into the boat. To race again seemed so natural: the right thing to do. I had spoken to Leslie Stretch, the CEO of Medallia, and the company had been so happy with the results of our partnership that they were keen to extend it.

The 24 hours after coming ashore were surreal. Other than inhaling every piece of fresh fruit and vegetable I could get my hands on, I found myself with back-to-back interviews and press conferences. I was featured on the front page of *The Times*, as well as in another five of our national papers. I had live interviews on the radio (one of which I hiccupped through) and on breakfast shows, as well as an international press conference at the Vendée Globe race village. I was surrounded by people, caring for me, telling me where to go and what to do. Initially, it was easier to let it happen, walking through the distracting cacophony in a daze. Two skippers, Jean Le Cam and Benjamin Dutreux, had turned up for my arrival, but none of the other skippers were present. Two skippers who had arrived ahead of me during the night waited until daylight to make their grand entrance once there were fans on the canal-side and their own entourages present outside of the curfew. I stood with the welcome groups, happy to see their joy at finishing the race, but feeling it a little weird that I was there before them. When Didac Costa arrived, he was greeted by the firemen of Les Sables d'Olonne, who formed a guard of honour, lighting flares and firing water from their trucks across the canal. It made me chuckle to think of my bin lorry honking its horn as I arrived the night before.

It was only when we came home that I experienced anything like the true sense of an ending. It was great to get back on the boat and sail out into the Bay of Biscay once again with Paddy, who had sailed to the race start with me four months ago. I needed to get back to Poole to complete the circle. I had no idea what to expect, not being fully aware of how many people stuck at home in lockdown had been following my race. My team told me I needed to light a flare as I came through the entrance to Poole Harbour, and at the time I questioned this with them, thinking it odd. I could see myself at the front of the boat, holding up a flare while some dog walker on the beach looked on in bewilderment. But as we turned around Durlston Head to sail across Swanage Bay towards Old Harry Rocks, the distinctive white chalk stacks that mark the entrance into Poole Harbour, three boats came racing towards us. I was slightly shocked to see that two of them were police, and my mind scurried around the possibility that I'd failed to fill in some vital piece of new Brexit or COVID paperwork. It soon became apparent, however, from their waves and honks, that they were part of a welcoming committee, and as they passed around the back of the boat, they shouted, 'We are your escort.' Soon they were joined by my team, other pleasure boats and a lifeboat. As we came down the channel, the beach on Studland was scattered with people waving and shouting, some with banners, and when we passed through the narrow entrance to the harbour I lit my flare while the crowd of folk who had gathered in the car park for the Sandbanks ferry waved and shouted. It was the same on the quay as I arrived at the marina. For me to be welcomed home in such a way was a huge consolation for the fact my family and many close friends were still not present, living too far away to travel legally and greet me. Apparently, my team had been inundated with requests for the precise time I would be arriving, so that people could take their one hour of exercise to welcome me home. Worried about creating an illegal gathering, my team had tried to discourage them. But still they came.

Representatives from local media met me on the dock, and I was interviewed once again about my race and how it felt to be back. Inevitably, the interviews would end with the same question I had been asked in France. This time I gave an answer.

'So Pip, what's next?'
'The Vendée Globe 2024.'

EPILOGUE

February 2024

The tenth edition of the Vendée Globe race will start on 10 November of this year, and once again I will be on the start line. Writing this book has taken me back to a time that seems so distant from my current position and yet the three intervening years have also flown by. By May 2021 I had signed a second deal with Medallia and we had bought *Bureau Vallée*, the small foil boat that came third in my 2020 race.

Over the past three years, I have built a British Ocean Racing team, based in Poole and comprising 14 members to cover all functions across the business, sponsorship, technical and performance areas. Building the team from scratch has not been easy; neither has expanding my one-woman show to a business capable of delivering performance race results. Joff has stayed on as our technical director; Lou now works full time, running operations and partnership management. Over the last three years we have recruited and trained staff, signed new sponsors, and delivered a programme of three or four international races a year, finishing the eighth ranked team in the world series at the end of our second year.

The Vendée Globe of 2020 was the most successful edition of the race to date and reached an audience of over two billion people during its four months of coverage. As a result, the number and calibre of hopeful participants in this year's race stands at 45 for a possible 40 places. Fourteen new-build boats have been launched in the last four years, so despite upgrading from *Superbigou* to the new boat, *Medallia*, on paper we still sit at 17th position in the fleet. I'd taken a leap of faith and changed my small foils to big ones, taking on a six-month refit that required additional fundraising to cover the costs and lost me six months of training time. The boat is a total beast: my top speed has been logged at 37.2 knots, it flies clean above the water on the new foils, and we have made this eight-year-old design relevant in the fleet once again. In the last solo race of 2023, I was beaten to a top ten position only in the last 20 miles of a 3,200-mile race.

With just eight months to go before the start of my next round-the-world race, I still have a big fundraising target to hit, a lot of training to do, one qualification race to finish, boat modifications to make, and not enough time to do it. But what a different campaign this one has been.

I have learned so many lessons in trust, growth and leadership by building a team from scratch. We are still small fry compared to the French mega-teams, but we punch hard above our weight and carry our own definitions of success always. I still don't get to be the carefree skipper, because of having taken on the responsibilities of being CEO of my growing company as well as feeling the weight of trust that comes with sponsorships. I still get stressed, and fight every day to make this campaign a reality.

In writing this book I've taken the time to remember who I was during my 2020 race, and all the lessons I've learned that make what I do today possible. I still love my sport; I feel freer and more equal on the water than I ever could on land. Outwardly, I have changed: I am older now, more confident, and with the team behind me we look like the professionals I was lining up against in those early days. But when I read my blogs from the race, it is plain to see that in my head and in my heart nothing has changed. I will always strive to be better, to achieve more, to make the most of opportunities. It's just that now I do it faster, and I have a small ability to help things happen for other people as well.

I have always believed that one of the greatest things about being a human being is our ability to learn, develop and adapt throughout our whole lives. Most of our adult lives these progressions are small, sometimes imperceptible day to day. But we learn routines and behaviours; we train our brains and our bodies for long-term gain. Very occasionally, the jumps are huge and obvious – and the 2023 Transat Jacques Vabre was one of those jumps.

Despite being my 22nd transatlantic crossing, I had no idea what to expect at the start of the race. I wasn't nervous, having worked quite hard at keeping my stress levels manageable with a pre-race routine that gave me time and space away from the hubbub and allowed my brain to think and feel other things. The delay due to Storm Ciarán didn't faze me particularly, other than the increased cost and logistical nightmare of our carefully laid plans being thrown in the air. But the truth is, I just didn't know what was going to happen. The huge investment we had made upgrading our IMOCA, *Medallia*, to bring it in line with 2024 generation boat performance was done. The big foils were there for all to see, a tangible, obvious outcome of skill, vision, hard work and collaboration. We had trained with them over the previous two months, going out in big breeze, pushing, feeling, learning, but never for more than four consecutive days offshore. Now we were going to push across the Atlantic, and weeks of stress-testing would find any weaknesses in the work we had done.

I had only had a snapshot of what the boat was capable of. I had experienced life on board at over 25 knots of boat speed. It was exhilarating, for sure. I had learned how to ramp up the performance and get the boat flying, full hull out of the water, and how to push for those photogenic moments of glamour and wonder. But neither my co-skipper, Nick, nor I had any idea what extended periods under those conditions would mean for the human beings on board. This was not just about pushing the boat to find weakness, but also about getting the first glimpses of what I might be capable of as a human being, alone for months at a time during the next Vendée Globe race.

We had made a huge step in the performance potential of *Medallia*. It was now my turn to make that step forward. I believed I could be capable of the increased physical and mental demands of sailing this new boat, but the truth is I just did not know. When we eventually set out on 7 November it was to sail a shortened course from the original, which would have taken us across the equator, round a remote Atlantic island, and back to the finish. Our time at sea was reduced by one week in a direct route to Martinique. We set sail in fairly familiar conditions for the North Atlantic in the autumn: straight into the path of an oncoming depression. Crossing an active weather front within 24 hours of leaving Le Havre, it meant big winds, big seas – often the conditions that break boats, crushing competitors' hopes and dreams before even leaving the Western Approaches.

I think one of the most challenging things about the race was the need to balance my objectives. This was a race. We had a 'new' boat to test; we wanted to demonstrate to all those that had invested in and supported us that it had been worth it. Furthermore, we needed to demonstrate to other potential sponsors that we represented a good prospect. It was an incredible opportunity to push the boat, and if things went wrong there would be two people to sort it out. However, the TJV is a qualification race for the Vendée Globe, and as a skipper qualifying under 'old boat' rules, I HAD to finish this race and bank the miles. There was the added pressure that the return race from Martinique to France, also a qualification race, would leave at the end of November, and as it was solo it carried double the miles of the TJV. To damage the boat in a way that would put me out of both races could mean the end to my Vendée Globe campaign. At one end of the spectrum was a safe race, a southerly route, never pushing the boat hard, taking a delivery-style approach to the course. At the other end was the need to prove both the boat and myself. If we never pushed, how would we know what additional work needed to be done to get us around the world the following year? I knew I was not alone in this conflict. Joff perhaps felt it more than me. He was aware of all the things that could go wrong; in the same way I see the potential for speed, he sees the potential for breakages. He wants to see the boat do well, but he hates to see it being pushed in the moment. We all feel it.

At the beginning of the race, it looked like there were two strategies opening up. One was a route to the south – on paper less fast, but with a lot less risk. The second was a route to the west after the Azores, which would be quicker but would involve bigger winds and sea states. We did not need to make a decision on which route to take until a few days into the race, and I didn't have an immediate feeling about which one I would choose. The deciding factor turned out to be the incurrence of a five-hour penalty for passing between the committee boat and the inner distance mark at the start (in truth, we passed some 50 metres away from the tug and never even saw the buoy), together with damage to our mainsail on the first night of the race. To take our penalty, we needed to stop, give the committee a position, then return to that position five hours later. We had until 30 degrees north to take it, and I decided we could use the time to fix the mainsail. We had already come up with a plan to lash the back of the sail together with carbon plate and Dyneema line. However, though the concept was right, the timing was not. I let the need to fix the main overtake my strategic view of the race. We took our penalty when the wind dropped for the first time, but it was the wrong time. The other boats around us were still sailing fast, the drop in wind having only been temporary. In my eagerness to get a fully functioning mainsail, I'd lost sight of the big picture. Once we started the main repair we had to finish it, and the whole thing took four hours, during which we were sailing dead downwind. Once the repair was done, it took us several hours to sail back upwind to our penalty gate. We had fixed the main, but we lost around eight to ten hours of ground on our fast-moving competitors, who were still heading south. I was kicking myself hard.

Our mainsail repair allowed us to use the main at full hoist and at two reefs, but the sail was still too weak to use at one reef. To gain the places we had lost, we would need to sail smart and hard. We made the decision to go west – to sail fast and push the boat – on day four of the race when we were lying 22nd, over halfway down the fleet. It wasn't a crazy flier: on paper, it was the faster route, but it represented more risk. In truth, I couldn't bear the thought of following the fleet around, clawing back small miles here and there, knowing that I could have done better. We exist to race, and that's what we needed to do.

Joining the big breeze in the west was intense. Nothing like anything I'd experienced before. Imagine being on a roller-coaster, as the cars are slowly shunted up the steep incline to the top of the ride. There is tension, but it's OK. When you get to the top, there is a huge drop in front of you. You fly down it, around corners, over small humps and back down again. You are strapped in, maybe screaming, the G-force pulling your body this way and that. It's exhilarating; the speed makes you giddy, but the ride is short, and at the end you can step off on to firm ground. Our 'roller-coaster' did not end. In the first ten minutes of acceleration, you have those same feelings: 'this is so incredible, this is crazy'. You holding on hard, watching the speed increase through 30 knots to 35. An Instagram moment – the perfect 30-second film to amaze and astound your friends. But it's not. Because this lasts longer than 30 seconds. Now you must find a way to live without a seat belt on a vehicle that is travelling at an average speed of over 20mph. You must stand up on the bucking, lurching surface, trim sails, make food, navigate, sleep and, in our case, bail out water from the leak in the back. Imagine a rally car co-driver taking off their seat belt and climbing into the back of the car to boil a kettle while the other continues to drive. This was our life.

The foil would lift us up, the bow rising into the air, and we would be left with one rudder in the water, so that *Medallia* was flying. The boat is designed to fall down at the back, so our flying was interspersed with the stern crashing down, rhythmically, as tonnes of weight smashed into the ocean, then lifted again repeatedly. This normal slamming, jarring rhythm we could almost predict. But occasionally, often when we achieved our maximum speeds, the bow came crashing down first. These nosedives were the most violent, and the most likely to damage a human being. Imagine a car crash, when the speed stops but the small human being carries on moving. I was thrown across the cabin twice from these nosedives, the second time still holding on to my freshly made bag of porridge, almost proud that not a drop spilt. It wasn't fun and you couldn't predict it. You just had to hold on, keeping your body in a defensive position, never dropping your guard, never assuming the next second is not the one to catapult you forward. I was wearing padded shorts, a hard hat at times, and spent as little time standing as I possibly could. When navigating, I'd sit on the floor cushioned by beanbags. When I attempted sleep, it was again on the floor with a nest of beanbags between me and the front of the boat, so that when we did nosedive I was forced into their soft protection.

But it is not just the physical challenges that made this tough. The noise was relentlessly loud: the rushing of the water, the slamming, the loud howling of the foils. It was impossible to hear a normal-level human voice. The sound gets inside your head; it is a constant reminder of pressure, and it never lets you relax.

For days on end, this was beyond brutal. Always managing the dual worries of 'can the boat handle it?' and 'how much can I handle?', the intensity was completely new, though I'd felt something similar on the last Vendée Globe race when I really started to push *Superbigou* hard in the south. Now, in the TJV, I was stretching the limits for myself and the boat, worrying constantly but also not willing to let this opportunity to perform as an athlete slip away from me. The truth is, we don't have to sail that hard. We can bring the foils in, we can use smaller sails. If it all gets too much, we can turn the bow downwind and everything just stops. But my question always is: *Who am I and why am I doing this?* A question that makes me put my foot on the gas.

We finished the race in 12th place, having taken ten places since making our decision to go west. We made more mistakes along the way, and I believe there was potential for us to finish in the top ten. I stepped off the boat more exhausted than I have ever been on any IMOCA race. Physically, I was a bit battered, but it was my brain that had taken the biggest pounding. I was mentally exhausted from pushing so hard and managing the stress that goes with that.

The boat had more than proved itself, as I knew it would. My team and all those with whom we collaborated could not have done a better job at upgrading our power and performance. I'd known the race was going to be tough, that sailing the boat in this new configuration would require something different from me. There was so much new to learn about the technical management of the boat: sail trim was different, sensations were different, even setting the autopilot up was different. When I set out, there was still the tiny demon sitting on my shoulder telling me I had finally stepped too far. I am a woman in my 50th year, late to the world of ocean racing and almost entirely self-taught and self-made. I did always believe I was capable of racing at this level, which is why I have pushed myself so hard, but when I started out solo racing in 2009, I never imagined the end result would be flying across the Atlantic in 2023.

It wasn't easy. None of this is easy. But together with Nick, my co-skipper, who supported me unequivocally all the way, we made a good start at bringing human performance in line with our incredible boat. Nick allowed me to make decisions as to how hard we would push, and I hugely appreciated his constant positive presence and support. He gave me space to make a huge leap forward in my own performance while feeling confident that I was not alone. But under such mental pressure there is always some part of your consciousness that is looking for the 'off ramp', and I have to work hard at keeping it under control. In the TJV, we only pushed the boat really hard for a few days. On the Vendée, I will be alone, and it will be for weeks at a time.

I have always said that at the end of each race or each race cycle, I ask myself three questions: Am I capable of more? Do I want to continue? Have I got the energy to go on? The answer is yes, yes and yes. I still laugh out loud at the speed, and I feel an intense pride in the fact that I am able to race this boat at this level. I love the energy, the tactics, the sport, and the fact that we are absolutely at the interface between the power of nature and human ingenuity. This sport makes me proud to be alive, proud to be me. It feeds my soul and makes me strong, and even if my body is bruised and my mind is exhausted, I cannot get enough of it.

ACKNOWLEDGEMENTS

The sad reality is I will not be able to thank every person to whom I owe gratitude on these two pages I have been granted to make my acknowledgements. This book is a small byproduct of my immense journey through life, towards what, at times, seemed like the unachievable goal of becoming a world-class sailor. My journey is far from over. Once one goal is achieved, the world ahead opens up, inviting a person to aspire to greater, tougher, harder things, and so I accept the challenge. I now run a professional ocean racing team based in the UK, and at the time of writing, we have broken into the top ten IMOCA teams in the world. Solo sailing is a team sport and I have not got to where I am alone. I owe so many thank yous to so many people, and the following are personal thank you mentions for just a few of the people who made my 2020 race possible:

Leslie Stretch, the man who could see my potential and the potential of the race, and who gave me the greatest opportunity of my life. Leslie changed the course of my career forever and has made me determined to give others opportunities in the future. He has demonstrated what leadership looks like.

Mark Mader for the years of synergy, support and partnership with Smartsheet. Pete Jones, who knows a maverick when he sees one and brought about our partnership with Yondr.

Professional sport is almost entirely reliant on commercial sponsorship to provide the necessary funds to deliver outright performance. I hope I have gone some way to demonstrating how far the ripples from a sport like ours can travel. We compete in the moment, but the race experience, the stories, the lessons and the values demonstrated on the water by each competitor, have an impact way beyond the end of our chosen event. We are one of the few sports in the world where the race stories live on to be told again and again. And where as much value and interest can be found for both sponsors and spectators in the stories of those who do not win, as in the ones who cross the finish line first. Our race around the world, and consequently the story I have been able to tell, would not have been possible without our great family of sponsors for the 2020 race:

Medallia, Smartsheet, Yondr, Codestone, WQI Marine, Poole Harbour Commissioners, One Sails, Helly Hansen, Marlow Ropes, Pro Marine Finance, Flag paints, Inspire, Composite Profiles, Actisense, Sungod, Store and Secure, Wessex Vans, Intergage, Barker Group, Biggin Hill Airport, Davies Chiropractors, SatCase, Saltwater Stone, Boatwork, Parkstone Yacht Club, Jangada Racing, Spinlock and every single person who donated any amount of time, money or wisdom to the campaign. I wish I could thank you all by name but we don't have enough pages.

In the meagre room I have left, I would like to name-check a few more people who made the biggest difference to my 2020 race:

Lou Adams, operations director, friend, my champion always, the recipient of a lot of my rants, an absolute rock at all times and in all ways. I would not have achieved half of what I have today without your strength and support. I don't give you enough credit ever; sometimes I don't have the words to explain how grateful I am.

Joff Brown, for being the safest, most conscientious pair of hands I could ever have put my boat in. Being a solo sailor, I want to do everything myself; trusting others to care as much as I do seems an impossible thing, yet with Joff, it was easy.

Paul Peggs, a wonderful friend who always knew what I was capable of and nagged me into entering the Vendée Globe race despite having no boat and no funding, then helped me make it happen.

Kerrie Gray, and everyone at Poole Harbour Commissioners, for giving my team a home and being proud of us.

Richard, Jeremy, Rupert, Sophie, Kass, Jon, Owain, Sabrina, Oli, Ash, Amelia, Paddy, Lucy, Charles, Sarah and Phil, who gave up their time to come out and help me learn how to sail *Superbigou* in the early days, often sticking bits back together as we went. Richard, who came and photographed us. A special mention to Charles, who rolls up his sleeves to the greatest of challenges, rebuilding gearboxes, climbing to the top of masts, modifying steering and keeping me sane by making me run miles and miles to remind me of the power of just putting one foot in front of another.

Paul and Helena, inspirational, positive, incredible people.

The many people who laid hands on tools, shifted kit and gave up their time to help me get to the start line, especially: Phil, Mark and Julie, Rob, Sabrina, Lorna, Millie, Sophie, Bobby, Jon, Becca, Oli, Richard, Nick, Sam, Michael, Lucy, Sally, Sarah, Chris, Paul, Helena, Ys, Christa, Katie, Isla, Clare, Rich, Mel, Yann, Amelia, John, Rupert, Mike, Paul and Paddy.

The people who fed me, reminded me to eat and looked under the lid of the campaign knowing it wasn't just about a boat and wanting to make sure I was still surviving; in particular my big sister Rachael, Lou, Sarah, Sabrina, Jon, Becca, Katie, Iain, Fi, Phil, Oli, Neil, Maggie and Em.

Chris, David, Edoardo, David, Tom, Paul and Marie, for helping me to find a voice, present in public, pitch a sponsorship proposal and navigate my way into a world of business that was an alien landscape.

All the journalists and editors who took an interest in our sport and gave me the opportunity to share some of what I was doing with the world, thank you for giving us airtime.

My parents for not worrying, or at least not showing me that they were worrying.

Our VG 2020 dream team, Joff, Lou, Isla, Hayley, Mikey, Paddy, Rob, Richard, Paul, Paul, Phil, Helena, Charles and Jose.

Beth, Millie and Flo, for fun fact Fridays.

And finally, only because we are at the end of the page and I can't go on endlessly; to the people who didn't just say, 'You should write a book', but who set me up to do it. Belinda, who could see the book in my head and introduced me to the right people to make it happen; Jane, who found me a publisher; and Wanda, an editor, who despite my lack of communication for weeks on end, never seemed to doubt I would spit the words out and worked with me to make it seem like sense.